Dec Calvinism

A Biblical Analysis and Refutation

Third Edition

Hutson Smelley

Deconstructing Calvinism
A Biblical Analysis and Refutation

Copyright © 2019 Hutson Smelley

Unless otherwise indicated, Bible quotations are taken from The King James Bible.

ISBN: 978-0-9861336-4-0

www.proclaimtheword.me

Other Works by the Author

Better with Jesus: A Mission 119 Guide to Hebrews
(2015)

Love, Romance and Intimacy: A Mission 119 Guide to
the Song of Solomon (2016)

Chasing Jonah: A Mission 119 Guide to Jonah (2018)

Living Hope: A Mission 119 Guide to First Peter (2019)

Table of Contents

Chapter 1

Calvinism on Trial

In our system of legal jurisprudence, to prevail in a civil action, the plaintiff's burden is typically a "preponderance of the evidence." The plaintiff must establish by evidence that every element of the claim sued upon is "more likely than not" true. Merely showing that the plaintiff's version of the events was possibly the way it happened fails to meet that burden. Instead, the plaintiff carries the evidentiary burden of taking it to the 51st yard line, showing the scales upon which the evidence is weighed tip in his or her favor.

The procedure of the modern courtroom provides a helpful analogy for the process that will be followed in this book for analyzing, evaluating, and ultimately, refuting Calvinism. Regardless of how you come out on Calvinism, there is an orderly, sensible approach for testing the five core principles of Calvinism against the evidence, chapter and verse, from the

Bible. This holds for any truth propositions about the Scriptures. We learn in the book of Acts that even when the apostle Paul preached, the "noble" people in Berea "searched the scriptures daily, whether those things [Paul said] were so." (Acts 17:11) A central purpose of this book is to test Calvinism against the evidence and see if "those things [are] so."

My observation is that propositions become true for three reasons. Some things become true because they are, in fact, true. And with propositions about God's special revelation, this means they are objectively true when tested against the Bible. But other propositions become true because we want them—indeed, sometimes desperately want them—to be true. And still others become true through much repetition. In the sphere of Bible propositions, this latter category refers to things that "preach well." Yet, many things that preach well (and frequently) are unquestionably false. Not all that glitters is gold. Only the first category—those propositions that are actually true—should matter here. For those propositions we look to evidence in the Bible, not to whether we want a particular proposition to be true or not, and not to whether it preaches well. The courtroom analogy is helpful here as we take on the task of weighing the evidence.

In recent years, Calvinism has again gained increasing popularity, especially finding a foothold in many seminaries and Bible colleges, which means that it trickles into the churches as these young people enter the ministry. As I listen to the preaching on the radio and interact with other preachers and teachers of the Word of God, I am frequently presented with strong Calvinist views. For so many, its principles are axiomatic rather than propositional. I intend to demonstrate that Calvinism cannot be established from evidence in the Bible. Not only that, no single verse in the Bible establishes even one of the five core principles of Calvinism.

Anyone who has delved just a little into Calvinism knows that its adherents posit long citations to proof texts for the

Calvinist principles they advocate. When its game day and the parties to a lawsuit come to present their case before the jury, the jury would be wrong to assume one party or the other had the right of it just because they brought a stack of documents or a line of witnesses to the courthouse. To determine whether the plaintiff meets the "more likely that not" burden, the jury must examine each individual piece of evidence, and consider it cumulatively, all against the backdrop of the context within which the dispute occurred. For us, that means taking the proffered Biblical evidence one verse at a time.

This book is about getting beyond the allegations, philosophical conjecture, and our theological commitments, and holding Calvinism to an evidentiary burden of proof. The reader is invited to sit as a juror and decide whether the Calvinists can meet their burden of proof. Let us put Calvinism on trial.

Starting at the Beginning

If you are selected to sit on the jury, you take an oath to consider the evidence without bias. When we approach the Scripture, we need to come to it like an unbiased juror. But at that point, of course, we all have a problem because we all have biases, whether we want to own up to it or not. However, there are two kinds of bias. The first reflects what we presently believe (our worldview) and is subject to change based on new information. Even if a belief is strongly held, this bias permits us to hear all the evidence before coming to a conclusion.

The second, however, is *willful bias*. This type of bias reflects a determination to protect what one believes at all costs, including ignoring contrary evidence (i.e., the proverbial "head in the sand" approach). I mentioned previously that some things become true simply because we want them to be true, and the willfully biased person clings desperately to their truth undaunted by and uninterested in the evidence, yet making a good show of hearing and interacting with the evidence. Peter addressed this when he spoke of those that scoff at the promise of Jesus' return, "saying, Where is the promise of his coming? for since the fathers fell asleep, all things continue as *they were* from the beginning of the creation." (2 Peter 3:4) Note that the scoffers point to supposed evidence, but Peter calls them out for their *willful bias*: "For this they willingly are ignorant of, that by the word of God the heavens were of old, and the earth standing out of the water and in the water: Whereby the world that then was, being overflowed with water, perished: But the heavens and the earth, which are now, by the same word are kept in store, reserved unto fire against the day of judgment and perdition of ungodly men." (2 Peter 3:5-7)

So when I speak here of sitting as an unbiased juror, I recognize we all have our biases. What I am urging is that we not be willfully biased. In this regard, please understand that I was an avid Calvinist for many years. I did not go to Bible college that way, but I came out that way. After being exposed to some alternative interpretations of key Calvinism verses, I challenged myself to try to make the very best arguments I could for a non-Calvinist position on some of those passages. This exercise should have sharpened my own arguments for Calvinism. But one key verse at a time, that exercise unraveled Calvinism for me. If you are disposed to Calvinistic leanings, then I would challenge you here at the beginning to simply do the same exercise as we walk through the evidence, but do it one verse at a time then move to the next one. All of us, as best we can, need to set aside our predispositions and examine the evidence. We should be satisfied with the verdict of Scripture and accept it as our verdict as well.

One unfortunate facet of the present trend toward Calvinism is that there is often confusion about what it means to be a Calvinist. One purpose of this book is to bring clarity to the issues for someone not already familiar with Calvinism. We must start with a clear understanding of precisely what

Calvinism is before we can meaningfully consider the evidence. It is unfortunate that some materials out there mess up at this first step.

We will see that there are five core principles, but each of those has different parts that must be considered. We must know each element of the five core truth propositions of Calvinism to properly assess the evidence. My approach will be very simple. I will first explain the basic principles commonly referred to as *Calvinism* with quotations from Calvinist writers so that the reader (juror) can check the sources and be sure that what is presented is a balanced, fair view of the traditional Calvinist doctrines. I will then demonstrate that the most popular proof texts (i.e., Bible passages offered to establish a point) for this belief system do not actually provide evidentiary support for it.

I note at this point that a decision had to be made between addressing every verse some Calvinists cite for what they believe, or focusing on the most significant verses—what we might call the foundation or pillar passages—and then a sampling of the other verses. I chose the latter to keep the book to a manageable length. Also, once the pillar verses tumble, the others tend to fit patterns that the sampling of other verses addressed will refute. After addressing the evidence proffered for Calvinism, I will give some consideration to how the Calvinist doctrines are contradicted by the plain teaching of the Bible.

What Matters Most

The subject is vast and this book could indeed cover numerous points concerning Calvinism. For example, there could be additional chapters on the history of Calvinism and the history and tenets of Arminianism.[1] All of these issues are more than

---

[1] Arminianism is named for James Arminius (1560-1609), although its

adequately addressed in other excellent books and it is simply not the purpose of this book to address them in any detail.[2] At the end of the day, whether Calvinism is Biblical is what matters most. If the Bible teaches Calvinism, then we should readily embrace it without question. As the authors of one Calvinist text have rightly observed:

> The question of supreme importance is not how [Calvinism] came to be formulated in five points, or why it was named Calvinism, but rather *whether it is supported by Scripture.* The final court of appeal for determining the validity of any theological system is the inspired, authoritative Word of God. If Calvinism can be verified by clear and explicit declarations of Scripture, then it must be received by Christians; if not, it must be rejected.[3]

If Calvinism is not Biblically supported, then it is no more than another philosophical system in the arena of human wisdom and ideas and we as the jurors must reject it. Having

---

formalization was at the hands of his followers after his death. In 1610, they drew up five points in response to Calvinism known as the Remonstrance, which Vance (see note 2) summarizes: (1) God has decreed to save those who shall believe on Jesus Christ and persevere in faith; leaving the unbelieving in sin to be condemned; (2) Jesus Christ died for all men, providing redemption if a man believe on him; (3) Man is in a state of sin, unable to of himself do anything truly good, but needs to be born again; (4) Man cannot without the grace of God accomplish any good deeds or movements, but this grace can be resisted; (5) Believers have power to persevere, but as to whether they can fall away, that must be more particularly determined out of the Holy Scriptures.

[2] For example, please refer to the outstanding treatise by non-Calvinist Laurence M. Vance, *The Other Side of Calvinism*, chapters 2, 3, and 4, Vance Publications, Fourth Printing (2007).

[3] David N. Steele, Curtis C. Thomas, and S. Lance Quinn, *The Five Points of Calvinism*, p. 17, P&R Publishing Company (2d ed. 2004).

explained the general approach and purpose of this book, several preliminary observations are in order.

Preliminary Observations

First, we need to consider something about words. Theology turns on words. Is God sovereign? Most evangelicals would give a resounding "yes." Are unsaved people depraved? Again, a resounding "yes." Is there a group of redeemed people described as *elect*? And once again, "yes." Probably most Christians who have thought about it would agree with these basic principles, but that does not settle anything. Two people can affirm God's sovereignty, but they may mean different things by their common use of the word. Likewise, two people could agree that unsaved people are depraved, but do they mean the same thing by depraved? Our definitions of terms like these are irrelevant and invalid unless they are in agreement with God's definitions. The following episode illustrates the point.

Two young ladies, about 15 years old, knocked on my door. They were very friendly, introduced themselves, and asked whether I had ever considered whether there might be further written revelation from God beyond the Old and New Testaments. We discussed that issue and then I asked them whether they believed Jesus Christ was deity, knowing that they did not. Of course, they quickly replied, "We do believe that Jesus is deity." Then I said, "Are you deity?" They were surprised by the question but admitted, "Yes, we are deity." And therein is the point. When I say Jesus is deity or divine, I mean that Jesus is the "I am" of the Old Testament, Jehovah. (John 8:58) When they said Jesus was deity, they certainly did not mean that he was Emmanuel, God with us.

So you see, the importance of how we define the words we use cannot be overstated. Those who are Calvinists, and those who are not, employ many of the same words to talk about theology, but do not mean the same thing. Calvinists often accuse non-Calvinists of not holding to the sovereignty of God. What they are actually saying is that non-Calvinists do not hold to the Calvinists' definition of the sovereignty of God. It remains to be seen whether their definition is in accord with the Holy Scriptures, but a further point should be made here. It is not enough to simply say that a word has a certain meaning—you have to be able to establish it from the lexical meaning(s) of the term and as used in the Bible. The following conversation from Lewis Carroll's classic *Through The Looking Glass* illustrates the point:

> "I don't know what you mean by 'glory'," Alice said.
>
> Humpty Dumpty smiled contemptuously. "Of course you don't — till I tell you. I meant 'there's a nice knock-down argument for you!'"
>
> "But 'glory' doesn't mean 'a nice knock-down argument'," Alice objected.
>
> "When *I* use a word," Humpty Dumpty said, in rather a scornful tone, "it means just what I choose it to mean — neither more nor less."
>
> "The question is," said Alice, "whether you *can* make words mean so many different things."
>
> "The question is," said Humpty Dumpty, "which is to be master — that's all."

My observation is that the definitions of key words are often assumed rather than established. This is not a Calvinist problem, but a more general problem for people of various theological persuasions and backgrounds. We have significant words like baptize, believe, repent, and wrath, just to name a few, on which central doctrines of the faith are grounded. Yet many who teach these doctrines never pause to establish that their definition of these words is actually correct. Recall my point earlier that some things become true by repetition; this falls into that category. If the definitions are wrong, then we are just injecting our theology into the individual words to ensure that we get out of the verses with those words what we want. This is a type of circular reasoning. Calvinists give definitions to certain words rather dogmatically. Since the correct meanings of words are at the heart of the issues under consideration, I will quote from several representative Calvinist sources in the chapters that follow so that the reader can understand what the Calvinists mean by the words they use, and where appropriate, we will take a closer examination of the Biblical use of key terms like *elect* to determine whether the Calvinists have rightly defined the terms or, instead, have simply employed a "Humpty Dumpty" argument.

One of my very best Bible professors was fond of saying that theology is about words and names. I addressed the issue of words above, but some comments about names are also appropriate. The issue at hand is what saith God, not what saith Calvin or anyone else. This is not to take away from the value of learning from other Christians, but my observation is that culturally in the United States we too often allow our thinking to be personality driven and this problem has surfaced in evangelicalism as well. Through books, radio, television, and conferences, certain people have achieved an elevated "hero" status among many evangelicals the way certain entertainers, politicians and sports figures have. They are inseparably identified with certain theological viewpoints and for many people these heroes are the final authority. I would further point out that we travel a foolish road when we listen primarily to one voice. This book is not about vindicating any particular historical perspective or any particular person's viewpoint, but seeking to understand whether the Calvinists' truth claims are scriptural or not.

A third preliminary observation is that not all Calvinists hold identical beliefs. Just as the word Baptist is worn by a diversity of groups, with some similarities but many differences, so too it is the case that not all Calvinists believe exactly the same things. Because it is beyond the scope of this book to try to address all of these differences, this book focuses on those principles that would be considered by most Calvinists to be the primary, traditional tenets of the system, even if they do not individually accept all of these traditional tenets. For this reason, this book footnotes references to several Calvinist texts. There will be no attempt at being exhaustive. Rather, the goal is to review representative examples of sources explaining the traditional tenets of Calvinism so that the definitions and principles can be understood from the pens of the Calvinists themselves. The reader is encouraged to independently review the cited texts.

A fourth point, which needs to be stressed here at the outset, is that the author will strive to maintain a Christian tone throughout this book. This book is written for edification. Christians should be able to discuss these points, write about them, and even constructively disagree about them, without engaging in sinful (unloving or prideful) conduct or *ad hominem* arguments. Indeed, the last chapter of this book is devoted to this very issue because of its importance, especially in the day of keyboard warriors addressing Calvinism (and various other issues) on blogs and social media. Charlie Bing's words on this issue are well taken:

> There are disagreements about some interpretations —sometimes passionate disagreements—but that is no cause to be unfair or mean-spirited. We are often too quick to label those with whom we disagree as "false teachers" or "heretics." The New Testament authors reserve the terms "false prophets" or "false teachers" for those who are maliciously undermining God's truth with blatant heresies. The New Testament only uses the term "false teachers" (psuedodidaskaloi) once where

they are equated with the obviously unsaved "false prophets" who teach "heresies" (2 Pet. 2:1). I do not think the terms "false teacher" or "heretic" in the biblical sense are deserved by any sincere Christian who holds a well-intentioned but erroneous interpretation of a Bible passage. Otherwise, I think we would all be false teachers teaching heresy, because we all differ in our interpretations of passages.[4]

Sadly, the Christians' assault weapon of choice is hurtful, mean-spirited words. Moreover, I find no Scriptural authority for Christians debating one another just for the sake of debating. There is a difference between a healthy dialogue and a debate where one person seeks to verbally beat down another.

Fifth, I hold without apology to the following orthodox Christian beliefs about the Bible: (1) The Bible was superintended by God through the pens of human authors and is inerrant in the original autographs; (2) The canon of Scriptures was completed with the Revelation, God having started in Genesis and finished in the Revelation with God and man dwelling together; (3) The Bible alone is our authoritative guide for all issues of life and godliness, and is wholly sufficient for this purpose; (4) The Bible should be interpreted in its plain, normal sense; (5) In the Bible, God has spoken with clarity. The clarity of Scripture is that quality of the Biblical text that, as God's communicative act, ensures its meaning is accessible to all who come to it in faith.[5] For all of these reasons, the answers to the questions raised by Calvinism are knowable and they are to be found in the Bible.

And sixth is the idea that one is either a Calvinist or an

---

4 Charles C. Bing, *Grace, Salvation, and Discipleship: How to Understand Some Difficult Bible Passages* (pp. 13-14). Grace Theology Press. Kindle Edition.

5 Mark D. Thompson, *A Clear and Present Word, The Clarity of Scripture*, pp. 169-170, Inter Varsity Press (2006).

Arminian. That is simply not the case. I am neither. Many people have the misconception that there are only two camps. This is the logical fallacy known as limited choice. It is akin to saying one must be a Democrat or Republican. A wise person once told me that there are three sides to most issues. I have found it a wise course to try to appreciate and understand the third side before making up my mind. As I will endeavor to demonstrate, it is possible to reject both extremes and take something of a middle ground approach between the two.

Let us be Biblicists first. "If the Bible is God's Word, and the evidence says it is, then once we line our thinking up with the thinking of the Bible, our positions become Bible positions and not opinions."[6]

Theology, Reason and the Hermeneutical Circle

The Bible not only provides information about God, but it is absolute truth and repeatedly emphasizes the "truth" nature of its revelation over against all competing claims. In Psalm 25:5, David wrote: "Lead me in thy *truth*, and teach me: for thou *art* the God of my salvation; on thee do I wait all the day." And again in the tenth verse of the same Psalm: "All the paths of the LORD are mercy and *truth* unto such as keep his covenant and his testimonies." Our God is called the "LORD God of *truth*" in Psalm 31:5. And in Psalm 33:4, we read, "all his works are done in *truth*." God is said in Psalm 51:6 to "desire *truth* in the inward parts" of man. Moreover, God's "law is the *truth*" (Psalm 119:142), God's "commandments are *truth*" (Psalm 119:151), and "his *truth* endureth to all generations." (Psalm 100:5) Paul would write in his letter to Timothy that God "will have all men to be saved, and to come unto the knowledge of the *truth*." (1 Timothy 2:4) Paul described certain corrupt men as being "destitute of the *truth*." (1 Timothy 6:5) It is not

---

[6] Lester Hutson, *Basic Bible Truths*, Morris Publishing, p. 13 (1999).

surprising that the Son of God claimed to be "the *truth.*" (John 14:6) And what we know about "the *truth,*" we learn by "rightly dividing the word of *truth.*" (2 Timothy 2:15)

In view of this, the rules of logic and sound deductive reasoning apply to truth claims about God.[7] As I already indicated, I take it as axiomatic that in the Bible God intended to communicate with clarity. God intended that we be able to understand that which He communicated about Himself, and that means that He intended that we be able to determine the truth as He revealed it. This does not mean that God has answered all of our questions in the Bible or that we can fully comprehend God or even that we will not grapple with certain passages, but it does mean that where He has spoken, He has not done so in logically irreconcilable contradictions.

Sound deductive reasoning is particularly important when we talk about the *inferences* we draw from the Bible that are not explicitly stated. Let me clarify about the distinction I am

---

[7] I have had it suggested to me that we cannot expect the truths of the Bible to always be logically consistent because, for example, the virgin birth defies logic. It would be more accurate to say that the virgin birth defies any naturalistic explanation. Only if we approach the virgin birth from a purely naturalistic worldview can we say that it defies logic. As evangelicals, of course, our worldview is not purely naturalistic and we see God moving in supernatural ways throughout human history as recorded in the Bible, and of course, the Scripture confirms a supernatural explanation of the Holy Spirit's role in the virgin birth. That the Bible's recorded miracles are supernaturally explained does not mean we are free to systematize our theology contrary to clear passages of Scripture and chalk away the contradictions to our inability to comprehend an infinite God. Obviously, we cannot fully comprehend God, but if we hold that God has revealed Himself in the Scriptures with clarity we cannot turn logic on its head simply because that is the only way to protect our theological commitments. Moreover, the example of miracles in the Bible like the virgin birth argues against tossing out logic to nurse our theological commitments. That God has revealed the miracles in such a way that we can understand them as miracles bolsters the point that God has spoken with clarity in the Bible.

making here. Many truths are Scripturally explicit. For instance, we do not merely infer that God is love; we have explicit statements in 1 John 4:8, 16 that "God is love." On the other hand, many *infer* (including me) that certain Old Testament references to the "angel of the Lord" are, in fact, references to the pre-incarnate Christ, but we do not have an *explicit* passage that says something like "the angel of the Lord is Jesus." (e.g., Zechariah 1:12) When we make these inferences, our footing relies upon the validity and soundness of our deductive reasoning.[8] Something I intend to demonstrate in this book is that Calvinism is completely inferential.

When it comes to systematizing theology, we are not only tasked with scrutinizing our deductive reasoning, but we must test our inferences against the balance of Scripture. As the authors of the hermeneutics classic, *Living By the Book*, explain: "By comparison we compare Scripture with Scripture. And that offers a great safety net, because the greatest interpreter of Scripture is Scripture itself... Remember,

---

[8] When we take what the Bible says and attempt to systematize certain truths, we are primarily engaged in deductive reasoning, that is, taking the premises we find in the Bible and deducing the conclusions that must necessarily follow. In order to be sound, a deductive argument must contain these elements: 1) The argument is formally valid, that is, it follows from the premises in accord with the rules of logic; 2) The argument is informally valid, that is, it avoids fallacies such as circular reasoning; and 3) The premises must be true. See J. P. Moreland & William Lane Craig, *Philosophical Foundations for a Christian Worldview*, IVP Academic, pp. 29-30 (2003). The cited text contains a fourth element that is not relevant here. As we consider the truth claims of Calvinism in the chapters that follow, it is appropriate that we consider whether their premises are true, whether their deductions follow from these premises in accord with the rules of logic, and whether they have used fallacious reasoning. God communicated His Word with an audience in mind, an audience that would apply basic deductive reasoning to His truth claims as well as the competing truth claims from other sources. If God did not intend the basic rules of deductive reasoning to apply, then He would not have so emphasized the "truth" nature of His revelation and appealed to His audience to know the truth and live by it.

although we have about forty different human authors, the sixty-six books are ultimately the result of one primary Author, the Holy Spirit, who coordinated the entire message. His Book is integrated. It hangs together."[9] Invalid and unsound deductive arguments typically result in a truth claim that contradicts a clear passage of Scripture. When we find that our inferences have led us to a logical contradiction within the Bible, then we are compelled to set aside our thinking and accept the witness of the Bible. To maintain as true a theological system that irreconcilably contradicts any verse of Scripture calls into question (1) the inerrancy of the Bible because now the Bible contradicts itself and (2) the clarity of the Bible because the rules of logic must be abandoned in order to "comprehend" the truths taught in the Bible. And we cannot gloss over such contradictions by simply calling them a "tension" or "two horns of a dilemma" and citing the incomprehensibility of God since we are talking about a Bible that God says is comprehensible. While it is certainly the case that we cannot expect to fully comprehend God (or even come close), we can and should seek to understand what God has intentionally revealed about Himself in His Word. And if our theology leads us to conclude that the Bible contains logically irreconcilable contradictions, we need to re-examine our theology and not play games with His Word.

In his soteriology treatise, David Anderson articulates how our systematic theology must be consistent with our Biblical theology in what he calls the *hermeneutical circle*:

> It is very important in our study of "salvation" to use our biblical theology to undergird our systematic theology. If we do not, we will be guilty of imposing our theological views upon the text or letting our systematic theology

---

9 Howard G. Hendricks and William D. Hendricks, *Living by the Book*, Moody Publishers, p. 237 (2007).

override our biblical theology. In good exegesis, the parts must add up to the whole, and then the whole will help us understand the parts (this is called the hermeneutical circle). But if one part is out of sync with the whole, then our understanding of the whole is faulty. We must be ever ready to adjust our understanding of the whole to correspond and complement our understanding of the parts, not vice-versa.[10]

Deductive reasoning should undergird our attempts to systematize theology, but we must always check ourselves against the hermeneutical circle. Jesus admonished those who tested him on issues like divorce or plucking an ear of corn on the Sabbath to consider whether their theological position comported logically with other Scriptures. Jesus would say, "have ye not read...." Jesus affirmed that what was written in the Old Testament was comprehensible and that their truth claims should be tested against it for logical consistency. I intend to demonstrate in this book that Calvinism sweeps aside valid, sound deductive reasoning to prop up a theological system that does not correspond and complement our understanding of the parts.

You Are What You Think

You might already be asking yourself, "Does it really matter?" That is an appropriate question because sometimes Christians dispute about doctrinal matters disproportionately to their relative importance. Some debate whether Jesus died on a Wednesday or a Friday, and I would contend that while this is an interesting issue for discussion, this is not a hill to die on and certainly not one over which to break fellowship. After all,

---

[10] David R. Anderson, *Free Grace Soteriology*, Xulon Press, p. 17 (2010).

we have widespread agreement the tomb is empty because our Lord resurrected early Sunday morning, and that unquestionably is more important. While everything the Bible teaches is important, some doctrines are addressed in great detail, while other issues are barely mentioned, or not mentioned at all, but merely surmised or inferred from what is said. What we believe about certain teachings in the Bible will directly impact how we live, but whether I believe Jesus was crucified on a Wednesday or Friday will not. The short answer as to Calvinism is that it matters a great deal. To see that is the case, I want to briefly introduce the concept of a worldview.

We read in the Proverbs: "Keep thy heart with all diligence; for out of it *are* the issues of life." (Proverbs 4:23) And again we read: "For as he thinketh in his heart, so *is* he...." (Proverbs 23:7) Our heart is that part of our immaterial person that is the seat of our thinking. The Bible sometimes uses the word "mind," but this is not to be confused with the physical organ we call the brain. What the Bible tells us is that we are what we think. That is no doubt why Paul exhorts us to "be ye transformed by the renewing of your mind." (Romans 12:2) A mind renewed on the Word should bring about a transformed life. Jesus explained that the heart is the ultimate source of the behaviors that defile us:

> Matthew 15:11 Not that which goeth into the mouth defileth a man; but that which cometh out of the mouth, this defileth a man. 16 And Jesus said, Are ye also yet without understanding? 17 Do not ye yet understand, that whatsoever entereth in at the mouth goeth into the belly, and is cast out into the draught? 18 But those things which proceed out of the mouth come forth from the heart; and they defile the man. 19 For out of the heart proceed evil thoughts, murders, adulteries,

fornications, thefts, false witness, blasphemies:
20 These are *the things* which defile a man: but
to eat with unwashen hands defileth not a man.

Conventional wisdom says you are what you eat, but Jesus' teaching is that **you are what you think**. And that being the case, it is an aid to understanding these issues to consider the term "worldview." In some circles, this term is frowned upon because it suggests having a view about everything in the world, but that is not what is intended here. Dr. G. Harry Leafe defined a worldview as "an orderly and related set of beliefs that form the basis of evaluating and integrating into our thinking what we come to believe and by which we consciously or subconsciously interpret and judge reality." Critically, while few people speak of it in these terms, everyone—Christian and non-Christian—has a worldview. Our worldviews are formed and shaped by ideas that we receive from various sources, including parents, cultural traditions, education, experience, and supposition.

Even the false things we believe affect what we do. Perception is just as influential as reality even though they may be very different. I toured an underground cavern once and came to a long passage that was completely dark and had a lowered ceiling so that I had to crouch down as I walked. After walking about 40 or so feet, believing I had cleared the portion with the lowered ceiling, I stood up. My worldview and reality quickly collided with the result of a sore noggin. I acted on the basis of a belief contrary to reality, much to my chagrin. So good and bad thinking both affect our behavior. That is why Paul warned about spiritual warfare for the Christian, which primarily takes place in the heart: "(For the weapons of our warfare *are* not carnal, but mighty through God to the pulling down of strong holds;) Casting down imaginations, and every high thing that exalteth itself against the knowledge of God, and bringing into captivity every thought to the obedience of Christ." (2 Corinthians 10:4-5) It matters what we believe.

Moreover, differences in worldviews can bring about conflict. No doubt that is why you have probably heard you should avoid talking about religion and politics. Certain areas of discussion tend to bring out our differences that other areas of discussion do not. Our tendency is to keep our relationships within the overlap of our worldviews, and when we are uncertain, we keep our dialogue shallow. Think of that person you see at church regularly but beyond some casual conversation when you see them on Sunday mornings, you have no further or deeper relationship to him or her. You play it safe, speaking of things you share in common such as views on the weather, last night's game, or how each other's children are doing in school. But if you were to stray from those things and ask probing questions, such as questions about origins, purpose, and eschatology, you may quickly find out that you are not on the same page as the other person. And the question is, why are you and the other person not on the same page? You go to the same church and outwardly have much in common, but you have different worldviews. There is a place of overlap, but also places of significant disjunction. This is why two reasonable and intelligent people can examine all of the same data and evidence and come out with different opinions on an issue. One may scratch his head befuddled at how anyone can see the issue differently based on the evidence, but the issue is not the evidence. It is a difference in worldviews.

Some of the chief components of our worldview are what we believe about God, reality, knowledge, ethics, mankind, and our personal preferences. It is beyond our present need to develop these categories except to recognize how critical what we believe about God (including a belief there is no God) is to our overall worldview. Is God a personal being? Does He have similar frailties and vices as humans? Does He know all things? Is He dynamically involved in my life? Does He care? There is obviously a tremendous difference between a God involved in our lives and the deistic view of a grand watchmaker that wound up the world and abandoned it. There is a difference between a God that loves all people and a God that loves only some people. If we have a deistic view of God, then we have no basis for prayer because we would be praying to a God that for all practical purposes abandoned us. But if God is dynamically involved in our lives, we have reason to petition God to move in our lives. If we view God as the ancients viewed their "gods" with a little "g" then we have little reason to ascribe to moral norms since the gods themselves were fraught with moral failures. But if God is holy, then He has a right to demand our holiness. Obviously, our views of God materially shape our worldview.

As Christians, we should seek to form Biblical worldviews—that is, worldviews where we interpret and judge reality on the basis of what the Bible says. We should be about the business of jettisoning much of the thinking that goes with the old man that we had before we trusted Christ, and replacing that with the thinking that goes with the new man, which thinking is God's thinking as revealed in the Bible. Indeed, Paul exhorted the Corinthians to develop worldviews with unity of purpose as to their church and its mission: "Now I beseech you, brethren, by the name of our Lord Jesus Christ, that ye all speak the same thing, and *that* there be no divisions among you; but *that* ye be perfectly joined together in the same mind and in the same judgment." (1 Corinthians 1:10) Similarly, Peter said to "arm yourselves likewise with the same mind" as Jesus. (1 Peter 4:1)

In forming a Biblical worldview, understanding God's redemptive plan for humanity is central. Were there no possibility of reconciliation with God presented in the Bible, it is doubtful any would read it, much less use it as a cornerstone of their worldview. But in fact, the Bible says a great deal about God's redemptive plan. The content of what the Bible says on this matter speaks volumes on the attributes and heart of God as well as mankind. Calvinism completely compasses God's redemptive plan and teaches that God saves a small percentage of humanity based on His elective determination before creation and passes over the rest. Since God's redemptive plan excludes most people, there is no basis for us to tell a lost person that God loves them, that Jesus died for them, that they should believe in Christ for salvation, or that there is hope beyond the grave. If the lost person is not elect, we would be misleading them if we said any of those things. Indeed, it is difficult to see how we could make any honest gospel presentation knowing most people are by God's purposes not savable. Not only that, since salvation hangs on God's elective determination before creation and not on a present decision for Christ, we must make this TULIP reality personal. We must come to grips with the fact that many of those we know, and perhaps some of those closest to us, have no possibility of being reconciled to God because they are not elect.

So again, we ask the question, "Does it really matter?" Yes, it indisputably does. Virtually every part of the Bible is affected by the nature of God's redemptive plan for humanity. That is the one lever in the Bible that the slightest movement greatly affects. And that in turn shifts our overall worldview since our view of God is the cornerstone of our worldview. You are what you think.

Chapter 2

Seeing the Big Picture

"Don't lose sight of the forest for the trees." This is the old adage that we can get so down in the weeds of an analysis that we lose sight of the big picture. Our goal in this book is take a deep dive on the principles of Calvinism, and then an exacting look at the proof texts for each of the five core principles. And so we need to start with a view of the big picture. We need to be able to re-calibrate our mental gauges, after we hone in on certain nuances and minutia, back to what the Calvinism big picture is. And from there we must back out to the even larger Biblical big picture. Calvinism is not just about election or depravity. It is a system of intertwined principles set within the larger context of the other truths of Scripture. Accordingly, before we dive into the proof texts for the five central principles, we will first get a big picture snapshot of Calvinism. I will also introduce the notion of the decrees of

God, a doctrine that is related to Calvinism and will serve to further enlarge our big picture view of Calvinism. Once we have the forest in view, we will be able to more effectively study the trees.

Five Tulip Principles

Often the five traditional core principles of Calvinism are referred to with the acronym, TULIP. Some Calvinists take issue with the use of TULIP, but the terminology is so popular that most people embrace it, at least for discussion purposes. The "T" stands for *total depravity*, the "U" for *unconditional election*, the "L" for *limited atonement*, the "I" for *irresistible grace*, and the "P" for *perseverance of the saints*. Our analysis of whether the Calvinist teachings are Biblically sound can only be as good as the definitions we begin with. In this introductory chapter, we will only quote representative examples from Calvinists as to what they mean by the use of these phrases. The purpose at this point is only to introduce the principles. In the subsequent chapters, we shall quote additional Calvinist sources and consider their primary proof texts, and ultimately, whether the principles are Biblically supported.

Total Depravity

Of *total depravity*, the Westminster Confession of Faith states as follows: "Man, by his fall into a state of sin, hath wholly lost all ability of will to any spiritual good accompanying salvation: so as, a natural man, being altogether averse from that good, and dead in sin, is not able, by his own strength, to convert himself, or to prepare himself thereunto."[11] One modern Calvinist text explains what is meant by total depravity:

---

[11] Chap. IX, sect. 3.

When Calvinists speak of man as being totally depraved, they mean that man's nature is corrupt, perverse, and sinful throughout. The adjective "total" does not mean that each sinner is as totally or completely corrupt in his actions and thoughts as it is possible for him to be. Instead, the word "total" is used to indicate that the *whole* of man's being has been affected by sin. The corruption extends to *every part* of man, his body and soul; sin has affected all (the totality) of man's faculties—his mind, his will, etc.

As a result of this inborn corruption, the natural man is totally unable to do anything spiritually good; thus, Calvinists speak of man's "total inability." The inability intended by this terminology is *spiritual inability;* it means that the sinner is so spiritually bankrupt that *he can do nothing pertaining to his salvation.*[12]

This means that a lost person is not capable, in and of himself, of placing faith in Jesus Christ, which is further clarified by the statement below:

Man is *totally depraved* in the sense that everything about his nature is in rebellion against God. Man is loyal to the god of darkness and loves darkness rather than The Light. His will is, therefore, not at all "free." It is bound by the flesh to the prince of darkness grim. *Total depravity* means that man, of his own "free will," will never make a decision for Christ.[13]

---

[12] *Supra* note 3, pp. 18-19.
[13] Duane Edward Spencer, *TULIP*, Baker Books, p. 34 (2d ed. 2007).

Indeed, we will see later that Calvinists teach that an unsaved man is incapable of doing anything pleasing to God, cannot understand anything about God, and cannot receive the gift of salvation apart from God first changing him (through regeneration) and gifting him with faith. Even non-Calvinists see God as the initiator of salvation; man cannot save himself, but is able to respond to the light of truth and the conviction of the Holy Spirit. The Calvinist speaks of inability, meaning a total lack of capacity to believe the truth. That is a significant difference.

Another term used in connection with the human condition of *total depravity* is *reprobation*; a person that is totally depraved could also be called *reprobate* if that person is not predetermined by God to be saved. "Reprobation is the sovereign decision of God before creation to pass over some persons, in sorrow deciding not to save them, and to punish them for their sins, and thereby manifest his justice."[14] This last definition relates *total depravity* to *unconditional election*, and will be clarified as we consider the latter concept. In summary, that a lost man is *totally depraved* means that his spiritual condition is such that he lacks the capacity to believe the gospel until God first enables him to believe and give him faith. This raises several questions about TULIP such as how and when God enables a person to believe, and whether God does so for all people, or only a sub-part of humanity, and if only for a sub-part of humanity, then why.

Unconditional Election

The "U" in TULIP stands for *unconditional election*. Grudem explains: "Election is an act of God before creation in which he chooses some people to be saved, not on account of any foreseen merit in them, but only because of his sovereign good

---

[14] Wayne Grudem, *Systematic Theology*, p. 685, Inter-Varsity Press (1994).

pleasure."[15] "The doctrine of election declares that God, before the foundation of the world, chose certain individuals from among the fallen members of Adam's race to be the objections of His undeserved favor. These, and these only, He purposed to save."[16] Similarly, the Baptist Confession of Faith of 1689 states: "Those of mankind who are *predestinated* unto Life, God, before the foundation of the world was laid, according to his eternal and *immutable Purpose*, and the secret *counsel* and good pleasure of *His will*, hath *chosen* in Christ to everlasting glory, out of His mere free grace and love, without any other thing in the creature as a *condition* or cause moving Him thereunto." Because of their *total depravity*, men need to be regenerated in order to believe, and God has unconditionally elected those He will regenerate:

> Election is grounded entirely in the free will of God and in His purpose for those whom He chose "in Christ Jesus" before the foundation of the world. His fore-knowledge is based upon His purpose, for His purpose is the manifestation of His sovereign will. Since man is incapable of giving himself life, opening his own eyes, or teaching himself spiritual truth, God must elect to act on a man's behalf. The work of regeneration, therefore, must precede faith and repentance and is the work of God. He must "open the heart" and cause His elect "to will and do" that which is pleasing to Him, otherwise none would believe.[17]

As Sproul explains, in the Calvinist system, the related term *predestination* refers to both *unconditional election* and *reprobation* together:

---

[15] *Supra* note 14, p. 670.
[16] *Supra* note 3, p. 27.
[17] *Supra* note 13, appendix on unconditional election.

In summary we may define *predestination* broadly as follows: From all eternity God decided to save some members of the human race and to let the rest of the human race perish. God made a choice—he chose some individuals to be saved unto everlasting blessedness in heaven, and he chose others to pass over, allowing them to suffer the consequences of their sins, eternal punishment in hell.[18]

Thus, traditional Calvinism teaches that all men are in a fallen condition such that they are not capable of believing the gospel. However, before creation and for His own purposes and out of His love, God chose some for salvation, enabling them to believe the gospel, and passing over everyone else (i.e., not enabling them, leaving them totally depraved forever). Those God chose for salvation are called the *elect*.

Limited Atonement

The "L" in TULIP stands for *limited atonement* and sometimes goes by other names such as *particular redemption*. By this term, the Calvinists mean that Christ's shed blood on the cross was only for the elect and fully secured their salvation:

Historical or mainline Calvinism has consistently maintained that Christ's redeeming work was definite in *design* and *accomplishment* — that it was intended to render complete satisfaction for certain specified sinners, and that it actually secured salvation for these individuals and no one else. The salvation which Christ earned for His people includes everything involved in bringing

---

[18] R.C. Sproul, *What Is Reformed Theology?*, p. 141, Baker Books (1997).

them into a right relationship with God, including the gifts of faith and repentance. Christ did not die simply to make it possible for God to pardon sinners. Neither does God leave it up to sinners to decide whether or not Christ's work will be effective. On the contrary, all for whom Christ sacrificed Himself will be saved infallibly. Redemption, therefore, was designed to bring to pass God's purpose of election.[19]

Similarly, Spencer summarizes this doctrine, distinguishing between the *efficiency* and *sufficiency* of the death Christ died:

Atonement is for the elect only, since Christ died only for those whom the Father gave Him to be His Bride. Only the saints or elect ones are ever said to be "beloved of God," for they alone are the objects of His saving grace. The Calvinist reasons that if Christ died for all, then all will be saved. If only the elect are to be saved, then Christ died for them, and them alone. Although it is true that the blood of Christ is surely *sufficient* in value to atone for all, still it is obviously *efficient* only for those who are saved by His unmerited favor.[20]

Putting together what we have seen so far from the Calvinists' point of view, apart from God, mankind is totally depraved, unable to do any spiritual good, including trusting Jesus. To remedy this, before the foundation of the world, certain individuals (i.e., the elect) were chosen by God to be enabled to believe, and for these and only these persons, Jesus died on the cross.

---

[19] *Supra* note 3, pp. 39-40.
[20] *Supra* note 13, appendix on limited atonement.

We should note that it is quite common for people to identify themselves as Calvinists but not hold to *limited atonement*. Such individuals are often referred to as *four point Calvinists*—they hold to TUIP, not TULIP, although anyone who only believes three or four points of TULIP Calvinism could be referred to as a three point Calvinist or four point Calvinist, as the case may be. In his book on limited atonement, four point Calvinist Robert Lightner explains the practical importance of this doctrine on our personal evangelism and whether we can preach with integrity to people that Christ died for their sins:

> This subject is of paramount importance to the ambassador for Christ. Unless Christ died for all men, the message of God's love and Christ's death must be given with tongue in cheek and with some reservation, because some may hear who are really not to be numbered among those whom God loved and for whom Christ died. Consistency and honesty would demand that the one who believes in limited atonement refrain from proclaiming God's universal offer of the good news of God's love and grace in Christ to all men indiscriminately, since in that view God did not extend grace to all nor did Christ die for all. Therefore, to tell all men that these things are true and that salvation is available for them is to speak that which is not true if the limited view be accepted.[21]

Obviously, Calvinism raises all kinds of practical and relevant questions that should not be casually ignored.

In fairness, I would further point out that, notwithstanding the quote above, many Calvinists holding to *limited atonement*

---

[21] Robert P. Lightner, *The Death Christ Died: A Biblical Case for Unlimited Atonement*, pp. 14-15, Kregel Publications (1998).

do evangelize, although it can also be said that some do not. Non-Calvinists often raise the question in response to Calvinism, "Why evangelize?" The question is a good one. Most Calvinists would say that they evangelize because God commands them to, and it is not their place to be concerned with who in their audience is elect or not. At the other extreme, some Calvinists, often referred as hyper-Calvinists, refuse to evangelize, participate in missions, or in extreme cases, even invite people to church. Obviously, it makes a difference what you believe.

Irresistible Grace

The fourth tenet of TULIP Calvinism, represented by the "I," is *irresistible grace*. Grudem defines *regeneration* as "a secret act of God in which he imparts new spiritual life to us. This is sometimes called 'being born again' (using language from John 3:3-8)."[22] In turn, the regenerated or born again person will be irresistibly drawn to God:

> Since it is the will of God that those whom He gave to His dear Son in eternity past should be saved, He will surely act in sovereign grace in such a way that the elect will find Christ irresistible. God does not *force* the elect to trust in His Son but rather gives them life. The *dead* human spirit finds the dead spirit of Satan irresistible, and all *living* human spirits find the God of the living irresistible. Regeneration (the work of God) must precede true repentance and faith.[23]

---

[22] *Supra* note 14, p. 699. Of course, not everyone would agree with this definition of *regeneration* or being *born again*.

[23] *Supra* note 13, appendix on irresistible grace.

Thus, for God's elect, there is a point in time when He regenerates them so that they are enabled to believe and are irresistibly drawn to Christ. By this means, God overcomes their total depravity for them in order to fulfill His purpose that they would be saved; God issues an inward call so that they can and will respond to the outward call, the gospel:

> The *gospel invitation extends a call* to salvation
> to every one who hears its message. It invites
> all men without distinction to drink freely of
> the water of life and live. It promises salvation
> to all who repent and believe. But this outward
> general call, extended to the elect and nonelect
> alike, will not bring sinners to Christ. Why?
> Because men are by nature dead in sin and are
> under its power. They are of themselves unable
> and unwilling to forsake their evil ways and to
> turn to Christ for mercy. Consequently, the
> unregenerate will not respond to the gospel call
> to repentance and faith. No amount of
> external threatenings or promises will cause
> blind, deaf, dead, rebellious sinners to bow
> before Christ as Lord and to look to Him alone
> for salvation. Such an act of faith and
> submission is contrary to the lost man's
> nature.[24]

Because the sinner is totally helpless to contribute anything to his salvation, God must do it all. God the Holy Spirit enables faith by changing a person's heart condition before salvation and the changed sinner will believe the gospel:

> Therefore, the *Holy Spirit*, in order to bring
> God's elect to salvation, extends to them *a
> special inward call* in addition to the outward
> call contained in the gospel message. Through

---

[24] *Supra* note 3, pp. 52-53.

this special call, the Holy Spirit performs a work of grace within the sinner, which inevitably brings him to faith in Christ. The inward change wrought in the elect sinner enables him to understand and believe spiritual truth; in the spiritual realm, he is given the seeing eye and the hearing ear. The Spirit creates within him a new heart or a new nature. This is accomplished through regeneration or the new birth by which the sinner is made a child of God and is given spiritual life. His will is renewed through this process, so that the sinner spontaneously comes to Christ of his own free choice. Because he is given a new nature so that he loves righteousness, and because his mind is enlightened so that he understands and believes the biblical gospel, the renewed sinner freely and willingly turns to Christ as Lord and Savior. Thus, the once dead sinner is drawn to Christ by the inward, supernatural call of the Spirit, who through regeneration makes him alive and creates faith and repentance within him.[25]

Because this special "inward call of the Spirit never fails to result in the conversion of those to whom it is made" it is often referred to by Calvinists as being "efficacious," "invincible," or "irresistible."[26]

Perseverance of the Saints

Finally, the "P" in TULIP stands for the *perseverance of the saints*, typically seen as a natural conclusion of the other four principles:

---

[25] *Id.*
[26] *Id.*

The logical conclusion of Calvinism is that since "salvation is of the Lord" and absolutely no part of it is dependent upon any *condition* found in the elect, but is wholly dependent upon the God who has *willed to save those whom He gave to His dear Son*, salvation can never be lost. The saints of God will surely persevere because He has given them His promise that no creature can take them away from Him (including themselves). We shall persevere because He wills to persevere![27]

Similarly, Grudem defines *perseverance*: "The perseverance of the saints means that all those who are truly born again will be kept by God's power and will persevere as Christians until the end of their lives, and that only those who persevere until the end have been truly born again."[28] While some Calvinists simply define this doctrine in terms of eternal security, for others the doctrine means much more, namely a life of fruitfulness and works consistent with one's position in Christ. Sproul says it is eternal security but his explanation reveals there is more to it than that since the believer cannot experience a "final apostasy":

A simple way to remember the essence of the doctrine of perseverance is to learn this ditty: "If we have it, we never lose it. If we lose it, we never had it." This is a "cute" way of affirming that full and final apostasy is never the lot of the Christian. Another shorthand expression of this doctrine is the aphorism "Once saved, always saved." This is sometimes called eternal security, since it calls attention to the enduring power of the salvation wrought for us and in us by the work of Christ.[29]

---

[27] *Supra* note 13, appendix on perseverance of the saints.
[28] *Supra* note 14, p. 788.
[29] *Supra* note 18, pp. 197-198.

The proof of whether one has stayed in the faith or fallen into a full and final apostasy typically comes down to a life of works vindicating one's position in Christ. Strong explains the doctrine in terms of "well-doing" and "constant activity":

> The Scriptures declare that, in virtue of the original purpose and continuous operation of God, all who are united to Christ by faith will infallibly continue in a state of grace and will finally attain to everlasting life. This voluntary continuance, on the part of the Christian, in faith and welldoing we call perseverance. Perseverance is, therefore, the human side or aspect of that spiritual process which, as viewed from the divine side, we call sanctification. It is not a mere natural consequence of conversion, but involves a constant activity of the human will from the moment of conversion to the end of life.[30]

Accordingly, the perceived absence of works or presence of continued sin might call a person's salvation into question. To be absolutely clear, this author is in full agreement with eternal security, but for many Calvinists the doctrine of perseverance of the saints goes beyond eternal security and encompasses what often goes under the phrase *lordship salvation.*

Eternal Decrees of God

In the pages that follow, I will devote a chapter to each of the foregoing TULIP principles, expanding the discussion of how Calvinists define these principles and inquiring whether their proof texts actually support the principles. In addition, we will also consider the doctrine often referred to as the *eternal decrees of God.* Spencer summarizes the doctrine this way:

---

[30] Augustus H. Strong, *Systematic Theology*, Judson Press, p. 881.

"Therefore, whatever comes to pass in any part of creation, at any time in history, does so because the omniscient God knew it as a possibility, willed it as a reality by His omnipotence, and established it in His divine plan or purpose."[31] Simply put, God predetermined every event without exception, including every person's thoughts, words, and actions. Obviously, if this is true, then our eternal destinies were determined before time began. For this reason, and because many Calvinist writers reference or rely upon the *eternal decrees of God*, we will explore what Reformed theologians call the *eternal decrees of God* and whether the doctrine is Biblically supported before moving on to addressing TULIP.

A Caution As We Proceed

Systematic Theology is an attempt to determine and articulate what the entire Bible says about various theological issues. The five core principles of Calvinism overviewed in this chapter present systematic statements that purport to articulate the collective teaching of the entire Bible on those issues. Unquestionably, there is value in studying Systematic Theology, but there is also a danger. Dave Anderson explains the tension between Systematic Theology and Biblical Theology:

> It is important when one begins a study in Systematic Theology to understand the tension with Biblical Theology. Whereas the latter takes a specific book and tries to determine the theology taught in that book, the former tries to take in to account the entire teaching God's Word on a particular doctrine. We might call Biblical Theology the "worm's view" and Systematic Theology the "bird's view." Of course, it should be intuitively obvious that a

---

[31] *Supra* note 13, p. 22.

proper system cannot be constructed without an accurate understanding of the theology of each book of the Bible as it stands on its own. The problem lies in the fact that no one person lives long enough to master the theology of each book of the Bible. Hence, systems of theology are developed before all the homework has been done. Each system seems to have some holes in it somewhere. That may sound discouraging or disillusioning to the beginning student, but from another point of view, the statement is encouraging. If mankind could completely systematize theology, that would be another way of saying that mankind can put God in a box, that the finite can fathom the infinite, that the ways of God are not mysterious after all.[32]

The danger is developing a Systematic Theology on soteriology (study of salvation) and becoming committed to it before mastering the books from which your Systematic Theology grounds its support. Students of seminaries and Bible Colleges frequently do exactly this because they are taught Systematic Theology at the same time or before courses in Biblical Theology, and even then, the Biblical Theology courses only overview the books of the Bible rather than taking deep dives. We would be on much more solid ground if we took a deep dive through several books of the Bible before becoming committed to a particular Systematic Theology, and that takes years of study. If we commit to our Systematic Theology first, then we face a great danger when we finally do take a deep dive in a book (maybe Romans) that we will only find what we decided a priori would be there. To do otherwise is to challenge or undermine the system we committed to, perhaps years earlier.

---

[32] David R. Anderson, *Free Grace Soteriology, Third Edition* (Grace Theology Press 2018), 351.

It is difficult to overstate the negative effects this approach has had on the issues studied in this book. It is very easy for a commitment to TULIP to become the interpretive grid for studying the Bible rather than a system that derives from studying the Bible. Once TULIP is the interpretive grid, the system becomes the willful bias I warned about in the first chapter and one's further study of the Bible is an exercise in circular reasoning since the grid guarantees a TULIP result.

As we proceed in this study, we will be putting on our Biblical Theology hats. We will take up the TULIP proof texts one-by-one and emphasis will be placed on the meanings of key words and the context of those proof texts. What do the key words in the verse mean? Why would Paul at this place in this book begin talking about TULIP? How does the proffered TULIP interpretation fit the immediate context and overall argument of the book? These are Biblical Theology questions and probing these types of questions will reveal that the proof texts provide no evidence to place on the scales.

Chapter 3

The Decrees of God

As a young man, I read an excellent book and I have never forgotten the words with which the book opens. At the beginning of Ray Bradbury's *Fahrenheit 451,* he quotes the famous Spanish poet Juan Ramon Jiminez: "If they give you ruled paper, write the other way." These words speak freedom. The book unfolds the story of Guy Montag, a fireman in a future where firemen do not put out fires, but start them, to burn books and, ultimately, to censor and control society. The story is powerful because we place such a high value on personal liberty, the ability to write outside the lines if we choose. Indeed, the pre-amble to our nation's Constitution states that liberty is a blessing: "We the People of the United States, in Order to form a more perfect Union, establish Justice, insure domestic Tranquility, provide for the common defence, promote the general Welfare, and secure the Blessings of Liberty to ourselves and our Posterity, do ordain and establish this Constitution for the United States of America."

Many people believe that God decreed everything that comes to pass, and indeed, they find it repugnant that it could be any other way: "A universe without decrees would be as irrational and appalling as would be an express train driving on in the darkness without headlight or engineer, and with no certainty that the next moment it might not plunge into the abyss."[33] This doctrine, if it is Biblical, raises the important question of what freedom, if any, we really have? *Webster's Third International Dictionary* defines freedom as "the quality or state of not being coerced or constrained by fate, necessity, or circumstances in one's choices or actions." This doctrine's proponents argue that freedom is maintained, so long as it is properly defined. We will look at that below, but you should consider at this point how you would articulate the meaning of freedom. As I indicated in the first chapter, how we define the words we use matters a great deal. I prefer another definition offered by *Webster's Third International Dictionary*: "the absence of antecedent causal determination of human decisions." But if God scripted the universe in every detail, then I certainly do not enjoy "the absence of antecedent causal determination" of my decisions. Whatever freedom I might be said to enjoy is necessarily circumscribed by God's decree of everything.

The Bible never promises the sort of freedoms our Constitution promises, but the Bible does speak of freedom or liberty. We are told that Jesus alone offers true freedom: "If the Son therefore shall make you free, ye shall be free indeed." (John 8:36) And again, we have liberty in Christ: "Stand fast therefore in the liberty wherewith Christ hath made us free, and be not entangled again with the yoke of bondage." (Galatians 5:1) Our liberty in Christ is liberty from bondage to sin to serve the living

---

33 Henry Clarence Thiessen, *Introductory Lectures in Systematic Theology*, WM. B. Eerdmans Publishing Company, p. 148 (1949). (quoting from another source quoting A.J. Gordon)

God: "As free, and not using your liberty for a cloke of maliciousness, but as the servants of God." (1 Peter 2:16) We have to ask what our liberty in Christ as believers really means if it all falls under the umbrella of an all-inclusive decree.

What is most peculiar about this profound truth claim is that God could so easily have explicitly stated that He predetermined everything, but no statement like that is found in the Bible. So where does it come from? More than anything, this concept is a philosophical conclusion about the sovereignty of God, and so you should consider the following question: What do we mean when we say God is sovereign? For those who hold to the doctrine that God predetermined everything without exception, God would not be sovereign if He had left out even one event from His decree of all things. They insist that only their viewpoint properly honors God as sovereign and that other views lessen God and elevate man. I would argue that we can reject the view that God decreed everything as unbiblical while maintaining that God is sovereign. Obviously, sovereign means different things to different people, just like freedom does. Again, how we define the words we use to talk about God matters. Our goal should be to determine whether the doctrine that God decreed everything is Biblical, i.e., whether it is taught explicitly or at least flows necessarily from what the Bible says. The only view that lessens God is the view that is not found in His special revelation to us in the Holy Scriptures.

To avoid any confusion at the outset, the view that God predetermined everything is not formally a part of TULIP Calvinism. Although it is a common view among Calvinists, it is more generally a part of Reformed theology. Obviously, if God predetermined everything, then He necessarily predetermined those He would save, and so we have good reason in our study of TULIP Calvinism to first inquire whether the Bible teaches the doctrine of the decrees of God. We will begin with an examination of the definition of the decrees of God.

How Reformed Theologians Define the Decrees

Louis Berkhof, a leading Reformed theologian of the 20th century, defines the decrees (or decree) in this way: "The decree of God is His eternal plan or purpose, in which He has foreordained all things that come to pass."[34] He continues by explaining that there is only one decree but because it covers many particulars, it is often spoken of in the plural, that is, as the decrees of God. It should not be surprising that this doctrine does not sit well with many believers. Culver harshly criticizes those that will not accept it: "Nothing in the scheme of Christian doctrine is so offensive to the secular spirit or so preposterous to the unbelieving mind as to propose that God has a plan for the whole universe down to such minute details as the hairs on one's head or the death of a sparrow (Matthew 10:29, 30) and is unfailingly executing the same."[35] Whatever one's reaction to the eternal decrees of God, the real issue is whether it is Biblical. And of course, if the decrees of God as Berkhof defined them are Biblical, then Berkhof or Culver or others should be able to point us to the passages that teach the doctrine and make quick work of the matter.

Lest anyone think Berkhof's view is singular among Reformed theologians, the definitions of others are quoted below, all sharing in common the conviction that God predetermines everything without exception:

> The decrees of God are His eternal purpose according to the counsel of His will, whereby, for His own glory, He hath foreordained whatsoever comes to pass.[36] (Dabney)

---

[34] Louis Berkhof, *Manual of Christian Doctrine*, Wm. B. Eeerdmans Publishing Company, p. 84 (1933).

[35] Robert Duncan Culver, *Systematic Theology*, Christian Focus Publications, Ltd., p. 122 (2006).

[36] R.L. Dabney, *Syllabus and Notes of the Course of Systematic and Polemic Theology*, The Banner of Truth Trust, p. 211 (2002).

By the decrees of God we mean that eternal plan by which God has rendered certain all the events of the universe, past, present, and future.[37] (Strong; also adopted by Culver[38])

The decree of God is his eternal, unchangeable, holy, wise, and sovereign purpose, comprehending at once all things that ever were or will be in their causes, conditions, successions, and relations, and determining their certain futurition.[39] (Hodge)

The decrees of God are *the eternal plans of God whereby, before the creation of the world, he determined to bring about everything that happens.*[40] (Grudem)

We may define the plan of God as his eternal decision rendering certain all things which shall come to pass.[41] (Erickson)

Commenting on the expansive scope of the decrees of God, Gordon Clark summarizes: "The material above shows clearly that God plans, decrees, and controls all events."[42] Spencer likewise makes clear that God's decrees go to everything without exception: "...whatever comes to pass in the history of mankind does so by virtue of the fact that it suited the eternal plan or purpose of God... Therefore, whatever comes to pass in any part of creation, at any time in history, does so because the omniscient God knew it as a possibility, willed it as a reality by His omnipotence, and established it in His divine

---

37 *Supra* note 30, p. 353.
38 *Supra* note 35, p. 123.
39 A.A. Hodge, *Outlines of Theology*, The Banner of Truth Trust, p. 200 (1999).
40 *Supra* note 14, p. 332.
41 Millard J. Erickson, *Christian Theology*, Baker Book House, p. 346 (1983).
42 Gordon Haddon Clark, *Predestination*, Lois A. Zeller and Elizabeth Clark George, p. 53 (1987).

plan or purpose."[43] And Erickson states: "The plan of God is all-inclusive."[44] Hodge provides an excellent summary "under several heads the Calvinistic doctrine on this subject":

> 1st. God foreknows all events as certainly future *because* he has decreed them and thus made them certainly future.
>
> 2nd. God's decree relates equally to all future events of every kind, to the free actions of moral agents, as well as to action of necessary agents, to sinful as well as morally right actions.
>
> 3rd. Some things God has eternally decreed to do himself immediately, e.g., creation; other things to bring to pass through the action of second causes acting under a law of necessity, and again other things he has decreed to prompt or to permit free agents to do in the exercise of their free agency; yet the one class of events is rendered by the decree as certainly future as the other.
>
> 4th. God has decreed ends as well as means, causes as well as effects, conditions and instrumentalities as well as the events which depend upon them.
>
> 5th. God's decree determines only the certain futurition of events, it directly effects or causes no event. But the decree itself provides in every case that the event shall be effected by causes acting in a manner perfectly consistent with the nature of the event in question.[45]

---

[43] *Supra* note 13, p. 22.
[44] *Supra* note 41, p. 353.
[45] *Supra* note 39, pp. 202-203.

We can readily see why consideration of this doctrine is so important. If God foreordained everything without exception, then He necessarily selected those who will be saved and spend eternity with Him and accomplished salvation for them. While many Calvinists would say that God did not select the rest of humanity for the lake of fire (so-called double predestination), the necessary implication from God selecting those He would save is that He made a decision not to select everyone. Whether you view it as God selecting the rest for the lake of fire, or merely passing over them as He selected those He would save, the net result for those that spend eternity in the lake of fire is the same. The Bible says God is love and God loves the world, and so this issue of the decrees of God merits our careful consideration. To support their view on God's decrees, Reformed theologians typically appeal to a philosophical argument[46] and then several purported proof texts. I will address the philosophical argument first, and then demonstrate that the Reformed theologians do not have a single verse that provides evidence supporting their doctrine of the decrees of God.

Foreknowledge and Foreordination

To appreciate their philosophical argument, we need to consider the concepts of *foreknowledge* and *foreordination.*[47]

---

[46] Certainly, some writers appeal to other philosophical arguments than the "divine foreknowledge" argument addressed in this text, but the author believes that this is the only one that superficially has some logical appeal. For instance, Hodge makes what he calls arguments from God's divine wisdom, divine immutability and divine benevolence, but in each of these Hodge uses circular reasoning, essentially assuming the existence of the decree of God and then reasoning the nature of the decree from the nature of God. Hodge, pp. 358-59. Consistent with the purpose and goals of this text, this chapter will be limited to the Calvinists' key philosophical argument and primary proof texts.

[47] Both of these are terms the Bible uses, though not often. *Foreknowledge* or a form of it occurs in Acts 2:23, Romans 8:29, 11:2, and 1 Peter 1:2, 20.

In the Reformed system, the words functionally mean the same thing. As we have already seen from their definitions of the decrees of God, the Reformed position is not that God merely foreknows all things, but that He foreordains or predetermines all things. In order to establish that God foreordains all things, they appeal primarily to a philosophical argument equating foreknowledge and foreordination. For Reformed theologians, these ideas are flip sides of the same coin.

Dabney writes, "God's foreknowledge is founded on His foreordination."[48] In other words, God foreknows everything because He first foreordained or decreed it. Hodge provides distinct definitions for these two terms:

> Foreknowledge is an act of the infinite intelligence of God, knowing from all eternity, without change, the certain futurition of all events of every class whatsoever that ever will come to pass.

> Foreordination is an act of the infinitely intelligent, foreknowing, righteous, and benevolent will of God from all eternity *determining* the certain futurition of all events of every class whatsoever that come to pass. Foreknowledge recognizes the certain futurition of events, while foreordination makes them certainly future.[49]

Notwithstanding his definitions, Hodge equates the two: "God foreknows all events as certainly future *because* he has decreed them and thus made them certainly future."[50]

Foreordain or a form of it occurs in Romans 8:29-30 and Ephesians 1:5, 11. The KJV uses "foreordained" in 1 Peter 1:20 but it is the same Greek term translated foreknew in other verses. These verses will be addressed in detail later in this book.

[48] *Supra* note 36, p. 216.
[49] *Supra* note 39, pp. 201-202.
[50] *Supra* note 39, p. 202.

Similarly, Strong also equates the two and does so for the very same reason, namely that God knows everything beforehand because He decreed it to happen: "Only knowledge of that which is decreed is foreknowledge.—Knowledge of a plan as ideal or possible may precede decree; but knowledge of a plan as actual or fixed must follow decree. Only the latter knowledge is properly *fore*knowledge."[51]

Hodge provides a philosophical argument for his view that "foreknowledge is equivalent to foreordination":

> God possessing infinite foreknowledge and power, existed alone from eternity; and in time, self-prompted, began to create in an absolute vacuum. Whatever limiting causes or conditions afterwards exist were first intentionally brought into being by himself, with perfect foreknowledge of their nature, relations, and results. If God then foreseeing that if he created a certain free agent and placed him in certain relations he would freely act in a certain way, and yet with that knowledge proceeded to create that very free agent and put him in precisely those positions, God would, in so doing, obviously predetermine the certain futurition of the act foreseen. God can never in his work be reduced to a choice of evils, because the entire system, and each particular end and cause, and condition, was clearly foreseen and by deliberate choice admitted by himself.[52]

In other words, God exercised complete foreknowledge before creating, and by creating only after contemplation of all He foreknew, God's creative acts predetermined every aspect of

---

[51] *Supra* note 30, p. 357.
[52] *Supra* note 39, p. 203.

the future of that creation. Strong offers essentially the same philosophical argument:

> In eternity there could have been no cause of the future existence of the universe, outside of God himself, since no being existed but God himself. In eternity God foresaw that the creation of the world and the institution of its laws would make certain its actual history even to the most insignificant details. But God decreed to create and to institute these laws. In so decreeing he necessarily decreed all that was to come. In fine, God foresaw the future events of the universe as certain, because he had decreed to create; but this determination to create involved also a determination of all the actual results of that creation; or, in other words, God decreed those results.[53]

Thus, Strong equates God's foreknowledge in creation with His decreeing everything that comes to pass. Similarly, although speaking in terms of "willing... into existence," Dabney also equates foreknowledge in creation with a decree:

> That is, the only way in which any object can by any possibility have passed from God's vision of the possible into His foreknowledge of the actual, is by His purposing to effectuate it Himself, or intentionally and purposely to permit its effectuation by some other agent whom He expressly purposed to bring into existence. This is clear from this fact. An effect conceived in *posse* only rises into actuality by virtue of an efficient cause or causes. When God was looking forward from the point of view of His original infinite prescience, there

---

[53] *Supra* note 30, p. 356.

was but one cause, Himself. If any other cause or agent is ever to arise, it must be by God's agency. If effects are embraced in God's infinite prescience, which these other agents are to produce, still, in willing these other agents into existence, with infinite prescience, God did virtually will into existence, or purpose, all the effects of which they were to be efficients.[54]

As Sproul explains, God foreknows because He decreed it all:

God knows not only all available options, but also which option will be exercised. He knows the end before the beginning. God's omniscience excludes both ignorance and learning. If there is ignorance in the mind of God, then divine omniscience is a hollow, indeed fraudulent, phrase. Learning always presupposes a certain level of ignorance. One simply cannot learn what one already knows. There is no learning curve for God. Since no gaps exist in his knowledge, there is nothing for him to learn.

* * *

It is said that God knows all contingencies, but none of them contingently. God never says to himself, "That depends." Nothing is contingent to him. He knows all things that will happen because he ordains everything that does happen. This is crucial to our understanding of God's omniscience. He does not know what will happen by virtue of exceedingly good guesswork about future

---

[54] *Supra* note 36, p. 212.

events. He knows it with certainty because he
has decreed it.[55]

Thus, the Reformed position is that God, knowing beforehand
all the possibilities for how the created universe would unfold
if He exercised His creative power, by choosing to so exercise
that power in a specific way foreordained everything that
would result from His exercise of creative power, and by virtue
of this foreordination, He also foreknows everything. In this
way, they equate foreknowledge and foreordination.

To the objector that posits that God did not foreordain
everything, Grudem provides a response from the Reformed
perspective:

> The problem with this position is that, even if
> God did not plan or cause things to happen,
> the fact that they are foreknown means that
> they will *certainly come about.* And this means
> that our decisions are predetermined *by
> something* (whether fate or the inevitable
> cause-and-effect mechanism of the universe),
> and they still are not free in the sense the
> Arminian wishes them to be free. If our future
> choices are known, then they are fixed. And if
> they are fixed, then they are not "free" in the
> Arminian sense (undetermined or uncaused).[56]

In what sense then does the Reformed theologian say that
people are free? As Grudem correctly notes, "The answer
depends on what is meant by the word *free.*"[57] Strong explains
the Reformed position and gives us an understanding of what
free means to them in that while God primarily decrees His
own acts, He secondarily decrees everything else:

---

[55] *Supra* note 18, pp. 171-72.
[56] *Supra* note 14, p. 348.
[57] *Supra* note 14, p. 330.

No undecreed event can be foreseen.—We grant that God decrees primarily and directly his own acts of creation, providence, and grace; but we claim that this involves also a secondary and indirect decreeing of the acts of free creatures which he foresees will result therefrom. There is therefore no such thing in God as *scientia media*, or knowledge of an event that is to be, though it does not enter into the divine plan; for to say that God foresees an undecreed event, is to say that he views as future an event that is merely possible; or, in other words, that he views an event not as it is.[58]

According to Strong, then, "free" simply means that our actions are secondarily or indirectly decreed. Grudem also addresses this issue of the sense in which people are free:

If God exercises providential control over all events are we in any sense free? The answer depends on what is meant by the word *free*. In some sense of the word *free*, everyone agrees that we are free in our will and in our choices. Even prominent theologians in the Reformed or Calvinistic tradition concur....

Thus, when we ask whether we have "free will," it is important to be clear as to what is meant by the phrase. Scripture nowhere says that we are "free" in the sense of being outside of God's control or being able to make decisions that are not caused by anything. (This is the sense in many people seem to assume we must be free...) Nor does it say we are "free" in the sense of being able to do right on our own

---

[58] *Supra* note 30, p. 357.

apart from God's power. But we are nonetheless free in the greatest sense that any creature of God could be free—we make *willing* choices, choices that have *real effects.* We must insist that we have the power of *willing* choice; otherwise we will fall into the error of fatalism or determinism and thus conclude that our choices do not matter, or that we cannot really make willing choices. On the other hand, the kind of freedom that is demanded by those who deny God's providential control of all things, a freedom to be outside of God's sustaining and controlling activity, would be impossible if Jesus Christ is indeed "continually carrying along things by his word of power" (Heb. 1:3, author's translation) If this be true, then to be outside of that providential control would simply be not to exist! An absolute "freedom," totally free of God's control, is simply not possible in a world providentially sustained and directed by God himself.[59]

As Grudem explains, we are not free in the sense that we can make uncaused choices, but the choices we make are "willing choices." We could describe this another way. Objectively, our choices are not at all free since God decreed or caused them, but they are subjectively free because in our minds we make our choices willingly. Along the same lines, Robert Reymond explains:

> How can the Reformed Christian speak of man's 'freedom' if God has decreed his every thought and action? The solution is to be found in the meaning of the word. Reformed

---

theology does not deny that men have wills (that is, choosing minds) or that men exercise their wills countless times a day. To the contrary, Reformed theology happily affirms both of these propositions. What Reformed theology denies is that a man's will is ever free from God's decree, his own intellection, limitations, parental training, habits, and (in this life) the power of sin. In sum, there is no such thing as the *liberty of indifference*; that is, no one's will is an island unto itself, undetermined or unaffected by anything.[60]

Accordingly, as most of the Reformed theologians recognize, so long as we define "freedom" in a certain way, then Reformed theology can maintain the absolute decree of God and freedom of man's will at the same time. The thing about freedom is that if you keep carving away at it, pretty soon it is no longer freedom no matter what you call it. How we define the words we use to talk about theology makes all the difference.

In summary then, Reformed theologians would not say that God primarily decreed the acts of free agents, but secondarily or indirectly did so because He created them (decreed their existence) with full knowledge of all of their acts. But as Grudem must concede, in their system, we are not free "in the sense of being outside of God's control or being able to make decisions that are not caused by anything," that is, we are not free in the sense of being able to make a decision that was not directly or indirectly scripted (recall the definition of freedom from *Webster's Third New International Dictionary* quoted at the beginning of the chapter, "the absence of antecedent causal determination of human decisions.").

---

[60] Robert L. Reymond, *A New Systematic Theology of the Christian Faith*, Thomas Nelson, Inc., p. 373 (1998).

Decrees of God and Sin

Any discussion of the decrees of God must account for whether the doctrine makes God, as the One who decreed all things, necessarily the initiator of sin. According to R. C. Sproul Jr., God desired and created sin but did not Himself sin: "God desired for man to fall into sin. I am not accusing God of sinning: I am suggesting that God created sin..."[61] Because this is such a point of contention, I will quote from several Reformed theologians responding to the issue. The comments in one Reformed systematic theology text are telling: "This is a very difficult question and it is important to discuss it with great prudence, *especially since there are no explicit Scripture passages to which we can point.*"[62] Strong responds to this issue making the point that most do, namely that God does not make creatures sin but makes creatures knowing they will choose to sin:

> They [i.e., the decrees] make God, not the author of sin, but the author of free beings who are themselves the authors of sin. God does not decree efficiently to work evil desires or choices in men. He decrees sin only in the sense of decreeing to create and preserve those who will sin; in other words, he decrees to create and preserve human wills which, in their own self-chosen courses, will be and do evil. In all this, man attributes sin to himself and not to God, and God hates, denounces, and punishes sin.

* * *

The decree to permit sin is therefore not an efficient but a permissive decree, or a decree to

---

[61] R. C. Sproul Jr., *Almighty over All: Understanding the Sovereignty of God* (Grand Rapids: Baker, 1999), 54.

[62] J. van Genderen and W. H. Velema, *Concise Reformed Dogmatics*, PR Publishing, p. 196 (2008).

permit, in distinction from a decree to produce by his own efficiency. No difficulty attaches to such a decree to permit sin, which does not attach to the actual permission of it. But God does actually permit sin, and it must be right for him to permit it. It must therefore be right for him to decree to permit it. If God's holiness and wisdom and power are not impugned by the actual existence of moral evil, they are not impugned by the original decree of it.[63]

Dabney explains, after first conceding that we cannot fully explain the relationship between God's decree and sin, that God does not author sin but authors the circumstances that will certainly cause our willing choice to sin:

That God is not, and cannot be the author of sin, is plain from express Scripture ... from God's law, which prohibits all sin; from the holiness of His nature, which is incapable of it; and from the nature of sin itself, which must be man's own free activity, or else is not responsible and guilty. But I remark, 1st, that so far as the great mystery of God's permission of sin enters into this objection, our minds are incapable of a complete explanation. But this incapacity is precisely the same, whatever scheme we adopt for accounting for it, unless we deny to God complete foreknowledge and power... God purposed to produce the free agents, to sustain their free agency untrammeled, to surround them with outward circumstances of a given kind, to permit that free agency, moved by those circumstances as occasional causes, to exert itself in a multitude

---

of acts, some sinful, not for the sake of the sin,
but for the sake of some good and holy results
which His infinite wisdom has seen best to
connect therewith. Last, in the sinful act, the
agency and choice is the sinner's alone; because
the inscrutable modes God has for effectuating
the certain occurrence of His volitions never
cramp or control the creature's spontaneity: as
consciousness testifies.[64]

Along the same lines, Clarence Thiessen explains the problem
by distinguishing between what God has efficiently caused and
what He has merely decreed to permit:

...there are two kinds of decrees: efficacious
and permissive. There are things which God
purposes that He also determines efficaciously
to bring about; there are other things which
He merely determines to permit.

* * *

On the assumption that God is the efficient
cause of all that is, some teach that He is the
Author of sin also...Not everything that is has
been efficiently caused by God...God is not the
Author of evil... But on the basis of His wise
and holy counsel, He decreed to permit sin to
come...[65]

So while claiming God decreed everything, Thiessen removes
God as the author of sin by saying He only "decreed to
permit" sin. But does this mixing of inconsistent terms bring
any clarity to the issue? Hodge also tries to explain away the
issue by mixing the notion of God's decree of everything with
free acts:

[64] *Supra* note 36, pp. 220-221.
[65] *Supra* note 33, pp. 148, 153.

The whole difficulty lies in the awful fact that sin exists. If God foresaw it and yet created the agent, and placed him in the very circumstances under which he did foresee the sin would be committed, then he did predetermine it. If he did not foresee it, or, foreseeing it, could not prevent it, then he is not infinite in knowledge and in power, but is surprised and prevented by his creatures. The doctrine of unconditional decrees presents no special difficulty. It represents God as decreeing that the sin shall eventuate as the free act of the sinner, and not as by any form of co-action, nor by any form of temptation inducing, him to sin.[66]

But the problem is that Hodge still has God placing the sinner in the decreed circumstances that are certain to bring about the sin, and calling it a "free act" does not change anything since, as we have seen, Reformed theology's definition of "free" is nothing more than an empty label. Berkhof responds along the same lines, but concedes, as he must, that it is not an entirely satisfactory response:

> ...It may be said, however, that the decree merely makes God the author of free moral beings who are themselves the authors of sin. The decree with reference to sin is not an efficient but a permissive decree. God did not decree to produce sin by direct divine efficiency. This consideration, it is true, does not fully remove the difficulty. The problem of God's relation to sin remains a mystery for us, which we cannot fully solve.[67]

---

[66] *Supra* note 39, p. 211.
[67] *Supra* note 34, p. 88.

Employing the same ideas as these other theologians, but writing in terms of first and second causes, Robert Reymond explains it this way:

> If we are to be biblical, it is important at the outset to affirm with no equivocation that God has ordained whatever comes to pass... But God is neither the author of sin nor the chargeable cause of sin. And we must insist upon this for three reasons. The first is simply this: The Bible teaches that 'God is light; in him there is no darkness at all' (1 John 1:5) and that he tempts no one to sin (James 1:13). The second reason is this: While he certainly decreed all things, God decreed that all things would come to pass *according to the nature of 'second causes,'* either (1) *necessarily,* as in the case of planets moving in their orbits, (2) *freely,* that is, voluntarily, with no violence being done to the will of the creature, or (3) *contingently,* that is, with due regard to the contingencies of future events, as in his informing David what Saul and the citizens of Keilah *would* do to him *if* David remained in the city of Keilah (1 Sam. 23:9-13). Therefore, *whatever sinfulness ensues proceeds only from men and angels and not from God.*[68]

As this point, the reader should take note of a recurring theme here. The Reformed theologians staunchly equate foreknowledge with foreordination in arguing philosophically for the decrees of God. Indeed, God foreknows everything because He decreed it all. But in dealing with the sin issue, they introduce new words like efficiently or permissive or secondarily to back away from the obvious result of their argument.

---

[68] Robert L. Reymond, *A New Systematic Theology of the Christian Faith,* Thomas Nelson, Inc., pp. 372-73 (1998).

R. C. Sproul also introduces new terms to try to answer the question, "Does this mean that *everything* that happens is the will of God?" in the affirmative, but he also backs away a bit by arguing that Augustine would have qualified the answer "in a certain sense."

> The "certain sense" of which Augustine spoke has often been articulated by a distinction between God's *decretive will* and his *permissive will.* This distinction is valid if used properly, but it is fraught with peril. It hints at a false dichotomy. The distinction is not absolute: what God permits, he *decrees* to permit. For example, at any given moment of my life, God has the power and authority to intrude providentially and to restrain my actions. In a word he can *prevent* me from sinning if he so chooses. If he chooses not to prevent me, he has clearly chosen to "permit" me to sin. This permission is not a divine sanction on my behavior. That he permits me to sin merely means that he chooses to allow it to happen rather than to intrude and prevent it. Because he chooses to let it happen in some sense he ordains or intends that it should happen.[69]

It is Sproul's last sentence that attempts to make the word *permit* mean *decree* "in some sense" that is problematic, a point we will return to shortly.

Refuting the Philosophical Argument

With this background, I will address the philosophical argument, which may be summarized as follows: (1) God has

---

foreknowledge and created the material universe, (2) therefore, every event in the creation is certain to occur in accordance with God's foreknowledge of the event before creation, (3) therefore, every event that comes to pass is fixed, (4) therefore, a causative agent fixed every event without exception, (5) that causative agent could only be God, and (6) therefore, God decreed (fixed) everything before creation.

While I agree God has foreknowledge, like so many things we will examine in this book, defining our words matters. God unquestionably, if we accept the Biblical witness, has foreknowledge concerning His creation. But Reformed theologians take this a step further and make God's foreknowledge so absolute in its breadth that it must include all of God's own future thoughts, words and actions. But if God's foreknowledge includes all of His thoughts, words and actions, then He is also bound by His foreknowledge. Since God is self-existent, there is no point in time when God did not already know every one of His future thoughts, words and actions. This means God is incapable of conceiving a thought he did not previously have at all points in time, speaking a word He did not always know He would speak at that precise moment, or performing a spontaneous action. But the God of the Bible experiences the moment, responds to events as they happen, and even expresses a change of mind.

This is not to say that God is wringing His hands wondering what will happen next. But instead, our view of His foreknowledge should start and end where the Bible does. We should not make inference upon inference that ultimately resolve God to a philosophical singularity no longer retaining the qualities of being a person. The Bible affirms God's foreknowledge about His creation, His determination that certain discreet future events will come to pass, and His ability to intervene in human events as He pleases. God can know how future events will unfold without His intervention, or with His intervention, and in His sovereignty reserves the right to intervene in human affairs in time as He pleases. There is no need to press the matter further, nor are we qualified to do so. There is no Bible verse that tells us God's own experience of life is scripted, nor that our lives are scripted. Rather than God's foreknowledge binding Him and us, it maintains our volition and His right to intervene as He pleases in His creation without leaving God in a state of uncertainty about things future. In this view of God's sovereignty, nothing comes to pass without God causing or permitting it, but there is no need for a comprehensive decree.

How the Reformed theologians deal with the issue of sin reveals the weakness of their philosophical argument. They must retreat from the strong words they use in their definitions like "decree" and "foreordain" in favor of weaker words like permissive and decretive, and yet still try, as Sproul does, to say it is a decree "in some sense." But we read in James 1:13 the following: "Let no man say when he is tempted, I am tempted of God: for God cannot be tempted with evil, neither tempteth he any man." Likewise, God wrote through Jeremiah: "They have built also the high places of Baal, to burn their sons with fire for burnt offerings unto Baal, which I commanded not, nor spake it, neither came it into my mind." (Jeremiah 19:5) We cannot admit the truth of verses like James 1:13 and Jeremiah 19:5 and also say that God decreed a discreet sin.

Redefining terms and creating new ones does not reconcile the logical inconsistency. We can, however, admit the truth of these verses and admit that God allowed the sin even though He could have intervened to stop it. There is no need, and no scriptural basis, to take it a step further and speak of a decree in any sense. Terminology like decree and foreordain say more than that God merely permitted something to happen. And Sproul's retreat position of "ordains or intends" is functionally equivalent. Ordains in this context is no different than foreordains, and intends suggests a desired consequence. In contrast to Sproul and the others quoted above, I am simply saying that God created humankind with volition, knowing in His foreknowledge that apart from His direct intervention we would sin, which He permitted because He intended to preserve our genuine volition. I would also point out that I am not saying that God did not predetermine any events (e.g., Christ's redemptive work, Revelation 13:8), but I am saying that the Bible does not confirm an all-encompassing decree nor can one be inferred.

Notwithstanding the foregoing, we should not lose sight of the fact that what really matters is what God says in the Bible. Obviously, if the Scriptures support the decrees of God, then we should be pleased to accept it, but if not, then the decrees of God should be summarily dismissed as just another religious philosophy in the arena of ideas.

Prophecy Proof Texts

We would expect from the vigor with which they argue the decrees of God that they could show us a single verse that states in no uncertain terms that God decreed everything. Instead, Reformed theologians always claim ample authority for their position but primarily rely on the instances in which God has provided a prophecy of a future discrete event or has articulated His control over a discrete event. Hodge defends this approach by arguing that if God foreordained one thing so that He could prophecy it, He had to foreordain everything:

> God has in the Scriptures foretold the certain occurrence of many events, including the free actions of men, which have afterwards surely come to pass. Now the ground of prophecy is foreknowledge, and the foundation of the foreknowledge of an event as certainly future, is God's decree that made it future. The eternal immutability of the decree is the only foundation of the infallibility either of the

foreknowledge or of the prophecy. But if God has decreed certain future events, he must also have included in that decree all of their causes, conditions, coordinates, and consequences. No event is isolated; to make one certainly future implies the determination of the whole concatenation of causes and effects which constitute the universe.[70]

Erickson likewise asserts that God's all-inclusive decree is implicit from the many things He has included in His plan:

The plan of God is all-inclusive. This is implicit in the great variety of items which are mentioned in the Bible as parts of God's plan. Beyond that, however, are explicit statements of the extent of God's plan.[71]

Their argument is really no argument at all—they simply state that if God decreed one discreet event He had to decree everything else in order to ensure that one event happens. That is unsubstantiated speculation. But to the extent that they argue that if God decreed some events we should infer generally that this is true of every thought, word and action, their argument is inductive. An inductive argument seeks to establish a generalized conclusion from specific occurrences. An example of an inductive argument would be if one argued that there are no instances in the Bible of angels appearing in the form of a woman, and therefore, angels can only appear in the form of a man. Without diverting our attention to angels, what I want you to see from this example is that inductive arguments do not establish anything absolutely. Rather, we speak of the relative strength or weakness of an inductive argument. If I am driving down the road and the first three cars I observe are red, my inductive argument that all the cars I will see on my trip will be red is exceedingly weak.

---

[70] *Supra* note 39, p. 206.
[71] *Supra* note 41, p. 353.

The Reformed theologians would have us believe that if they amass enough verses showing God's supernatural intervention in human affairs, then we can conclude from these discrete occurrences that God foreordained everything. Such inductive reasoning seeks to draw a conclusion about trillions upon trillions of events from just hundreds, and is analogous to my red car example. But actually it is much weaker than that because relatively few Bible verses speak of any "decree." Any verse that provides a prophetic utterance of some future event is merely assumed to be part of the decree. Because such argumentation is too weak to support the conclusion, and because I fully agree that the Bible is full of prophecies that will all be fulfilled and that God routinely intervenes in human affairs, there will be no attempt here to address these purported proof texts. These verses provide no evidence that God foreordained everything without exception before creation in a decree.

General Proof Texts

The logical place to start our inquiry is with Bible verses that mention a decree. In the KJV, there are 57 occurrences in 55 verses. Of these 57 occurrences, 47 of them refer to the decrees of men. Of the remaining 10 occurrences, we read that God decreed the rain in creation (Job 28:26), the boundaries of the seas (Job 38:10; Jeremiah 5:22), the position of the stars (Psalm 148:6; Proverbs 8:29), the destruction of Israel (Isaiah 10:22; Zephaniah 2:2), to punish Nebuchadnezzar (Daniel 4:17, 24), and in reference to the city boundaries being extended (Micah 7:11). Although we should expect such a profound truth claim as the Calvinist's decrees of God to have a single explicit proof text—somewhere in the Bible that God says he decreed everything before creation—it does not. Indeed, this particular claim is so far reaching that its absence from the Bible in explicit terms speaks volumes. It would be like God never explicitly saying that salvation is by grace, or that Jesus was resurrected, and leaving us to try to cobble this profound truth together inferentially from scattered verses in the Bible. Yet that is not at all God's pattern. We have a tremendous amount of special revelation from God from the creation to the New Heavens and the New Earth, but no verse that God decreed everything. Just as we will see with every part of TULIP Calvinism, the decrees of God is purely inferential, resting on human reasoning and not Bible evidence, all in the name of their concept of sovereignty.

We turn then to those very few verses that are typically cited as support for the doctrine of the decrees of God. As we will see, none of these verses even come close to suggesting, explicitly or by inference, that God foreordained everything without exception in a decree prior to creation. Instead, properly understood in their specific contexts, these are just additional examples of God moving with regard to discrete events. And as we begin this journey through the Calvinist's evidence, you will see a simple pattern. I will exegete the verse in context to understand its meaning. That is the key. Over and again we will see that (1) the verses say nothing explicitly about any ancient decree of everything and (2) understood in context the verses do not permit any reasonable inference of such a decree.

> Job 23:13 But he *is* in one *mind*, and who can turn him? and *what* his soul desireth, even *that* he doeth. 14 For he performeth *the thing that is* appointed for me: and many such *things are* with him.

These verses are part of Job's response[72] to his supposed comforters and follow his insistence that he has not sinned:

---

[72] A comment is in order here. Job's comforters express an incorrect theology throughout the book and therefore it would be dubious to build doctrine on their words. Job is also struggling throughout the book to square his experience with his theology.

"Neither have I gone back from the commandment of his lips; I have esteemed the words of his mouth more than my necessary *food*." (Job 23:12) Job's comforters believe that his situation can only be a result of his sin. One of the purposes of the book of Job is to correct the belief that if someone experiences sickness or other bad events in their life it must have occurred as a result of sin. But at this point in the book, Job also does not understand why he is experiencing so many bad things in his life since he insists he has not committed some terrible sin. Although Job does not believe his troubles came as a result of personal sin, he does believe that God is the source of his troubles; he does not know what we know, namely that Satan is behind it.

Job comments in verse 13 that when God purposes to do something, no one can change His mind or stop Him from doing it. Further, in verse 14, Job continues the thought and states that God will accomplish what He has decreed for Job. What Job has in mind are the bad things that have happened to him that he has attributed to God. He believes God has caused these things to happen and states that God will perform these things that God appointed for him. Job says nothing about when these things were appointed, but we know that these events stem from Satan's interaction with God in the first two chapters. Also, Job is not saying that every aspect of his life was appointed; he is only commenting about the affliction he is experiencing. Accordingly, there is no support in Job's words for a supposed decree of God before the foundation of the world of all events without exception.

> Psalm 115:3 But our God *is* in the heavens: he hath done whatsoever he hath pleased.

This verse is the Psalmist's response to the hypothetical and sarcastic question of the Gentile nations in Psalm 115:2: "Wherefore should the heathen say, Where *is* now their God?" The Psalmist responds that God is in heaven. Of course, the import of the Gentile's sarcasm is that the God of Israel is impotent. But the Psalmist responds, "he hath done whatsoever he hath pleased." This says nothing of a decree, much less a decree prior to creation of everything without exception. Instead, the Psalmist merely confirms that God is capable of doing whatever He pleases and has done so, which is in contrast to the Gentile's idols made of silver and gold that have no power, as the rest of the Psalm confirms. What we learn from Psalm 115 is that God is omnipotent, but we find no evidence here of any precreation all-inclusive decree.

> Psalm 135:6 Whatsoever the LORD pleased,
> *that* did he in heaven, and in earth, in the seas,
> and all deep places.

The context of this verse is God's greatness and His deserving praise, in particular for His selection of Israel as His "peculiar treasure." In the immediately preceding verse, the Psalmist states: "For I know that the LORD *is* great, and *that* our Lord *is* above all gods." Thus, like Psalm 115:3, a contrast is being made between God and the false gods. The living God is omnipotent. He can do as he pleases anywhere in the universe. The Psalmist follows this general statement with some discrete examples, but neither in this verse nor the ones that follow does he mention a decree or even hint that God foreordained everything without exception, or anything at all. That God is omnipotent and able to do as He pleases does not establish His foreordination of everything without exception prior to creation.

> Proverbs 16:33 The lot is cast into the lap; but
> the whole disposing thereof *is* of the LORD.

This verse presents a real pillar in defense of the purported decrees of God. But what does this proverb tell us? Men cast lots and cannot control the outcome. At most, this verse tells us that God determines the outcome of lots (stones or pebbles thrown like dice). In view of Israel's historic use of lots to determine God's will (e.g., to distribute the land to the tribes, to make certain decisions), it is likely that this proverb is not teaching that God always dictates the outcome of lots, but does so in certain circumstances when people use lots to determine God's will in a matter, such as in Jonah 1:7 when the lots indicated that it was because of Jonah that the ship was in a storm. (See also Acts 1:26) In other words, the proverb sets up a contrast between men who cannot control the lots and God who can. But even if the proverb teaches that God always controls lots, it does not say He decreed either the outcome of the lots or of every event without exception before the foundation of the world.

> <u>Isaiah 14:26</u> This *is* the purpose that is purposed upon the whole earth: and this *is* the hand that is stretched out upon all the nations. <u>27</u> For the LORD of hosts hath purposed, and who shall disannul *it*? and his hand *is* stretched out, and who shall turn it back?

These verses in Isaiah can only evidence the decrees of God if the context is ignored. We may ask, what has God "purposed upon the whole earth" in verse 26? The answer is in the preceding two verses: "The LORD of hosts hath sworn, saying, Surely as I have thought, so shall it come to pass; and as I have purposed, *so* shall it stand: That I will break the Assyrian in my land, and upon my mountains tread him under foot: then shall his yoke depart from off them, and his burden depart from off their shoulders." We are told that God has purposed to "break the Assyrian in my land." The Assyrians were the world superpower at the time so that God's breaking down of the Assyrians, also the subject of other Old Testament prophesies like that of Nahum, is "purposed upon the whole earth." God can surely do that which He has purposed against Assyria since it is His "hand that is stretched out upon all the nations," an expression of God's power. We are told in verse 27 that God has purposed to deal with Assyria and Isaiah asks rhetorically, who can stop God? Of course, what God has purposed against Assyria He can surely bring to pass, and historically He did. Once again, the supposed support for the decrees of God is wanting. Isaiah's words here say nothing of a general decree of all things, nor even of the timing of God's decision against Assyria. In any event, these verses only concern God deciding to cause a discrete event in history regarding Assyria.

> Isaiah 46:10 Declaring the end from the beginning, and from ancient times *the things* that are not *yet* done, saying, My counsel shall stand, and I will do all my pleasure: 11 Calling a ravenous bird from the east, the man that executeth my counsel from a far country: yea, I have spoken *it*, I will also bring it to pass; I have purposed *it*, I will also do it.

Here, God is speaking against Israel's idolatry. In contrast to dumb and impotent idols, God has real power. He says in verse 9, "Remember the former things of old: for I *am* God, and *there is* none else; *I am* God, and *there is* none like me." Continuing the thought, God speaks through Isaiah in verse 10 and states that only He can declare the end from the beginning, the things that are not yet done. These statements, "declaring the end from the beginning" and "from ancient times the things that are not yet done" are in parallel and convey the same idea. Only God can foretell future events before they occur. Notice that nothing is said here about foreordaining or decreeing future events, but only foretelling them. Is God saying that He has decreed everything from ancient times or the beginning? No. The next verse tells about God's sure counsel ("My counsel shall stand") and has to do with a discrete event. God will call a "ravenous bird from the east," that is, a nation to come in judgment against His people. God says that He has spoken it and will be it to pass, for "I have purposed it, I will also do it." These words are not saying anything about a pre-creation decree of all things, but a specific purpose of God regarding bringing a country in judgment against His people.

> Daniel 4:35 And all the inhabitants of the earth *are* reputed as nothing: and he doeth according to his will in the army of heaven, and *among* the inhabitants of the earth: and none can stay his hand, or say unto him, What doest thou?

Nebuchadnezzar was a prideful man that attributed his kingship and the extent and prosperity of his kingdom to himself. To remedy Nebuchadnezzar of his sinful attitude, God gave him the mind of a beast "till thou know that the most High ruleth in the kingdom of men, and giveth it to whomsoever he will." (Daniel 4:25) After seven years of grazing, Nebuchadnezzar had a change of heart and confessed the sovereignty of God. Verse 35 quoted above is a part of Nebuchadnezzar's confession. We should first note what Nebuchadnezzar does not say. In particular, he says nothing about a decree or its timing or foreordination. What he does say is that God does as He wishes in heaven (i.e., among the angels) and on earth and none can stop Him, a sharp contrast to the pagan gods of Babylon that are placated or manipulated by men. That God does as He wishes in heaven and on earth hardly proves that He has foreordained every event without exception from before creation. The only way to make such a hermeneutical leap is to approach the text with an agenda. If we let God speak for Himself, He says nothing here about a decree or foreordination. Moreover, that God brought to pass (we are not told how) Nebuchadnezzar's rise to power is only a discrete event in history. To draw the conclusion that because God brought this one event to pass that He causes everything to happen in accordance with a pre-creation decree does not logically follow.

> Daniel 11:36 And the king shall do according to his will; and he shall exalt himself, and magnify himself above every god, and shall speak marvellous things against the God of gods, and

shall prosper till the indignation be accomplished: for that that is determined shall be done.

The Reformed take on this verse is yet another example of trying to draw a conclusion about the totality of history from a discrete event. Without a doubt, in this verse God reveals to Daniel (and to us) something about a future king (i.e., the Anti-Christ). This king is going to "prosper till the indignation be accomplished." The phrase "that that is determined" has reference to the accomplishing of the time of indignation. Thus, there is a discrete event in the future that God has said will come to pass. This tells us what few would dispute, namely that God does determine certain discrete events. But again, you cannot draw the conclusion that because God determined some discrete events in history that He did decreed everything without exception before creation.

> <u>Matthew 10:29</u> Are not two sparrows sold for a farthing? and one of them shall not fall on the ground without your Father. <u>30</u> But the very hairs of your head are all numbered.

These two verses say nothing of any decree or timing of a decree, but rather, speak to God the Father's love for people. To see the context, consider 10:28: "And fear not them which kill the body, but are not able to kill the soul: but rather fear him which is able to destroy both soul and body in hell." Jesus is saying that we should not fear men, but God, because men can only destroy the body (temporary), but God can send the whole person to hell (eternal). In this context, Jesus points out that God's love for His creation is of such magnitude that even a sparrow cannot fall to the ground without His taking notice. In contrast to the birds, God's attention to people is such that He even knows the number of hairs on the heads of everyone in the world. This indicates God's love for people, which is a ground for comfort. For this reason, Jesus concludes in 10:31: "Fear ye not therefore, ye are of more value than many sparrows." Once again, the proof texts prove nothing of the decrees of God. These verses speak to God's love and omniscience, but say nothing of any decrees.

> Acts 17:26 And hath made of one blood all nations of men for to dwell on all the face of the earth, and hath determined the times before appointed, and the bounds of their habitation;

This verse is a pillar proof text for the decrees of God. To get the proper context for this verse (part of Paul's sermon in Athens), we need to look at the preceding two verses: "God that made the world and all things therein, seeing that he is Lord of heaven and earth, dwelleth not in temples made with hands; Neither is worshipped with men's hands, as though he needed any thing, seeing he giveth to all life, and breath, and all things." (Acts 17:24-25) Paul is addressing an Athenian crowd, and to them he says that God is the creator, that He is not an idol made by men's hands, and that He is the source of life. Then, in verse 26, Paul tells them that God created all men, Greeks and everyone else, to dwell on the earth. Paul is addressing their Greek pride in these verses. For the God Paul preaches is not just a God of one particular people, but all peoples; He is not just a God over Greece or some other country, but all countries. Indeed, God established national boundaries ("bounds of their habitation"). Moreover, God is a sustainer of life, having provided for the seasons ("the times before appointed"), which are tied to the harvests. Paul's statement is similar to what he says in Acts 14:17, "Nevertheless he left not himself without witness, in that he did good, and gave us rain from heaven, and fruitful seasons, filling our hearts with food and gladness." The Greek term *kairos* is used in both verses. The appointed times in view in Acts 17:26 are the seasons. The verse says that God appointed the seasons, a fact we know from Genesis 1, and that He determines the boundaries of nations. The verse does not teach that God foreordained everything, nor does it say anything about the timing of a decree.

> Ephesians 1:11 In whom also we have obtained an inheritance, being predestinated according to the purpose of him who worketh all things after the counsel of his own will.

Some argue that the last clause of this verse means that God predetermined all things, but the verse does not say God predetermined anything. The verse does not say God "decreed all things" or that God "decreed all things before creation," but that God "worketh" or accomplishes "all things." Moreover, God's "counsel" also cannot be equated to God's "decree," for otherwise men could not refuse God's counsel. Yet, the Bible records: "But ye have set at nought all my counsel, and would none of my reproof." (Proverbs 1:25; see also Proverbs 1:30, Luke 7:30) This verse is referencing God's working to reconcile things to Himself in Christ from the prior verses (see Ephesians 1:9-10), and not to a decree of all things. Like all of the other verses we have examined, this one does not even come close to saying God decreed everything before creation.

Concluding Thoughts on the Decrees of God

I suggested in chapter 1 that we put Calvinism on trial, scrutinize the evidence, and accept the verdict of Scripture. Although it is not formally part of TULIP Calvinism, I have included the decrees of God in the analysis because of its close relationship to the TULIP. The first evidence submitted for this doctrine was a philosophical argument that equates foreknowledge with foreordination, leading to the conclusion that God authors sin, which of course the Bible expressly rejects. We then noted that none of the verses in the Bible that actually use the term "decree" say that God decreed everything. And then there was a series of verses that do not even mention the word "decree" and, instead, only speak of God bringing to pass certain discrete events, generally without any reference to when God purposed that the events would occur. Since these proof texts do not say anything about a decree of all things before the foundation of the world, nor can such a decree be inferred, they fall far short of demonstrating that God decreed everything. Moreover, as I pointed out before, the absence of a single Bible verse that simply states that God decreed everything is a glaring omission for such a profound truth claim as the decrees of God. The verdict must be rendered against this doctrine.

The better view is to accept God's foreknowledge of His creation because the Bible teaches this doctrine and not add to it. We should be content to say, without taking it a step further and insisting on a decree nowhere found in Scripture, that God created with foreknowledge and intervenes in His creation as He pleases and, therefore, everything that comes to pass was either caused or permitted by God. The practical implication of refuting the Reformed doctrine of the decrees of God is that our lives are not scripted for us. Our thoughts, words and actions matter a great deal and God is just to hold us responsible for our actions because we were created with genuine volition. The greatest responsibility we have is determining what to do about the revelation of Jesus Christ, to accept Him as the Son of God who died for our sins, was buried, and rose again, or to reject Him. Whatever our decision will be, nowhere in the Bible is it taught that God forced our hand. God has invited us into the family. "And the Spirit and the bride say, Come. And let him that heareth say, Come. And let him that is athirst come. And whosoever will, let him take the water of life freely." (Revelation 22:17)

Chapter 4

Total Depravity

John 3:16 is probably the most famous verse in the New Testament, if not in the entire Bible. Those familiar words are a clarion call of the love of God for lost sinners: "For God so loved the world, that he gave his only begotten Son, that whosoever believeth in him should not perish, but have everlasting life." The verse is at the same time remarkably profound in its implications and immediately comprehensible in its application. One preacher I know comments that this verse is so simple that a kindergartner can comprehend it. But for many Calvinists, the verse is not simple at all. If it could be understood by those God did not choose in eternity past to save, then it could be believed and they could trust Christ for eternal life. And since that would wreak havoc on their theology, it must be maintained that the non-elect cannot even comprehend the gospel message. They cannot truly understand John 3:16.

What a profound truth proposition this is. The human mind is capable of understanding advanced mathematics, employing complex engineering to build everything from smart phones and tablets to large buildings and stadiums, unraveling the workings of subatomic particles, and composing sophisticated musical compositions, among other things, but John 3:16 is beyond the pale. Unlike advanced mathematics, the gospel of Jesus Christ does not seem to be a complex message. Consider the following succinct definition of the gospel: "Saving faith is the belief in Jesus Christ as the Son of God who died and rose again to pay one's personal penalty for sin and the one who gives eternal life to all who trust Him and Him alone for it."[73] If the Calvinists are correct, this message is beyond the comprehension of an unsaved person unless God regenerates the unsaved person and then gives him faith in Jesus Christ. So we might ask, what then makes the gospel incomprehensible to the unsaved man? Surely, it is not the historical facts of the death, burial and resurrection of Jesus. So what part of this message is incomprehensible?

While we should not interpret Scripture on the basis of our experience, we should expect that our experience will confirm what the Bible teaches. But what I have found is that even people who reject the gospel message seem to understand it and certainly claim to understand it. Instead of inability to comprehend or believe, it is invariably pride or some other attachment to sin that causes people to reject the good news. The Bible says: "And this is the condemnation, that light is come into the world, and men loved darkness rather than light, because their deeds were evil." (John 3:19) Obviously, anecdotal observation does not prove anything, but the view that unsaved people cannot comprehend the gospel does not pass the smell test for reasonableness in our experience. The Calvinists would respond, of course, that the difference between the gospel and scientific truths is that the gospel is

---

[73] J.B. Hixson, *Getting the Gospel Wrong*, p. 84 (2008).

spiritual truth that can only be comprehended by spiritual (i.e., regenerate or saved) people. It remains to be seen if the Bible draws that distinction and teaches that people cannot understand the gospel.

If total depravity is true, then its implications are far reaching and strike at the very heart of our beliefs about human anthropology and soteriology. For those that are not "elect," the gospel is information that they do not know and cannot grasp. The non-elect person can hear or read the words of the gospel, memorize and quote them back, but is entirely incapable of understanding or responding in faith. As I noted in the prior chapter regarding the decrees of God, we should expect to find at least one Bible verse that plainly says God decreed everything. Now, we have another truth claim, equally profound. Surely the Calvinists should be able to muster a single verse in the Bible that plainly states that the unsaved man cannot comprehend the gospel and cannot believe. We will see below that they have no such verse, and once again their position is purely inferential, but first, we will take a more detailed look at how total depravity is defined in their own writings.

How the Calvinists Define Total Depravity

The Calvinist concept of total depravity means, among other things, that apart from God's regeneration, a person lacks the capacity to understand and believe the gospel. It is not that the person hears the gospel, considers it, comprehends it, and rejects it. Rather, he hears the words, but because he is so hopelessly and helplessly lost and unable to move toward God in the slightest, he cannot comprehend it and can only reject the message unless God first makes him spiritually alive by "regeneration," in which case the person not only comprehends the message but cannot reject it, for it is now compelling to him. Only the "elect" receive this "regeneration" and accept the gospel message (we will address the elect in the next chapter). This doctrine throws a new light on a substantial portion of the Bible. Much of the Bible is reduced to stories about God "going through the motions." Gospel presentations no longer seem sincere since some in the audience cannot accept it and others cannot reject it.

The issue before us, of course, is whether this is a Biblical view of man. In some sense, the question is how lost is man? Or asked another way, how fallen is man? If you say that man is totally depraved, what does that mean? The Calvinists often say the issue is whether man is depraved, but that is not really the issue since many non-Calvinists would agree that man is depraved. As I have commented before, theology is often about words, and here the issue is what the Bible teaches about (i.e., how God defines) the depravity of man. Now, let's turn to the Calvinists' own recitation of this doctrine so that the reader can be assured that the foregoing summary of this doctrine is accurate.

Spencer defines the concept of total depravity in terms of man's natural capacity to please God and expressly states that because of total depravity a person can never "make a decision for Christ":

> *Total depravity* means that man in his natural state is incapable of doing anything or desiring anything pleasing to God. Until he is "born again" of the Holy Spirit and given a living human spirit, man is the slave of Satan ("the Prince of the power of the air") who drives man to fulfill the desires of the flesh that are in enmity with God. In the sight of God the "best hearted man" holds only evil thoughts because they are oriented to doing *human* good for the glory of himself or Satan but never for the glory of the Creator....
>
> Man is *totally depraved* in the sense that everything about his nature is in rebellion against God. *Total depravity* means that man,

of his own "free will," will never make a
decision for Christ.[74]

One might ask whether this means that man is experientially
as bad as he can possibly be. Calvinists are careful to
distinguish total depravity from absolute depravity, that is, the
idea that unsaved man will always sin to the fullest extent
possible:

> When Calvinists speak of man as being totally
> depraved, they mean that man's nature is
> corrupt, perverse, and sinful throughout. The
> adjective "total" does not mean that each
> sinner is as totally or completely corrupt in his
> actions and thoughts as it is possible for him to
> be. Instead, the word "total" is used to indicate
> that the *whole* of man's being has been
> affected by sin. The corruption extends to
> *every part* of man, his body and soul; sin has
> affected all (the totality) of man's faculties—his
> mind, his will, etc.[75]

The writers just quoted would further explain depravity by
saying that man is spiritually depraved, that is, "the natural
man is totally unable to do anything spiritually good" and, as a
consequence, "he can do nothing pertaining to his salvation."[76]
Strong also differentiates the doctrine from absolute
depravity, but still defines man as incapable of any good:

> ...that every sinner is: (a) totally destitute of
> that love to God which constitutes the
> fundamental and all-inclusive demand of the
> law; (b) chargeable with elevating some lower
> affection or desire above regard for God and
> his law; (c) supremely determined, in his whole

---

[74] *Supra* note 13, pp. 33-34.
[75] *Supra* note 3, pp. 18-19.
[76] *Supra* note 3, p. 19.

inward and outward life, by a preference of self to God; (d) possessed of an aversion to God which, though sometimes latent, becomes active enmity, as soon as God's will comes into manifest conflict with his own; (e) disordered and corrupted in every faculty, through this substitution of selfishness for supreme affection toward God; (f) credited with no thought, emotion, or act of which divine holiness can fully approve; (g) subject to a law of constant progress in depravity, which he has no recuperative energy to enable him successfully to resist.[77]

When we read that the Calvinists insist that a lost person cannot do anything good, at least not without bad motives, obvious questions arise. Can a lost person sincerely love their spouse or their children? Apparently the answer for many Calvinists is no:

Finally, sin results in inability to love. Since other people stand in our way, representing competition and a threat to us, we cannot really act for the ultimate welfare of others if our aim is self-satisfaction. And so suspicions, conflicts, bitterness, and even hatred issue from the self-absorption or the pursual of finite values that has supplanted God at the center of the sinner's life.[78]

Second, because man is totally or pervasively corrupt, he is *incapable of changing his character or of acting in a way that is distinct from his corruption.* He is unable to discern, to love, or to choose the things that are pleasing to God.[79]

---

[77] *Supra* note 30, p. 839.
[78] *Supra* note 41, p. 619.
[79] *Supra* note 68, p. 453.

It is helpful at this point to relate this concept of total depravity to the decrees of God that was the subject of the prior chapter and unconditional election that is the subject of the next chapter. The reader should note in what follows the use of the term reprobation, which is that aspect of God's decrees that certain men would remain totally depraved for their entire lives. Reprobation and election are twin doctrines in the Calvinists' system that fall under the larger umbrella of *predestination:* "While God's decree is His purpose as to all things, His predestination may be defined to be His purpose concerning the everlasting destiny of His rational creatures. His election is His purpose of saving eternally some men and angels. Election and reprobation are both included in predestination."[80] Berkhof states that "[p]redestination is simply ... the purposes of God respecting His moral creatures" and that it "includes two parts, namely, election and reprobation."[81] He defines election as follows: "It may be defined as God's eternal purpose to save some of the human race in and by Jesus Christ." He then explains reprobation in light of election:

> The doctrine of election naturally implies that some of the human race were not elected. If God purposed to save some, He also purposed not to save others... Reprobation may be defined as that decree of God whereby He has determined to pass some men by with the operation of His special grace and to punish them for their sin to the manifestation of His justice. From this definition reprobation appears to be really a twofold purpose namely, (a) to pass by some in the bestowal of regenerating and saving grace; and (b) to assign them to dishonour and to the wrath of God for their sins.[82]

---

[80] *Supra* note 36, pp. 223-24.
[81] *Supra* note 34, pp. 90-91.
[82] *Supra* note 34, p. 91.

Thus, the Calvinist system teaches that God, as part of His decree of all things that would come to pass, elected certain people for salvation, whom He will enable ("with the operation of His special grace" He will undo their total depravity) to believe, and passed over the others. Since they were passed over, they remain forever reprobate or totally depraved, destined to make the only choice they are capable of, namely to reject the gospel and spend eternity in the lake of fire.

Grudem provides similar, but more detailed, definitions. "Election is an act of God before creation in which he chooses some people to be saved, not on account of any foreseen merit in them, but only because of his sovereign good pleasure."[83] "Reprobation is the sovereign decision of God before creation to pass over some persons, in sorrow deciding not to save them, and to punish them for their sins, and thereby to manifest his justice."[84] Although Grudem remarks that God passed over people "in sorrow," there is no adequate explanation in the Calvinist system for why God passed over anyone if it caused Him sorrow. In other words, if God pre-selected certain individuals for salvation, why did He not do so for everyone? No Calvinist suggests that God could not have elected everyone. The fact is that these concepts reveal philosophical difficulties for the Calvinists, many of which they simply chalk up to a mystery we should be content not to understand. On many occasions, I have been told that the real issue is not why God did not save everyone, but why He saved anyone at all. This is, of course, just punting the difficult question. But if they have no scriptural support for their position, then the mystery is quickly removed.

With this background in mind, we will turn to addressing the common proof texts for the doctrine of total depravity. It should be noted that Calvinists' writings frequently support total depravity by a string cite of scripture passages rather than

---

[83] *Supra* note 14, p. 670.
[84] *Supre* note 14, p. 685.

any extended Biblical analysis. In reality, the entire TULIP structure, although it boasts much support, actually rests on a small handful of what might be deemed their "pillar" passages. Those who accept the TULIP interpretation of the pillar total depravity passages often find the doctrine all over the pages of the Bible. For this reason, it would be impossible here to address all the verses in which Calvinists may find total depravity. Instead, the goal below will be to first address the three pillar texts for total depravity before examining some of the other proof texts.

Pillar Proof Text: Romans 3

The central question presented by the Calvinist doctrine of total depravity is whether lost people can understand the gospel and trust Christ without God giving them their faith. I often hear people discuss Calvinism primarily in terms of election, but the issue driving Calvinism is total depravity, not election. Obviously, if people cannot believe because of their depravity, then necessarily no one will ever be saved through faith in Christ unless God picks people for salvation and gives them faith, overcoming their depravity. Probably the Calvinists' favorite total depravity passage is from Romans 3. The two key verses are below:

> Romans 3:10 As it is written, There is none righteous, no, not one: 11 There is none that understandeth, there is none that seeketh after God.

Calvinists draw at least three conclusions from this passage. First, an unsaved man cannot do anything righteous or good with righteous or selfless motives, and that includes placing faith in Christ. Second, an unsaved man cannot comprehend God's Word, and in particular, the gospel. Third, an unsaved man cannot seek God in response to His revelation, and in particular, by placing faith in Christ. From these verses, they find conclusive evidence for total depravity. Because this passage is such a critical part of the Calvinist arsenal, it will be addressed in detail.

First of all, we should observe that these verses do not explicitly say what Calvinists claim from them. Calvinists read the phrase "there is none righteous" to mean "no one can do a righteous thing." They read the phrase "there is none that understandeth" to mean "no one is capable of understanding the gospel." And they read the phrase "there is none that seeketh after God" to mean "no one is capable of seeking God." Since the passage obviously does not contain the words Calvinists infer, the question is whether total depravity can be validly deduced from what the verses actually say.

Second, we must be careful to view this proof text—as we should for all proof texts—in context. And here, that means in the overall context and flow of Paul's argument in Romans 1-3, to see if the Calvinist inferences are justified. The following is a high level outline of Paul's argument from 1:16 through the end of chapter 3.

- The gospel is the power of God unto salvation to those that believe (1:16-17)

- People suffer God's temporal wrath (degradation of humanity) as a result of sin (1:18-32)

- Even the moralizers (self-righteous) are not exempt from God's wrath because they also sin (2:1-5)

- God is the equitable judge presently dealing with all people (2:6-11)

- God's future judgment will likewise be equitable (2:12-16)

- Jewish people will have no advantage in the day of judgment simply because they are Jewish (2:12-29)

- Jewish people were privileged in being the recipients of the Scriptures (3:1-8)

- But the Scriptures condemn all humanity incapable of achieving salvation on its own (3:9-20)

- We can only receive God's righteousness by faith (3:21-31)

Paul's statement in Romans 1:16 is the foundational thesis of the whole epistle: "For I am not ashamed of the gospel of Christ: for it is the power of God unto salvation to every one that believeth; to the Jew first, and also to the Greek." Paul argues from Romans 1:18 through 3:20 that every Jewish person and every Gentile person without exception are sinners and therefore guilty before God, unable to achieve their own justification. Then, beginning in Romans 3:21, Paul addresses the solution to mankind's sin problem, namely the grace of God found in Jesus Christ. A little closer look at Romans 1 will help.

There, Paul describes the downward spiral of sin, with references to God giving people over to their depravity in response to their initiating sinfulness and rebellion. We read in Romans 1:24: "Wherefore God also gave them up to uncleanness through the lusts of their own hearts, to dishonour their own bodies between themselves." Then in Romans 1:26: "For this cause God gave them up unto vile affections: for even their women did change the natural use into that which is against nature." Although Paul makes reference to them being "without understanding" (v. 31), he could not be more plain that they marched their way down the spiral of sin comprehending what they were doing and where it would lead them. Paul writes that they "are without excuse" (v. 20), "knew God" but "became vain in their imaginations" (v. 21) and "became fools" (v. 22), "changed the truth of God into a lie" (v. 25), "did not like to retain God in their knowledge" (v. 28), and although they were "knowing the judgment of God" for their conduct "not only do the same, but have pleasure in them that do them" (v. 32).

Indeed, it is in response to their desire not to have God in their knowledge that God gave them over even further to their depravity: "And even as they did not like to retain God in their knowledge, God gave them over to a reprobate mind, to do those things which are not convenient." (Romans 1:28) Far from teaching that unsaved people are born incapacitated from believing, Paul expressly teaches that they can understand and that it is only in response to their rebellion that God gives them over further to their own depravity. At no point in Romans 1 does Paul say that people reach a point of inability to believe the gospel. What Paul explains in Romans 1 is humanity's sliding all the way down in its depravity as humanity excludes God from the equation. We must keep in mind that while Paul speaks in the plural, this picture applies to us individually.

Romans 3:9 and the beginning of 3:10 form a bridge between Paul's preceding argument and what follows: "for we have before proved both Jews and Gentiles, that they are all under sin; As it is written...." The phrase "before proved" refers to the preceding passages beginning in 1:18 where Paul explained, "both Jews and Gentiles ... are all under sin." Then, at the beginning of verse 3:10, Paul writes, "as it is written," indicating that what follows is provided as Scriptural evidence for his extended argument that "Jews and Gentiles ... are all under sin." Paul would demonstrate that all humanity is "guilty before God" (3:19); they cannot be justified based on their "deeds of the law" but instead only have "knowledge of [their] sin" (3:20). Verses 3:10-12 stress what man does not do (what is lacking) and 3:13-17 stress what man does do, revealing his depravity. And 3:18 ("there is no fear of God before their eyes") effectively summarizes the preceding accusations. Critically, these verses speak of what man does or does not do, and his inability to achieve his own justification, but not of man's ability to respond to God. That is why Calvinists need to rewrite phrases like "there is none that seeketh after God" to something like "there is none capable of seeking after God."

Paul's explicit purpose is to scripturally support his argument that "both Jews and Gentiles... are all under sin." But what does "under sin" mean? If "under sin" means "only capable of sinning," then Calvinists might have a theological leg to stand on. As we so often find in studying the Bible, however, it answers the exegetical questions it raises. Paul makes some comments in Romans 6 that are especially helpful here. In Romans 6:14, Paul writes: "For sin shall not have dominion over you: for ye are not under the law, but under grace." The phrase "under sin" does not mean "only capable of sinning" any more than "under the law" means "only capable of keeping the law" or "under grace" means "incapable of sinning." Paul states that they "were the servants of sin" but have now been "made free from sin" and "servants of righteousness." (Romans 6:17, 18) They formerly served sin and had no allegiance to righteousness, but "now being made free from sin... become servants to God." (Romans 6:20, 22) They were "under sin" in the sense that sin had them in its grip. However, Just as Christians, as servants of righteousness, are capable of acting contrary to their position by sinning, so also non-regenerate people, as a servants of sin, capable of acting contrary to their position.

Paul's purpose, then, is not to establish that unsaved people can only sin, but that no one can live in such a way as to achieve their own justification under the law (i.e., by keeping God's standards), which in the passage at hand refers broadly to the Old Testament revelation God gave to the Jewish people. The notion of being under sin, against the backdrop of Romans 1 and consistent with Romans 6, is that (1) every person sins and (2) they will continue to slide down the spiral of their own depravity so long as they remain under sin.

> Romans 3:9 What then? are we better *than they?* No, in no wise: for we have before proved both Jews and Gentiles, that they are all under sin; 10 As it is written, There is none righteous, no, not one: 11 There is none that understandeth, there is none that seeketh after

God. 12 They are all gone out of the way, they
are together become unprofitable; there is
none that doeth good, no, not one. 13 Their
throat *is* an open sepulchre; with their tongues
they have used deceit; the poison of asps *is*
under their lips: 14 Whose mouth *is* full of
cursing and bitterness: 15 Their feet *are* swift
to shed blood: 16 Destruction and misery *are* in
their ways: 17 And the way of peace have they
not known: 18 There is no fear of God before
their eyes. 19 Now we know that what things
soever the law saith, it saith to them who are
under the law: that every mouth may be
stopped, and all the world may become guilty
before God. 20 Therefore by the deeds of the
law there shall no flesh be justified in his sight:
for by the law *is* the knowledge of sin.

Paul links together a series of Old Testament quotations as
support that both Jews and Gentiles are "all under sin" and
therefore "guilty before God." Romans 3:10-12 borrows from
Psalm 14:2-3, Romans 3:13 borrows from Psalm 5:9, Romans
3:14 borrows from Psalm 10:7, Romans 3:15-17 borrows from
Isaiah 59:7-8, and Romans 3:18 borrows from Psalm 36:1. Paul
selects Old Testament verses that describe discreet unsaved
groups of people completely given over to sin—they have slid
all the way down in their depravity just like Paul described in
Romans 1. Paul shows us the end of the line, as it were, for
those who persist in their own strength leaving God out of the
equation. Anyone who would set out to achieve their
justification in their own strength must understand they are
cannot execute their own escape from sin. All of humanity is
tried and found guilty apart from a right relationship with
God, and their behavior will vindicate God's judgment.

Paul first quotes from Psalm 14 (Romans 3:10-12), a Davidic
psalm that speaks to the future Tribulation period when God's
people are persecuted. It is clear that Psalm 14 did not speak to

events current to David since it speaks, for example, of God's people being eaten like bread, which did not happen to Israel during David's reign. Rather, Psalm 14 speaks to the rampant anti-Semitism that reaches its zenith during the Tribulation period. Although David speaks in Psalm 14:1-3 regarding corruption in universal terms, he then mentions God's people in verse 4, righteous people in verse 5, those who take refuge in the Lord in verse 6, and deliverance for Israel in verse 7. It is evident that David is contrasting two groups of people during the future Tribulation period, the people of God and their persecutors. The conduct of Israel's persecutors shows us a group of people wholly given over to their depravity.

Indeed, they sank so far that the cry of their heart is that "there is no God." (Psalm 14:1) It should come as no surprise that they do not understand or seek God since that is the nature of being atheists. As is common in the Psalms and Proverbs, the notion of lacking understanding (14:2) is simply another way to describe a fool (14:1). The Proverbs tell us that the fear of the Lord is the beginning of wisdom, but these people have no fear of the Lord at all. Borrowing from Psalm 14, Paul describes their utter foolishness in their total self-reliance, but he is not saying that from birth they are incapable of understanding God, incapable of doing a good thing, incapable of understanding the gospel, or incapable of seeking God, and indeed, if that were the case, why would God be found looking "from heaven upon the children of men, to see if there were any that did understand, and seek God." (Psalm 14:2) Rather, Paul explains *what men do* without God, for in reliance only on their own resources and leaving God out of the equation, "they are all gone out of the way, they are together become unprofitable; there is none that doeth good, no, not one." (Romans 3:12) The incapacity to understand the gospel that Calvinists teach is nowhere found in Psalm 14, nor does it even fit Paul's argument in Romans 3. Calvinists say that man is born with total inability. In contrast, Paul teaches a deepening progression into depravity (the effect of being "under sin") that takes us further from God.

Likewise, Psalms 5:9 and 10:7 (Romans 3:13-14) also provide no support for the Calvinist concept of total depravity, but are additional Old Testament illustrations of Romans 1 theology in application. Paul quotes the absolute language in Psalm 5:9 in 3:13, but in the context of that Psalm, this verse is a statement by David about a specific group of his enemies in his time these many centuries ago. Like Psalm 14, Psalm 5:9 uses universal language but only addresses the conduct of a very small subset of the human race in rebellion against God. Similarly, Psalm 10 describes how wicked people behave, and in Psalm 10:7 their speech is addressed. Paul borrows language about speech from both Psalms to emphasize the effects of sin's dominion over unsaved humanity apart from the righteousness that comes by faith that he addresses later in the chapter. Once again, we have a picture, not of where man begins, but where depravity will take him if he continues in rebellion against God. And this shows again that humanity is under sin and thus guilty before God. Critically, however, Romans 3:13-14 only describes their manner of speech, not their capacity to understand the gospel or respond to God. Moreover, note that Psalm 10:4 (just before the language Paul borrows for Romans 3:14) says of "the wicked" under consideration that they "through the pride of [their] countenance, will not seek after God." It is not that they cannot seek God because they are reprobate, but because of pride that they do not seek God.

Paul next appeals to Isaiah 59:7-8 (Romans 3:15-17), whose language in isolation is absolute, but in context speaks of sinful Israel living in rebellion to God, and again illustrates Romans 1 by adding another charge to the indictment of unsaved humanity as being under sin and therefore guilty before God. Paul speaks to their violence in thought and deed. But once again, Romans 3:14-17 describes what people given over to their depravity do, yet says nothing of a total inability to comprehend the gospel and respond to God. We see the pattern continue that Paul addresses *conduct* and not *capacity*.

And finally, Paul summarizes the charges with a quotation from Psalm 36:1 (Romans 3:18), wherein David makes the general statement that wicked people do not fear God, and in the context of the Psalm, seems to have David's enemies in mind. Note that David does not say that wicked people cannot know God, but that they do not fear Him as they should, which is a different matter. Moreover, the reason there "is no fear of God before his eyes" is not that he cannot understand God's revelation, but that his pride is in the way, as the subsequent verse in Psalm 36 states: "For he flattereth himself in his own eyes, until his iniquity be found to be hateful." (Psalm 36:2) This mirrors what Psalm 14 expressly teaches—pride, not incapacity, is the reason people do not seek God. Nothing in Paul's Old Testament quotations suggest anything about a capacity to grasp the gospel and place faith in Christ. Instead, his final quotation returns us to the issue of pride; recall, it was unsaved man's becoming vain in his imagination and rebelling against the God he knew (Romans 1:21) that initiated the Romans 1 downward spiral. Romans 3:10-18 pictures the plight of unsaved humanity given over to its depravity, unable to manage their own escape from being "under sin," for which they are guilty before God.

At this point in the analysis, we do well to recall the hermeneutical circle from the first chapter of this book. We should not expect Paul to teach that people are incapable of seeking or responding to God when the appeal of God in Scripture is that people would seek him:

> Deuteronomy 4:29 But if from thence thou shalt *seek* the LORD thy God, thou shalt find him, if thou *seek* him with all thy heart and with all thy soul.

> 1 Chronicles 16:11 *Seek* the LORD and his strength, *seek* his face continually.

> Isaiah 55:6 *Seek* ye the LORD while he may be found, call ye upon him while he is near.

Jeremiah 29:13 And ye shall *seek* me, and find me, when ye shall *search* for me with all your heart. 14 And I will be found of you, saith the LORD: and I will turn away your captivity, and I will gather you from all the nations, and from all the places whither I have driven you, saith the LORD; and I will bring you again into the place whence I caused you to be carried away captive.

Hosea 5:15 I will go and return to my place, till they acknowledge their offence, and *seek* my face: in their affliction they will *seek* me early.

Amos 5:4 For thus saith the LORD unto the house of Israel, *Seek* ye me, and ye shall live.

Zephaniah 2:3 *Seek* ye the LORD, all ye meek of the earth, which have wrought his judgment; seek righteousness, seek meekness: it may be ye shall be hid in the day of the LORD'S anger.

Acts 17:26 And hath made of one blood all nations of men for to dwell on all the face of the earth, and hath determined the times before appointed, and the bounds of their habitation; 27 That they should *seek* the Lord, if haply they might feel after him, and find him, though he be not far from every one of us:

Hebrews 11:6 But without faith it is impossible to please him: for he that cometh to God must believe that he is, and that he is a rewarder of them that diligently *seek* him.

Calvinists insist there is no inconsistency between God's constant appeal for people to seek Him and their belief that unsaved people cannot seek God apart from irresistible grace. We will deal with irresistible grace in a later chapter, but it suffices to point out here that the Bible plainly teaches that God's appeal for people to seek Him is not in vain: "I have not spoken in secret, in a dark place of the earth: I said not unto the seed of Jacob, Seek ye me in vain: I the LORD speak righteousness, I declare things that are right." (Isaiah 45:19) To the extent that most expositors take Cornelius as unsaved prior to his meeting with the apostle Peter in the book of Acts, he provides a specific example of an unsaved individual that sought God (Acts 10:2,22), as does the Ethiopian eunuch (Acts 8). And again, the reason some people do not seek God is not because they cannot do so, but because of their pride: "The wicked, through the pride of his countenance, will not seek *after God*. God *is* not in all his thoughts." (Psalm 10:4) That is what Paul said in Romans 1:21 and 3:18.

In view of the foregoing analysis, let's return to the three inferences Calvinists draw from Romans 3:10-11: (1) an unsaved man cannot do anything righteous or good with righteous or good motives, and that includes placing faith in Christ; (2) an unsaved man cannot comprehend God's Word, and in particular, the gospel; and (3) an unsaved man will never seek God, and in particular, by placing faith in Christ. As we have seen, read in the contexts of the earlier material in Romans and the Old Testament passages quoted, Paul addressed what non-regenerate people lack or do because they are under sin, not their capacity to respond to God or to comprehend the gospel. Indeed, Paul says no more and no less than that all, Jew and Gentile, are "under sin" and "have sinned, and come short of the glory of God." As long as they remain under sin, they are condemned as a part of sinful humanity being progressively given over to their depravity. All of this is not to say that unsaved man can save himself; God is the initiator by bringing the truth of the gospel, and when a person trust's Christ, God is the one doing the saving. Their greatest need is to be freed from sin, and the solution is deliverance found only in Christ by faith: "But now the righteousness of God without the law is manifested, being witnessed by the law and the prophets; Even the righteousness of God *which is* by faith of Jesus Christ unto all and upon all them that believe: for there is no difference." (Romans 3:21-22)

Paul provided a shorter version of the same argument in Galatians 3:21-22, again using the phrase "under sin" and referring to the solution to the problem, namely faith in Jesus Christ: "*Is* the law then against the promises of God? God forbid: for if there had been a law given which could have given life, verily righteousness should have been by the law. But the scripture hath concluded all <u>under sin</u>, that the promise by faith of Jesus Christ might be given to them that believe." It is interesting that Paul does not tell the Galatians that some can believe and others cannot, but simply that the righteousness required by God is available by faith and will be given to them that believe. We can conclude with certainty that Romans 3:10-18 does not teach total depravity (i.e., total inability).

<u>Pillar Proof Text: 1 Corinthians 2:14</u>

Probably the Calvinists' next favorite passage for the notion that an unsaved person cannot comprehend the gospel and therefore cannot believe is 1 Corinthians 2:14. If you look at how Calvinists interpret Romans 3 and then how they interpret this verse and others I will address below, what becomes apparent is that any time a verse mentions an inability to do something, Calvinists invariably draw the inference that they cannot believe the gospel even though the passages never mention the gospel.

> <u>1 Corinthians 2:14</u> But the natural man receiveth not the things of the Spirit of God: for they are foolishness unto him: neither can he know *them*, because they are spiritually discerned.

In this verse, the Calvinists find the concept directly taught that unsaved man (the "natural man") is not able to receive "the things of the Spirit of God," namely the gospel. But as we shall see, the entirety of 1 Corinthians 2 has nothing whatever to do with total depravity. Instead of addressing total depravity, Paul is making an argument about the current spiritual condition of his Christian audience that is reflected in their divisions and strife. Paul is speaking to the saved people in the church of Corinth about his desire to teach them the deeper things of God. We can summarize Paul's argument in 2:1 through 3:3 as follows: (1) when Paul came to Corinth, he did not speak in words of human wisdom, but simply preached the gospel and demonstrated the power of God (2:1-5); (2) but Paul does teach a type of wisdom to mature believers (2:6-8); (3) this wisdom was received by direct revelation from the Spirit and could not be obtained in any other way (2:9-16); (4) this wisdom of God cannot be understood by a natural person because it involves deep spiritual matters (2:13-15); and (5) because the Corinthians are carnal, Paul cannot yet teach them this wisdom (3:1-3). Paul is comparing the capacity of the Corinthian believers for the deeper things of God with the limitations faced by a natural or unsaved man. The gospel is not even in view. It is the meat of the Word that Paul is concerned about so that he can move them on to maturity.

Paul says this in the first two verses of the chapter: "And I, brethren, when I came to you, came not with excellency of speech or of wisdom, declaring unto you the testimony of God. For I determined not to know any thing among you, save Jesus Christ, and him crucified." Paul did not come to them with man's wisdom but with the gospel and "a demonstration of the Spirit and of power." (1 Corinthians 2:4) But even though Paul did not come to Corinth in "excellency of speech or of wisdom" he does teach a different type of wisdom to mature or "perfect" believers: "Howbeit we speak wisdom among them that are perfect: yet not the wisdom of this world, nor of the princes of this world, that come to nought." (1 Corinthians 2:8) Paul explains why the wisdom he speaks about is directed to the mature believers. This was a hidden wisdom (1 Corinthians 2:9) that could not be naturally deduced, but only received by direct revelation from God. Paul states:

> 1 Corinthians 2:9 But as it is written, Eye hath not seen, nor ear heard, neither have entered into the heart of man, the things which God hath prepared for them that love him. 10 But God hath revealed them unto us by his Spirit: for the Spirit searcheth all things, yea, the deep things of God.

Natural observation will not allow us to learn God's wisdom ("eye hath not seen"), neither can it be learned from men ("nor ear heard"), nor can we deduce God's wisdom from our own minds ("neither have entered into the heart of man"). Instead of being naturally deduced, this knowledge was revealed "unto us by his Spirit." This is not just another wisdom in the arena of ideas, but indeed, "the deep things of God." It is important to notice that the "us" in verse 10 is the same as the "we" in verse 8, namely a reference to Paul and probably the other apostles, not all believers.

Paul confirms again in 2:11 that only the Spirit of God knows the deep things of God: "For what man knoweth the things of a man, save the spirit of man which is in him? even so the things of God knoweth no man, but the Spirit of God." Then Paul says of himself and the select others to whom God made special revelation: "Now we have received, not the spirit of the world, but the spirit which is of God; that we might know the things that are freely given to us of God." (1 Corinthians 2:12) The common misinterpretations of chapter 2 arise from taking the "us" and "we" to indicate Christians generally rather than Paul and the other apostles, individuals specially selected by God for the purpose of revealing His wisdom by special revelation. Paul is saying that he received direct revelation from God, much as he also said in Galatians 1, and as Jesus promised to the apostles in John 16:13.

Paul continues in 2:13 and explains that he is about the business of teaching what was revealed to him by God's Spirit: "Which things also we speak, not in the words which man's wisdom teacheth, but which the Holy Ghost teacheth; comparing spiritual things with spiritual." We must remember at this point how Paul started off. He spoke of his first and primary mission of preaching the gospel and not "excellency of speech or of wisdom," but then made a contrast and explained that there is a type of wisdom that he teaches to perfect or mature believers, namely "the deep things of God." This wisdom that he teaches to the mature believers was received by direct revelation from God. And it is this wisdom that he teaches to mature believers that is being referred to in 2:13 when Paul says "which things also we speak, not in the words which man's wisdom teacheth." Where Paul is heading is that just as this wisdom could not be naturally deduced, but only received by direct revelation from God, it can only be taught to spiritually mature people, for it is wisdom "which the Holy Ghost teacheth; comparing spiritual things with spiritual."

This brings us to the Calvinist stronghold, 1 Corinthians 2:14: "But the natural man receiveth not the things of the Spirit of God: for they are foolishness unto him: neither can he know *them*, because they are spiritually discerned." This verse begins with "but," indicating that it is in contrast to the prior statements Paul made about the source of his teachings and his statement that he teaches certain things to mature believers. The "deep things of God" cannot be understood by the natural man because they are spiritual matters, but Paul is not speaking about the gospel here. We must remember that Paul is writing to a church made up of people who have already professed faith in the gospel. There is no need for Paul to address whether or not they have the capacity to believe the gospel because they already have. What they have not done is matured as believers, and that is the issue he is speaking to, as he will explicitly state in the opening verses of chapter 3.

Ignoring that contextually it is doctrine fit for mature believers and not the gospel that Paul has in mind, Calvinists extricate the phrase "for they are foolishness unto him: neither can he know them, because they are spiritually discerned." They insist that the gospel is foolishness to the unsaved person in the sense that he hears it but cannot comprehend it. However, it is because they are "natural" that the ramifications of God's deeper truths are lost on them, and in that sense they cannot "know them." Since it is the deeper things of God in view here, and not the gospel, this does not mean that the natural man cannot become a believer by faith and, as he matures, come to know these deeper truths Paul wants to teach the Corinthians. As we will see in chapter 3, the saved but immature and carnal believers in Corinth face the same limitations as the unsaved person when it comes to grasping the ramifications of the deep things of God for their lives, and that is Paul's whole point in teaching what he does in chapter 2.

What we have in chapter 2 is Paul contrasting the natural man with the mature believer. But of the spiritual or mature believer, he says they "judgeth all things." (1 Corinthians 2:15) The "all things" refers to the content of Paul's teaching that he received by direct revelation. The mature person has the ability to evaluate these things and understand the ramifications for their lives. Paul concludes: "For who hath known the mind of the Lord, that he may instruct him? But we have the mind of Christ." (1 Corinthians 2:16) The answer to Paul's rhetorical question is no human being naturally knows the mind of the Lord. As he has already taught, only the Spirit knows the deep things of the Lord and those to whom God has made direct revelation, like Paul. Paul and some other select men could say that they had received "the mind of Christ" by this direct revelation. As was Paul's manner to teach this content to mature believers, he desires to teach it to the Corinthians.

Accordingly, in chapter 3, Paul makes the point he was building up to in chapter 2, namely that the Corinthians are characteristically carnal, and just as their outward conduct looks no different than that of unsaved people, they face the same spiritual limitations the unsaved man has with regard to learning the deeper teachings reserved for the mature believers. "And I, brethren, could not speak unto you as unto spiritual, but as unto carnal, even as unto babes in Christ. I have fed you with milk, and not with meat: for hitherto ye were not able to bear it, neither yet now are ye able. For ye are yet carnal: for whereas there is among you envying, and strife, and divisions, are ye not carnal, and walk as men?" (1 Corinthians 3:1-3) If Paul were merely teaching man's wisdom, it could be taught to anyone, but because it is God's wisdom delivered to Him by special revelation, those that would hear Paul's teaching must have a certain level of spiritual maturity. Paul's audience is walking in a sinful lifestyle ("carnal"), which is a reflection of their spiritual maturity. Thus, Paul must feed them milk and not meat. Paul is not teaching the Christians in Corinth about the capacity of an unsaved man to understand the gospel, which has no relevance whatsoever to their situation, but is speaking to those prideful spiritual babies in Corinth about their own condition and inability to learn the deeper things of God available only to the mature. Thus, in its context, there is no support at all for the Calvinists' total depravity in 1 Corinthians 2.

I would further note that what Paul says here in 1 Corinthians is the same issue addressed in Hebrews 5 to believers who had reached a relative level of maturity and then backslidden in the face of persecution. The author of Hebrews desired to teach them deeper truths about the priesthood of Melchisedec: "Of whom we have many things to say, and hard to be uttered, seeing ye are dull of hearing. For when the time ye ought to be teachers, ye have need that one teach you again which be the first principles of the oracles of God; and are become such as have need of milk, and not of strong meat...But strong meat belongeth to them that are of full age." (Hebrews 5:11-14) In Hebrews 6, the author stated his desire to leave behind the basics and "go on unto perfection" (6:1). He recognized that his audience's spiritual immaturity limited his ability to teach them "meat." That is Paul's issues in the 1 Corinthians passage. In both places, the issue is not the gospel but moving immature believers to a place of being able to learn the deeper truths of God. Natural man and the spiritually immature cannot do that.

Pillar Proof Text: Ephesians 2:8

Since Calvinists argue that the unsaved person is incapable of understanding the gospel or believing in Christ, it follows that in order for a person to ever believe, God must give faith to them. This point is critical. The doctrine of total depravity absolutely excludes the possibility of anyone believing in Christ apart from God giving that person his belief. Since people can only be saved through faith in Christ, we should expect ample Biblical proof that God gives people their faith. What we actually have is one primary proof text, namely Ephesians 2:8-9, that Calvinists cite as explicit support, and a small handful of verses from which they infer that God must give people saving faith. Now, let's see if the Bible actually affirms that God gives people their faith.

> Ephesians 2:8 For by grace are ye saved through faith; and that not of yourselves: *it is* the gift of God: 9 Not of works, lest any man should boast.

Calvinists take the terms "that" and "gift" in Ephesians 2:8 to refer to the word "faith" that precedes it in the verse or to refer to both the grace and the faith. Based on this conclusion, they teach that totally depraved man is only able to receive salvation when God gives him the faith he needs. I would first point out that, syntactically, we cannot take the pronoun "that" to refer only to faith. Harold Hoehner recognized this in his commentary on Ephesians: "A serious objection to this is that the feminine noun [faith] does not match the neuter gender of the pronoun [that]."[85] Hoehner concludes that "[r]ather than any particular word it is best to conclude that [the pronoun] refers back to the preceding section... the concept of salvation by grace through faith."[86] Charlie Bing similarly explains in reference to the Calvinist position that "that" refers to faith:

> Let's lay aside the theological problems with such a view and just deal with the text. That interpretation assumes that the word "that" (touto) in verse 8 refers to "faith" as the gift of God (the words "it is" in v. 8 are not in the Greek text but are supplied by translators). However, if "that" refers to "faith," it would have to be in the feminine gender, as is true of abstract nouns like faith. But it is in the neuter gender. So what does "that" refer to? Obviously, it refers to salvation by grace. A survey of the commentary tradition on this verse will find that many, and maybe most, agree with the view that "that" does not refer to "faith." This fits the context perfectly from chapter 1 through 2:1-10, which is about how God has saved us by His grace. The neuter pronoun translated "that" is used elsewhere in Ephesians to refer to a phrase or clause that immediately precedes it (cf. 1:15; 3:1). The parallelism of "not of yourselves" in verse 8 and "not of works" in verse 9 seals the argument that salvation by grace is in view as the gift of God.[87]

---

85 Harold W. Hoehner, *Ephesians, An Exegetical Commentary* (Grand Rapids: Baker Academic 2002), 342.

86 *Supra* note 85, p. 342-43

87 Bing, *Grace, Salvation, and Discipleship: How to Understand Some Difficult Bible Passages*, 175-176.

Consider the following: "...*it is* the gift of God: Not of works, lest any man should boast." Calvinists typically argue that the "gift" must include the faith, for if our faith was not itself given to us by God then we would boast in our works, specifically the *work of believing.* Calvinists argue that believing or faith is a work, and since salvation is not by works, the only way for anyone to be saved apart from works is for God to give them faith. But is believing a work? Is Paul really concerned that one of the Ephesians would boast because of his believing, or is Paul concerned that one of them would boast of their salvation?

I would submit that common sense dictates that Paul is telling his audience that their salvation in Jesus Christ is the gift, received simply by believing, and therefore not a ground for boasting. And the Scriptures confirm common sense here, for Paul explicitly states in his epistle to the Romans that faith is not a work: "To declare, *I say,* at this time his righteousness: that he might be just, and the justifier of him which believeth in Jesus. Where *is* boasting then? It is excluded. By what law? of works? Nay: but by the law of faith. Therefore we conclude that a man is justified by faith without the deeds of the law." (Romans 3:26-28) And in Romans 4:4-5, Paul covers this ground again: "Now to him that worketh is the reward not reckoned of grace, but of debt. But to him that **worketh not, but believeth** on him that justifieth the ungodly, his faith is counted for righteousness." Moreover, Paul in other places used the words "gift" or "free" to emphasize the truth that is already inherent in the term "grace," namely that it is not earned. (see, e.g., Romans 5:15-16)

As Roy Zuck wrote in his hermeneutics text, "An obscure or ambiguous text should never be interpreted in such a way as to make it contradict a plain one."[88] To teach that the "gift" in Ephesians 2:8 refers to their faith, rather than the salvation

---

[88] Roy B. Zuck, *Basic Bible Interpretation, A Practical Guide to Discovering Biblical Truth,* Victor (Colorado Springs: Victor 1991), 111.

itself, is not likely in view of the syntax and is inconsistent with common sense and other clear statements to the contrary by Paul. The plain sense of what Paul tells the Ephesians is that salvation is a gift to be received by faith, and because it is a gift, there is no room for boasting in having received it. There is no support here for total depravity, and indeed on a proper interpretation, Ephesians 2:8 flies in the face of the Calvinist doctrine by teaching that God's grace is available to everyone that exercises faith.

The Unsaved Cannot Believe

In addition to the pillar proof texts we have just considered, Calvinists cite several other verses for the proposition that unsaved people cannot believe the gospel. I will address the more common proof texts below.

> John 8:43 Why do ye not understand my speech? even because ye cannot hear my word. 44 Ye are of your father the devil, and the lusts of your father ye will do. He was a murderer from the beginning, and abode not in the truth, because there is no truth in him. When he speaketh a lie, he speaketh of his own: for he is a liar, and the father of it.

The Calvinists' argument from this verse is that Jesus is telling his audience that they are incapable of comprehending his message and therefore incapable of positively responding. We will see that this passage teaches exactly the opposite. The reader would do well to carefully review all of John 8:12-59. Jesus is speaking at the Temple to non-believing and antagonistic Pharisees and others in the crowd. The key to the passage is Jesus' forgiveness of the adulteress' sins at the beginning of the chapter, which only God can do, and then his claims to be the "I am," Jehovah God of the Old Testament (see verses 24 and 58). The opposition Jesus is facing is from those that refuse to accept him as the unique God-man, the Christ. They have heard him teach that he is the Son of God, but they do not want to accept his words so they persist in asking him who he is: "Then said they unto him, Who art thou? And Jesus saith unto them, Even *the same* that I said unto you from the beginning." (John 8:25) It is to this group who refuses to accept Jesus' identification of himself and keeps asking the question he already answered that Jesus says, "Why do ye not understand my speech?" Jesus answers his own question: "even because ye cannot hear my word."

In context, the point Jesus is making is not that they cannot comprehend his words, but just the opposite. They understand it perfectly well but reject it as blasphemy, and so they keep pressing the same question about who he is. This is evident from the context already examined and the meaning in John's writings of the term "hear." The Greek term is *akouo* (Strong number 191) and its normal lexical meaning is simply to hear. John uses the term 58 times in his gospel. Although it sometimes simply means to hear (e.g., John 4:1), it often carries the connotation of hearing with a response, and sometimes of being able to bear or accept what was said. For instance, John clearly uses "hear" to carry the sense of responding in John 1:37, 40, 5:24-25, 28, 9:31, 10:16, and 11:41-42 (and in many other verses). Likewise, consider his use of "hear" in John 6:60 when, like the passage under consideration, it is those who do not accept Jesus' words whose hearing is in issue: "Many therefore of his disciples, when they had heard *this*, said, This is an hard saying; who can <u>hear</u> it?" By this, his disciples were asking Jesus who could bear or accept what he had said because it was "an hard saying."

This meaning best fits the context of the passage under consideration. When Jesus provides the answer to his sarcastic question about their understanding his teaching, Jesus says, "ye cannot hear my word" meaning that they understood it but would not accept the truth of what he was saying. Notably, some newer translations recognize this; the NET, for example, translates the phrase as "It is because you cannot accept my teaching." In any event, they obviously understood Jesus loud and clear since they took up stones to try to murder him in John 8:58-59. Since Jesus' statement actually acknowledges that they do understand his word, this passage expressly refutes total depravity rather than supporting it.

> Romans 8:7 Because the carnal mind *is* enmity against God: for it is not subject to the law of God, neither indeed can be. 8 So then they that are in the flesh cannot please God.

Calvinists sometimes offer these verses to support total depravity, but the passage has nothing to do with the capacity of unsaved people to believe the gospel. Instead of teaching that unsaved people cannot believe, this passage confirms that people cannot live completely in accordance with the righteousness reflected in the law and, therefore, cannot please God morally. Paul wrote to believers, and this passage occurs in a subsection (8:1-11) emphasizing our deliverance from the law of sin and death (8:2 explicitly says this). While our position is "in the Spirit" (Romans 8:9), our condition depends on how we choose to live. Believers will choose to either walk in the flesh or walk in the Spirit, and our mindset (thought life) will follow our condition. Those believers who walk "after the flesh do mind the things of the flesh; but they that are after the Spirit the things of the Spirit." (Romans 8:5) And, in turn, our mindset affects whether we enjoy the benefits of being set free from the law of sin and death.

Paul writes, "For to be carnally minded is death; but to be spiritually minded is life and peace." (Romans 8:6) The "death" here has nothing to do with the eternal destiny of non-believers, but the present experience of defeat and despair that carnally minded believers have. The reason they experience "death," Paul explains, is because a mindset on the things of the flesh is at odds with God ("the carnal mind is enmity against God"). (Romans 8:7) This should come as no surprise. The person living for purely physical things in a world that is passing away are at odds with God. Recall James' words to believers, "know ye not that friendship with the world is enmity with God?" (James 4:4) The person living for the world has enmity with God because his "carnal mind...is not subject to the law of God, neither indeed can be." (Romans 8:7) We must understand as believers that we cannot have it both ways. We cannot fulfill the righteousness of the "law of God" and have our minds in submission to God's standards while having a mindset focused on the flesh.

Now, we get to the linchpin of this passage for Calvinists. Paul writes, "So then they that are in the flesh cannot please God." (Romans 8:8) The position of being "in the flesh" reflects a non-believer (cf. Romans 8:9). Paul says a non-believer cannot please God, and in the context of the immediately preceding material, Paul means the non-believer is always at enmity with God because they cannot have a mindset that submits to the righteousness of God's law. And Paul's point for believers is that they have a choice to walk in the flesh or walk in the Spirit, and why would they ever want to walk in the flesh, experience death, and be at odds with God.

Now, the Calvinist takes "cannot please God" out of context. Paul says non-believers "cannot please God" in that they cannot submit their minds to the standards of righteousness in God's law, but the Calvinist reads "cannot please God" to mean "cannot believe the gospel" or "cannot respond favorably to God." But the passage does not say an unsaved person can never do anything good or never satisfy any part of the law; it says he cannot keep his thinking in submission to God's standards of righteousness in the law. And this is a far cry from saying he cannot believe the gospel. While the unregenerate cannot please God morally, God is pleased when sinners are saved by believing the gospel: "For after that in the wisdom of God the world by wisdom knew not God, it pleased God by the foolishness of preaching to save them that believe." (1 Corinthians 1:21) The inference Calvinists force over this passage to establish total depravity is completely unjustified.

> Ephesians 4:17 This I say therefore, and testify in the Lord, that ye henceforth walk not as other Gentiles walk, in the vanity of their mind, 18 Having the understanding darkened, being alienated from the life of God through the ignorance that is in them, because of the blindness of their heart: 19 Who being past feeling have given themselves over unto lasciviousness, to work all uncleanness with greediness.

This passage is sometimes used to support total depravity. Having just written about Jesus' gifts to the church (Ephesians 4:11-12) for the edification of the saints and God's desire that believers grow in their knowledge of His Son and mature into Jesus' likeness, and having warned them against false doctrine, Paul admonishes them not to live ("walk") like lost people, in ignorance and blindness to God's standards. Because Paul speaks of the lost having their "understanding darkened" and having "blindness of their heart," Calvinists assert that the unsaved cannot comprehend the gospel and believe. Of course, there is no reason in the flow of Paul's argument for him to jump ship from the issue of godly living and write to the Ephesian believers about the capacity of unsaved people to believe the gospel.

In any event, Paul tells us that the lost are separated from God "through the ignorance that is in them" (4:18), not incapacity, which contrasts with Paul's admonition in 4:13 to grow in the knowledge of God's Son. The "ignorance" they have is not because they cannot comprehend but because of the "blindness of their heart" (4:18). But Paul does not associate their blindness with not being elect; he expressly says it is rooted in their sinfulness (4:19). They are blameworthy for their condition because they "have given themselves over unto" it. In contrast to their ignorance, Paul says to the believers in Ephesus, "ye have not so learned Christ. If so be that ye have heard him, and have been taught by him, as the truth is in Jesus." (Ephesians 4:20-21) Paul did not say to them that God enabled them to comprehend the gospel or "un-darkened" their understanding, but simply that they had learned Christ.

The problem the lost have is alienation from God because of sin, and sin blinds people to the truth and keeps them in ignorance, but the light of the gospel can break through the darkness. The solution to the problem is Christ and the truth he offers, the truth that removes the ignorance so that through faith the alienation from God can be removed. We do well to remember Paul's teaching in Romans 1:21, where he describes the downward spiral of sin and relates it to the darkening of the heart: "Because that, when they knew God, they glorified him not as God, neither were thankful; but became vain in their imaginations, and their foolish heart was darkened." Paul plainly teaches that the darkening followed their knowing God but choosing not to glorify him as God. The subject passage in Ephesians essentially teaches the same truth, saying nothing about any total inability to come to Christ in faith.

God Must Give the Unsaved Their Faith

Calvinists argue that God has to give people the faith they need to be saved. We examined in Ephesians 2:8-9 their pillar proof text for this principle, but there are many others they offer as "evidence" for this principle. The first in our list (Lamentations 3:26) is so weak as to fall into the category of being entirely frivolous as an offer of proof.

> Lamentations 3:26 It is good that a man should both hope and quietly wait for the salvation of the LORD.

According to some Calvinists, this verse expresses humanity's condition. Since a person can do zero toward their salvation, all they can do is wait patiently for God to do it all, if so be that they are elect. In context, however, the book of Lamentations is what its title suggests. It is a set of lamentations written, probably by the prophet Jeremiah, after the destruction of Jerusalem by the Babylonians. The salvation to wait for as they mourn or lament the destruction is God's reversal of what has become of Jerusalem (a condition described in detail in the book) and the rest of the nation. Thus, it is physical and not spiritual deliverance that is being written about. This verse obviously has nothing to do with total depravity. And even if the context were salvation, how could a totally depraved person incapable of seeking or understanding God have the spiritual wherewithal to "both hope and quietly wait for the salvation of the LORD"? There is no evidence here for total depravity.

> John 1:11 He came unto his own, and his own received him not. 12 But as many as received him, to them gave he power to become the sons of God, even to them that believe on his name: 13 Which were born, not of blood, nor of the will of the flesh, nor of the will of man, but of God.

Calvinists often cite John 1:13 for the proposition that salvation from the death penalty of sin is zero percent man ("nor of the will of the flesh, nor of the will of man") and one hundred percent God ("but of God"), which they take to mean God must give us our faith or no one would ever be saved. I have included John 1:11-12 above for context. John 1:12 repeats what is stated throughout the Bible and especially in John's Gospel, namely that salvation is available "to them that believe on his name." What John 1:13 says is that the new birth is sourced in God, and verse 12 says it is given ("to them gave he power to become the sons of God") to those that "believe on his name." The passage does not say that God gives the belief to them, but gives the new birth to those that believe. Verse 13 does not support total depravity, and indeed, as with many purported proof texts for Calvinism, this passage teaches just the opposite. Moreover, a read through the entirety of John's Gospel reflects that Jesus repeatedly asked people to respond in faith either to his words or his works. And indeed, John wrote the book "that ye might believe that Jesus is the Christ, the Son of God; and that believing ye might have life through his name." Everything about this book assumes people have a choice to believe.

> 1 Timothy 2:25 In meekness instructing those that oppose themselves; if God peradventure will give them repentance to the acknowledging of the truth; 26 And *that* they may recover themselves out of the snare of the devil, who are taken captive by him at his will.

Sometimes Calvinists offer this verse as proof that an unsaved person cannot repent "to the acknowledging of the truth," that is, to the gospel, unless God gives the repentance to them. As even most Calvinists will acknowledge, those that make this argument are taking this passage far out of context. The epistle we call 2 Timothy is a "pastoral epistle" that Paul writes to a young preacher named Timothy to help him in his daily church ministry. Paul is not advising Timothy about evangelizing, but about dealing with believers who have been snared by the devil, taken spiritually captive to bad doctrine. For that situation, Paul tells Timothy to humbly instruct them in proper doctrine. And it is concerning these gone astray believers that Paul says God may grant them repentance to the truth, i.e., sound doctrine. This passage simply has nothing to do with the gospel, total depravity or the unsaved at all.

Made Unable to Believe

Calvinists also cite certain proof texts that allegedly demonstrate that God makes people unable to believe. This points out a great contradiction that is important for us to see. Our role as the jurors is to see if the evidence shows what the Calvinists are trying to prove, and at this stage we are focused only on total depravity. The Calvinist needs scriptural evidence that lost people cannot comprehend and believe the gospel unless God gives them faith. But if that is the truth proposition under consideration, why would God need to make anyone unable to believe. If people are born totally depraved and apart from the regeneration of the Holy Spirit are unable to comprehend the gospel and believe, then what reason in the world would there be for God to make them more unable to believe than they already are? This evidence draws a relevance objection. And as we shall see, like the proof texts already considered, these also do not teach total depravity as Calvinists define the term.

> Matthew 11:25 At that time Jesus answered and said, I thank thee, O Father, Lord of heaven and earth, because thou hast hid these things from the wise and prudent, and hast revealed them unto babes. 26 Even so, Father: for so it seemed good in thy sight.

Even though the passage does not mention the elect or reprobate, Calvinists would say that this verse teaches that the non-elect cannot believe because God has "hid these things from [them]." But if that is what the text means, then it has absolutely nothing whatsoever to do with total depravity. On the Calvinist reading, the verse says nothing about the ability of the non-elect to comprehend the gospel and believe, but instead, that God has actively engaged in preventing the non-elect from understanding. There is a tremendous difference between saying that unsaved man, by his nature, cannot comprehend and believe, and saying that God actively prevents them from believing, thus hiding the truth from people. And of course, the text says nothing about when this happened, but it does seem impossible that God could have hidden the truth from them before they were born, or for that matter, before creation when the supposed decrees of God were made. As we shall see, the Calvinists' interpretation is incorrect and the passage actually refutes total depravity.

We should first note the larger context. At the beginning of Matthew 11, some of John the Baptist's disciples come to Jesus to ask if he is the Messiah. Jesus affirms that he is, that his works were those prophesied to be done by the Messiah, and further, that John the Baptist would fulfill the Old Testament prophecies about Elijah preceding the Messiah if he were accepted as such. At that point, Jesus addresses the response of the generation to which John and he preach:

> <u>Matthew 11:15</u> He that hath ears to hear, let him hear. <u>16</u> But whereunto shall I liken this generation? It is like unto children sitting in the markets, and calling unto their fellows, <u>17</u> And saying, We have piped unto you, and ye have not danced; we have mourned unto you, and ye have not lamented. <u>18</u> For John came neither eating nor drinking, and they say, He hath a devil. <u>19</u> The Son of man came eating and drinking, and they say, Behold a man gluttonous, and a winebibber, a friend of publicans and sinners. But wisdom is justified of her children. <u>20</u> Then began he to upbraid the cities wherein most of his mighty works were done, because they repented not: <u>21</u> Woe unto thee, Chorazin! woe unto thee, Bethsaida! for if the mighty works, which were done in you, had been done in Tyre and Sidon, they would have repented long ago in sackcloth and ashes. <u>22</u> But I say unto you, It shall be more tolerable for

> Tyre and Sidon at the day of judgment, than for
> you. 23 And thou, Capernaum, which art exalted
> unto heaven, shalt be brought down to hell: for
> if the mighty works, which have been done in
> thee, had been done in Sodom, it would have
> remained until this day. 24 But I say unto you,
> That it shall be more tolerable for the land of
> Sodom in the day of judgment, than for thee.
> 25 At that time Jesus answered and said, I thank
> thee, O Father, Lord of heaven and earth,
> because thou hast hid these things from the
> wise and prudent, and hast revealed them unto
> babes. 26 Even so, Father: for so it seemed good
> in thy sight.

Jesus gives an illustration of the characteristic reaction of the generation in verses 16 and 17. His point is that in view of the revelation they received, they have not properly responded. Instead, they criticize him and John the Baptist, but for opposite reasons, which demonstrates that they are disingenuous. Following on this general assessment, Jesus upbraids Chorazin and Bethsaida for not repenting at his works and even declares that Tyre and Sidon would have repented had they witnessed the same. Of course, Tyre and Sidon did not repent and will be judged (11:24), and we know from other passages that their inhabitants will spend eternity in the lake of fire. According to the Calvinists, they were predestined to this and were, in fact, unable to repent. But Jesus rejects the Calvinists' position and instead teaches that had they seen the signs he did for "exalted" Chorazin and Bethsaida, they would have repented, which is consistent with his criticism of the generation's improper reaction in 16 and 17 (the criticism implies they could have responded differently). This is a direct Biblical rejection of the TULIP views of total depravity and election.

Since Jesus directly refutes the Calvinists' total depravity in 11:21, he would surely not teach it just a few verses later. What is stated in 11:25 must be seen in this context. Also, it is apparent that Jesus is speaking sarcastically; those called "wise and prudent" are really the arrogant or prideful (like "exalted" Chorazin), and those called "babes" are the humble (not literal infants). In reference to those that saw his works but would not accept him as Messiah and in reference to those that offered conflicting "wisdom" about John the Baptist and Jesus, he says to the Father, "I thank thee, O Father, Lord of heaven and earth, because thou hast hid these things from the wise and prudent, and hast revealed them unto babes." This is not a commentary on their ability to believe, but their refusal to humble themselves and believe. God has openly revealed the truth about Jesus Christ, but by the very nature of that revealed truth, arrogance and pride are barriers to believing. The sense in which God has hidden the truth is simply that it requires humility to accept God's message, and when one humbles himself the truth is no longer hidden. That is why Jesus follows up with an invitation, a statement about his own humility, and a call to take his yoke and learn of him: "Come unto me, all ye that labour and are heavy laden, and I will give you rest. Take my yoke upon you, and learn of me; for I am meek and lowly in heart: and ye shall find rest unto your souls. For my yoke is easy, and my burden is light." (11:28-30) The invitation is to humble oneself and find rest. This passage does not support total depravity, but instead, directly refutes it because Jesus teaches that everyone is capable of believing whether or not they have done so (e.g., Tyre and Sidon).

> Jude 4 For there are certain men crept in unawares, who were before of old ordained to this condemnation, ungodly men, turning the grace of our God into lasciviousness, and denying the only Lord God, and our Lord Jesus Christ.

This verse might better go under the heading of unconditional election, but nevertheless often finds itself in proof text lists for total depravity. The idea Calvinists see here is that certain men were made by God to be false teachers so that they would be condemned by God. As with the last verse, we have to wonder whether the Calvinists are trying to prove total depravity or something else? If they are trying to prove total depravity, then why did God need to ordain them to anything? For by virtue of not being in the elect they will be condemned, and most Calvinists will argue that God did not select anyone for hell, but rather, He simply did not select them for heaven. Those that cite this verse seem be arguing that as part of God's decree of all things He decreed these men to be false teachers (i.e., God decreed sin) and be condemned to hell for it. As I have pointed out several times, words matter a great deal, and the key word here is "ordained." The word "ordained" has as its primary meaning to be written about beforehand, as it is used in Romans 15:4 and Ephesians 3:3. It is the Greek verb *prographo,* taken from the Greek verb *grapho* that generally means to write (we get our word graph from it). The lexicon BDAG gives the primary meaning as "to write in advance or before, write beforehand" and secondary meaning as "to set forth for public notice, show forth/portray publicly, proclaim or placard in public." As shown below, these definitions make perfect sense of the text.

Charles Spurgeon, himself a Calvinist, remarked that the Word of God is like a diamond, which is only to be properly cut with another diamond. Jude 14-15 states: "And Enoch also, the seventh from Adam, prophesied of these, saying, Behold, the Lord cometh with ten thousands of his saints, to execute judgment upon all, and to convince all that are ungodly among them of all their ungodly deeds which they have ungodly committed, and of all their hard *speeches* which ungodly sinners have spoken against him." And then Jude 17-18 states: "But, beloved, remember ye the words which were spoken before of the apostles of our Lord Jesus Christ; how that they told you there should be mockers in the last time, who should walk after their own ungodly lusts." These false teachers that are the primary subject of the little book of Jude are not said to have been predetermined to be false teachers and condemned. Rather, Enoch and the Lord's apostles prophesied generally that such false teachers would come, and by inspiration of God certain prophecies were written and became Scripture. Jude 4 simply teaches that we were warned in advance (*prographo*) about these sorts of false teachers. There is no support here for the concept that some people are totally depraved in the sense of a total inability to believe the gospel.

> 1 Peter 2:8 And a stone of stumbling, and a rock of offence, even to them which stumble at the word, being disobedient: whereunto also they were appointed.

Some Calvinists argue that this verse says certain people were predestined not to believe and are therefore not capable of doing so. Yet again, we have a purported proof text that certainly does not say that unsaved people cannot believe the gospel. Moreover, even if the interpretation taken by some Calvinists were correct, then people reject Christ not because they are unable to believe or God passed them over as He was electing some for heaven, but because He predestined them to reject Christ. Thankfully, such notions are not found in this passage or anywhere else in the Bible.

The proper interpretation turns first on the meaning of the Greek term translated "appointed," and then of course on the context in which this verse appears in Peter's epistle. The Greek term is *tithemi* (Strong number 5087), which appears in the New Testament 96 times. There is not a single instance in which it clearly has the sense of predestine, but rather, it is typically translated as put, set, laid, or make, as the context dictates. BDAG gives its primary meaning as "to put or place in a particular location." It is occasionally translated as appointed. (e.g., 1 Thessalonians 5:9; 2 Timothy 1:11; Hebrews 1:2) Peter used the term only three times. (1 Peter 2:6, 8; 2 Peter 2:6; translated lay, appointed, and making, respectively) In our English language, it is a simple matter to check a dictionary and find that the term appoint is typically defined along the lines of "to fix, set, or arrange." According to BDAG, the term can have the meaning of "to assign to some task or function." Neither the Greek term nor its translation here in 1 Peter 2:8 mean predestination. With this background, let's look to the context.

The term at issue, *tithemi*, was used by Peter in 2:6 (quoting Isaiah 28:16) and again in 2:8 (quoting Isaiah 8:14). In 2:6, he wrote about God appointing, placing or setting the chief corner stone, Jesus, in Sion. In other words, Jesus was placed by God in a position of honor and those who believe in Jesus are likewise exalted or honored by God ("shall not be confounded," i.e., dishonored or put to shame). To set up the contrast, Peter quoted Isaiah 8:14 in verse 8 and addressed the consequences for those that reject the Word of God. We should note here what follows in Isaiah 8:15: "And many among them shall stumble, and fall, and be broken, and be snared, and be taken." Isaiah prophesied that many people would reject the living stone, Jesus Christ. The point is that these disobedient people are confounded or put to shame or debased because of their disobedience in rejecting the Word of God about Jesus Christ. For that reason alone, they are assigned a position of dishonor and condemnation. This says nothing about anyone being unable to believe or predestined not to believe, but instead, Peter merely explained the consequences of their disobedience. There is no support for the Calvinists' total depravity here.

Total Depravity by Analogy

Finally, we come to those proof texts that Calvinists rely upon that may be generally categorized as "analogy" proof texts. Where lost people are analogized to being "dead" in some way or being a "corrupt tree" or a source of "evil treasure," many Calvinists infer an inability to comprehend the gospel and believe even though none of the verses explicitly say so.

> Ephesians 2:1 And you hath he quickened, who
> were dead in trespasses and sins; 2 Wherein in
> time past ye walked according to the course of
> this world, according to the prince of the
> power of the air, the spirit that now worketh in
> the children of disobedience: 3 Among whom
> also we all had our conversation in times past
> in the lusts of our flesh, fulfilling the desires of
> the flesh and of the mind; and were by nature
> the children of wrath, even as others.

We do well to first notice what this passage does not say. It does not say that some group of people cannot believe the gospel. It says nothing of God passing over them before creation. Instead, Paul simply confirms to the Ephesians that before their salvation experience, they were "dead in trespasses and sins." The way the Calvinist argument usually goes begins with a question: "What can a dead man do?" To this question, they respond, "nothing, because he is a spiritual corpse." As such, he cannot even believe. The logical flaw here is referred to as circular reasoning; this occurs when the person making the argument assumes as a premise that which he seeks to prove. The Calvinists assume what they are seeking to prove by how they treat the definition of "dead." Specifically, they conflate the concept of what is means to be physically dead with Paul's use of dead in Ephesians 2:1, which unquestionably does not refer to physical death. But that is not how language works. Paul uses the term figuratively to refer to their former spiritual condition.

Many important Bible words have figurative uses and literal uses, and the figurative use is not just the literal definition with a spiritual application. The Greek word *hupsoō* is used literally in 1 Timothy 2:8 of "lifting up holy hands," but figuratively to mean "exalt" in verses like 2 Corinthians 10:5, 11:20 and 1 Peter 5:6 ("that [God] may exalt you in due time"). There is a big difference in meaning between being physically elevated and being advanced in position or rank, which involves no physical movement at all. Similarly, the Greek *helkuō* literally means to drag or draw, as in John 18:10 (Peter "drew" his sword), John 21:6 (to "draw" in their fishing nets), Acts 16:19 (forcibly move Paul and Silas to the marketplace), and James 2:6 (rich people "draw you before the judgment seats"). But when it is used figuratively, there is no compulsion involved, but instead it has the sense of enticing or wooing, as in John 6:44-45 (God drawing people by His word) and Song of Solomon 1:4 (in the LXX, drawing or wooing his wife). We similarly have the Greek verb *pleroō*, which literally means to fill or fulfill, as in Matthew 1:22, 2:15, 17 (fulfilling a prophecy) and John 12:3 (filling a room with an odor). But when used figuratively, it has a starkly different meaning of being influenced or controlled, as in Luke 2:40 (by wisdom), John 16:6 (by sorrow), Acts 5:3 (by Satan) and Ephesians 5:18 (by the Spirit). Similarly, the word sober means not inebriated, but is only used figuratively in the New Testament to have the sense of being alert and prepared (e.g., 1 Thessalonians 5:5).

All of this is to say that it is a fallacy to conflate a word's literal meaning with its figurative use, or to simply make a spiritual application of the literal meaning. The word *nekros* is a noun that literally means dead, but when used figuratively it very fluid, but does not speak to inability. Even in the English language we use the word "dead" figuratively and it has nothing to do with the total inability associated with being physically dead (e.g., that party is dead). In the New Testament we see figurative uses that do not mean inability, as in Matthew 8:22 ("let the dead bury their dead"), Romans 6:11 (to believers, "reckon ye also yourselves to be dead indeed unto sin") and James 2:17 ("dead" faith). Romans 6:11 is helpful in understanding Ephesians 2:1. Paul writes in Romans 6:11: "Likewise reckon ye also yourselves to be dead indeed unto sin, but alive unto God through Jesus Christ our Lord." The concept here is separation, just as it is in Ephesians 2:1: "you...were dead in trespasses and sins." They were alive to the world (Ephesians 2:2) but dead unto God. Why? Because they were completely oriented to the world and the things of the flesh. But does this mean they cannot respond to the gospel?

The dead man in Luke 16:24 not only could speak to Abraham, but had sufficient spiritual capacity to understand why he was in torment and begged that someone be sent to his brothers to testify to them of the truth so that they might not have to endure the same fate. Moreover, if the dead man can do nothing, then he cannot even sin or reject the gospel, so even the Calvinist must admit that dead men can do something. But can a dead man turn to God? Jesus said so in his parable about the prodigal son: "For this my son was dead, and is alive again; he was lost, and is found. And they began to be merry." (Luke 15:24) The better view of the meaning of "dead in trespasses and sin" is not as a description of unsaved man's capacity to comprehend and believe, but of his condition before God. Adam became "dead in trespasses and sin" after the Fall, and yet at the same time he was able to converse with God. (Genesis 3:1-19) His condition did not render him totally incapable of understanding the things of God, but it did separate him from the life of God, which we see represented in the physical act of his expulsion from Eden and his preclusion from the tree of life.

The term "dead" does not indicate total inability, and in the greater context of Ephesians 2, Paul answers how dead people are delivered from death and made alive, namely through faith: "For by grace are ye saved through faith; and that not of yourselves: it is the gift of God." (Ephesians 2:8) As to the phrase "by nature the children of wrath," we are not to understand that they can only do that which deserves the wrath of God. Although sin comes naturally to them, they can act out of accord with that nature and even "do by nature the things contained in the law" in their lost state. (Romans 2:14) This Calvinist idea that an unsaved person can do no good whatsoever, including responding favorably to the gospel, is simply not found in this passage or anywhere else in the Bible.

> Matthew 7:16 Ye shall know them by their
> fruits. Do men gather grapes of thorns, or figs
> of thistles? 17 Even so every good tree bringeth
> forth good fruit; but a corrupt tree bringeth
> forth evil fruit. 18 A good tree cannot bring
> forth evil fruit, neither *can* a corrupt tree bring
> forth good fruit.

These verses are part of the famous Sermon on the Mount.
Some Calvinists appeal to these verses to establish that
unsaved man cannot do anything good, including responding
to the gospel, from the words, "neither can a corrupt tree
bring forth good fruit." First, note that the context is false
prophets, as verse 15 makes clear: "Beware of false prophets,
which come to you in sheep's clothing, but inwardly they are
ravening wolves." These false prophets do not wear placards
giving away who they are, but instead, they are clandestine.
They wear "sheep's clothing." The fruit Jesus is telling us to
look for cannot be all of their conduct because in sheep's
clothing they will fool us. The whole point is that you cannot
tell who they are by what you see. What is on the outside is a
disguise to cover what is on the inside. The fruit is specifically
limited to their words, for that is what false teachers do that
gives them away; they say "God said...." when God did not say.
It is obvious that the fruit of prophets is prophecy, and
therefore evil fruit must be false prophecy. In Jesus' parallel
teaching in Matthew 12, that it is the teaching or words that is
in view cannot be disputed:

> Matthew 12:31 Wherefore I say unto you, All
> manner of sin and blasphemy shall be forgiven
> unto men: but the blasphemy against the Holy
> Ghost shall not be forgiven unto men. 32 And
> whosoever speaketh a word against the Son of
> man, it shall be forgiven him: but whosoever
> speaketh against the Holy Ghost, it shall not be
> forgiven him, neither in this world, neither in

the world to come. 33 Either make the tree good, and his fruit good; or else make the tree corrupt, and his fruit corrupt: for the tree is known by his fruit. 34 O generation of vipers, how can ye, being evil, speak good things? for out of the abundance of the heart the mouth speaketh. 35 A good man out of the good treasure of the heart bringeth forth good things: and an evil man out of the evil treasure bringeth forth evil things. 36 But I say unto you, That every idle word that men shall speak, they shall give account thereof in the day of judgment. 37 For by thy words thou shalt be justified, and by thy words thou shalt be condemned.

That false teachers walk about in sheep's clothing and must be discovered by their words is confirmed in several places in the Bible. Moses warned the children of Israel to test a prophet's words. (Deuteronomy 13:1-5, 18:20-22) Jeremiah struggled against false prophets that claimed to speak words from God but lied. (Jeremiah 13; Lamentations 2:14) Other prophets also addressed those that lied to the people. (Micah 3:5-6; Zephaniah 3:4; Zechariah 13:2-5) According to Jude, false teachers "crept in unawares" (Jude 4), they "speak evil of dignities" (Jude 8), "speak evil of those things which they know not" (Jude 10), "ran greedily after the error of Baalam for reward" (Jude 11), will be judged for their words (Jude 15), "their mouth speak great swelling words" (Jude 16), and they are "mockers" (Jude 18). The ultimate false prophet is the beast from the land in Revelation 13 who also wears sheep's clothing ("had two horns like a lamb") but teaches false doctrine ("spake as a dragon"). Rather than a sweeping statement about how to pick out true believers from those with false professions, this passage is limited to recognizing false teachers and warns us to test their words.

Total Depravity and Scripture

As we have seen, the Bible simply does not teach, and in fact refutes, the Calvinist doctrine of total depravity aka total inability. In studying theology systematically, we are attempting to pull together all of the truths of the Bible about a certain issue. If our systematized theology is contrary to any passage of Scripture, then we have to re-evaluate and adjust our theology (apply the hermeneutical circle from chapter 1). As Dave Anderson explains of systematic theology:

> Finally, let us remember, Systematic Theology is like a spreadsheet. Changes in one of the major points of the system will most likely cause changes in other points of the system as well. This could be good. It could lead to a new system with a greater degree of consistency, coherence, congruity, and comprehensiveness. But if it leads to increased contradictions or fails to incorporate all the evidence, perhaps the proposed change is invalid.[89]

I will set out below several additional teachings from the Bible that are irreconcilable with total depravity and, accordingly, force us to reject total depravity on the evidence.

First of all, fundamentally, total depravity means that no unsaved person ever seeks God, despite the consistent appeal of Scripture that we seek God: "Seek the LORD, and his strength: seek his face evermore." (Psalm 105:4) Calvinists say that even though God, over and again, appeals to people to seek Him, unsaved people cannot do so. As one Calvinist explains:

> God deals with man according to his *obligation*, not according to the measure of his ability.

---

[89] David R. Anderson, *Free Grace Soteriology, Third Edition* (Grace Theology Press 2018), 32.

> Before the Fall, man had both the obligation and the ability to obey God. As a result of the Fall, he retained the former but lost the latter. Man's inability to obey, arising from the moral corruption of his nature, does not remove from him his obligation to love God with all his heart, soul, mind, and strength, and his neighbor as himself. His obligation to obey God remains intact. If God dealt with man today according to his ability to obey, he would have to reduce his moral demands to the vanishing point. Conversely, if we determined the measure of man's ability from the sweeping obligations implicit in the divine commands, then we would need to predicate *total ability* for man, that is to say, we would all have to adopt the Pelagian [Arminian] position, for the commands of God cover the *entire* horizon of moral obligation.[90]

But where is there any suggestion in the Bible that God deals with unsaved people solely on the basis of their obligations and not their ability. Moreover, this response does not answer the question—why would God just go through the motions of calling people to Him knowing they cannot respond? Nor does it logically follow that if people could respond to God's appeal to seek Him that one must be an Arminian (this is the fallacy of limited choice addressed in chapter one).

We have to ask ourselves, are not God's constant appeals to us to seek Him more consistent with an ability to do so than an inability? The answer is obviously yes, and in any event, God did not leave us to sheer speculation on this point, but affirmatively answers the question of whether we are able to seek Him: "I have not spoken in secret, in a dark place of the earth: I said not unto the seed of Jacob, Seek ye me in vain: I the LORD speak righteousness, I declare things that are right.

---

90 *Supra* note 66, pp. 454-55.

Assemble yourselves and come; draw near together, ye that are escaped of the nations: they have no knowledge that set up the wood of their graven image, and pray unto a god that cannot save." (Isaiah 45:19-20) And again, in reference to Judah in captivity: "Then shall ye call upon me, and ye shall go and pray unto me, and I will hearken unto you. And ye shall seek me, and find me, when ye shall search for me with all your heart." (Jeremiah 29:12-13)

Indeed, the witness of the Bible is that people can seek God. To the polytheistic Greeks in Athens, Paul said: "[God] hath made of one blood all nations for to dwell on all the face of the earth.... That they should seek the Lord, if haply they might feel after him, and find him, though he be not far from every one of us." (Acts 17:26-27) In reference to non-believing Israel, Paul confirms that they have a zeal for God, which is inconsistent with the Calvinist teaching that unsaved people never seek God: "Brethren, my heart's desire and prayer to God for Israel is, that they might be saved. For I bear them record that they have a zeal of God, but not according to knowledge." (Romans 10:1-2) Paul goes further than that. To see the background for what Paul teaches, remember that Moses taught Israel that they had the ability both to understand and do the commandments of the Law: "For this commandment which I command thee this day, it is not hidden from thee, neither is it far off. It is not in heaven, that thou shouldest say, Who shall go up for us to heaven, and bring it unto us, that we may hear it, and do it? Neither is it beyond the sea, that thou shouldest say, Who shall go over the sea for us, and bring it unto us, that we may hear it, and do it? But the word is very nigh unto thee, in thy mouth, and in thy heart, that thou mayest do it." (Deuteronomy 32:11-14) Building on this Old Testament truth, Paul confirmed that unsaved Jews had the ability to come to Jesus, for like the Mosaic Law, Paul's teaching about righteousness by faith was not hidden from them: "For Moses describeth the righteousness which is of the law, That the man which doeth those things shall live by them. But the righteousness which is of faith speaketh on this wise, Say not in thine heart, Who shall ascend into heaven? (that is, to bring Christ down from above). Or, Who shall descend into the deep? (that is, to bring up Christ again from the dead). But what saith it? The word is nigh thee, even in thy mouth, and in thy heart: that is, the word of faith, which we preach." (Romans 10:5-8)

If Paul had said no more, we could conclude without reservation that total depravity must be rejected as inconsistent with the plain teaching of the Bible. But, Paul puts the last nails in the coffin on total depravity when he states that faith comes by hearing, and hearing by the Word of God: "But they have not all obeyed the gospel. For Esaias saith, Lord, who hath believed our report? So then faith cometh by hearing, and hearing by the word of God." (Romans 10:16-17) If faith came as a gift from God, surely this would have been the place to mention it. To try to salvage total depravity, the Calvinist might argue that the unsaved person cannot "hear" the Word of God in the sense that Paul uses that term here, that is, they might try to redefine "hearing" to front-load their theology into the term since it certainly is not in the passage. But that will not work because in this same passage, Paul confirms that they have heard: "But I say, Have they not heard? Yes verily, their sound went into all the earth, and their words unto the ends of the world." (Romans 10:18) So did Israel reject Jesus because it did not hear and know? On the contrary, they rejected God's Word out of sheer disobedience: "I say, Did not Israel know? First Moses saith, I will provoke you to jealousy by them that are no people, and by a foolish nation I will anger you. But Esaias is very bold, and saith, I was found of them that sought me not; I was made manifest unto them that asked not after me. But to Israel he saith, All day long I have stretched forth my hands unto a disobedient and gainsaying people." (Romans 10:19-21) When people rebel against God, sin is always at the root of it: "But exhort one another daily, while it is called today; lest any of you be hardened through the deceitfulness of sin." (Hebrews 3:13)

Paul's teachings in Romans 10 reject total depravity, and so do Jesus' teachings. Remember how Jesus castigated some of the cities he ministered to in Israel for not responding to revelation that would have caused Sodom to respond. (Matthew 11:21-24) In what we often call the parable of the sower, which might better be called the parable of the soils, Jesus said: "And he said unto them, Know ye not this parable? and how then will ye know all parables? The sower soweth the word. And these are they by the way side, where the word is sown; but when they have heard, Satan cometh immediately, and taketh away the word that was sown in their hearts." (Mark 4:13-15) Of the four types of soils, only the first type is representative of unsaved people. Paul said faith comes by hearing, and that by the Word of God. Jesus confirms that unsaved people that reject the Word not only hear it, but have it "sown in their hearts" before it is taken away by Satan. This, of course, parallels precisely what Paul said in Romans 10:8 about the Word being in their hearts and yet rejected. The parallel passage in Luke makes it clear that Jesus is describing what happens when unsaved people reject the Word: "Now the parable is this: The seed is the word of God. Those by the way side are they that hear; then cometh the devil, and taketh away the word out of their hearts, lest they should believe and be saved." (Luke 8:11-12) Obviously, if these people are totally depraved as Calvinists define it, then the devil could not possibly take the word from their hearts and prevent them from believing and being saved. Perhaps Jesus was not a Calvinist!

What Jesus said in the parable of the sower reminds us of Paul's statements in 2 Corinthians 4:3-4:

> 3 But if our gospel be hid, it is hid to them that are lost: 4 In whom the god of this world hath blinded the minds of them which believe not, lest the light of the glorious gospel of Christ, who is the image of God, should shine unto them.

Once again, it is not total depravity that keeps the lost from believing, but blindness brought about by the "god of this world," that is, Satan. Obviously, Satan could never blind an elect person from believing since, according to TULIP, God will in His timing regenerate them and give them faith. But in what way could he blind a non-elect person from believing since, according to the Calvinists, they are incapable of believing anyway? If the TULIP is true, there is no sense in which Satan can blind a person from believing so that they die lost. The fact is that any blinding brought about Satan is ultimately irrelevant since the elect still get saved and the non-elect still go to the lake of fire for eternity.

The immediate context of Paul's statements in 2 Corinthians 4:3-4 about blindness is his statements in 2 Corinthians 3 about the blindness of Israel:

> 12 Seeing then that we have such hope, we use great plainness of speech: 13 And not as Moses, which put a vail over his face, that the children of Israel could not stedfastly look to the end of that which is abolished: 14 But their minds were blinded: for until this day remaineth the same vail untaken away in the reading of the old testament; which vail is done away in Christ. 15 But even unto this day, when Moses is read, the vail is upon their heart.

Paul shares the gospel in "great plainness of speech," not veiling it in any way, unlike Moses' veiling of the glory of God that shone from his face temporarily. As in Moses' day, there remains a veil over Israel's heart when the Old Testament is read. If there were any argument to be made for total depravity, we would expect that the veil must be removed in order for people to believe. Paul says exactly the opposite: "Nevertheless when it shall turn to the Lord, the vail shall be taken away." (2 Corinthians 3:16) The Greek particle *an* translated in 3:16 as "it" is typically used suppositionally and translated, for instance, as "whosoever." Paul is saying that he preaches the gospel in great plainness of speech, and when a Jewish person turns to Christ, the veil is removed.

So it is that faith comes by hearing, and hearing by the Word of God, and we have this testimony about Jesus: "That was the true Light, which lighteth every man that cometh into the world." (John 1:9) And with reference to his disciples who would preach and live out the Word of God, Jesus said: "Ye are the light of the world. A city that is set on an hill cannot be hid. Neither do men light a candle, and put it under a bushel, but on a candlestick; and it giveth light unto all that are in the house. Let your light so shine before men, that they may see your good works, and glorify your Father which is in heaven." (Matthew 5:14-16) The world is a dark place, but the truth can pierce through the darkness, and if people reject the light, it will be because they prefer the deeds of darkness and not because they were incapable of receiving the light: "And this is the condemnation, that light is come into the world, and men loved darkness rather than light, because their deeds were evil." (John 3:19) So everyone must make a choice. Jesus said this in Matthew 7:13-14:

> 13 Enter ye in at the strait gate: for wide is the gate, and broad is the way, that leadeth to destruction, and many there be which go in thereat: 14 Because strait is the gate, and narrow is the way, which leadeth unto life, and few there be that find it.

If the TULIP is to be believed, then it seems that the reprobate would be born on the wide road to destruction and be unable to get off the road. Jesus paints a different picture— that of a choice faced by everyone to choose to enter through the wide gate or the narrow one.

One final note: many and perhaps most Calvinists believe that several passages in the Bible address what they would call "spurious faith," meaning the fake faith of those that are professors but not possessors of eternal life. James 2:14-26 is a favorite passage they would cite as a warning against those who never truly believed. As a result, these Calvinists see books like James and Hebrews as addressing a mixed audience of believers and non-believers and warning them against the danger of deluding themselves into thinking they are Christians when in fact their faith is fake or spurious. It is beyond the scope here to address their misunderstanding of these books, but if they are right, why would these Bible authors write to unsaved people? Since lost people, in their depravity, cannot comprehend the things of God—even the gospel—then why write New Testament epistles to lost people? Surely James and the author of Hebrews knew they were writing to people that could not understand their words.

What we believe has implications. As I pointed out at the beginning of this subsection in the quote from Dave Anderson, small changes to our systematic theology in one place, like working in a spreadsheet, have consequences elsewhere. Total depravity creates tremendous inconsistencies with the rest of the Bible that cannot be convincingly resolved.

An Alternative Viewpoint

Since Calvinism is so often discussed in terms of the acronym TULIP, it seems well to present an alternative view in the form of an acronym. A fitting replacement for TULIP is NULIF (pronounced "new life"), which stands for the following: naturally sinful, unconditional grace, limitless atonement, invitation, and forever. In this and the chapters that follow, I will present these alternatives to the TULIP. The first to consider is *naturally sinful*, an alternative to *total depravity*.

As we have seen, Calvinists hold that lost people not only sin, but indeed are incapable of doing anything good and pleasing to God. They can neither respond favorably to the gospel nor understand it. Although the Bible does not teach total depravity as Calvinists define that term, it does teach that people are depraved. They are under sin and therefore naturally sinful. Every person is born with a propensity to sin and in fact does commit personal sin. Indeed, the person who claims to have never sinned is a liar: "If we say that we have not sinned, we make him a liar, and his word is not in us." (1 John 1:10) Over and again, unsaved people are referred to in Paul's writings as sinners. God loved sinners, and Christ died for them: "But God commendeth his love toward us, in that, while we were yet sinners, Christ died for us." (Romans 5:8) The apostle would even refer to himself as a sinner: "This is a faithful saying, and worthy of all acceptation, that Christ Jesus came into the world to save sinners; of whom I am chief." (1 Timothy 1:15) Every last person is convicted a sinner: "For all have sinned, and come short of the glory of God." (Romans 3:23) Paul refers to the unsaved condition as being "dead in trespasses and sins" (Ephesians 2:1) and the unsaved are "by nature the children of wrath" (Ephesians 2:3).

Does this mean that the unsaved man can never act contrary to his sinful nature or propensity? What about the Christian, whom Paul calls righteous? "For as by one man's disobedience many were made sinners, so by the obedience of one shall many be made righteous." (Romans 5:19) Jesus' sacrifice made a way for "sinners" to "be made righteous." Indeed, the one Christ saves is a new creature: "Therefore if any man be in Christ, he is a new creature: old things are passed away; behold, all things are become new." (2 Corinthians 5:17) John writes: "Whosoever is born of God doth not commit sin; for his seed remaineth in him: and he cannot sin, because he is born of God." (1 John 3:9) The saved man has the righteousness of God in Christ: "For he hath made him to be sin for us, who knew no sin; that we might be made the righteousness of God in him." (2 Corinthians 5:21) The unsaved are called "unrighteous," the saved are called "righteous," and the two should not be unequally yoked together: "Be ye not unequally yoked together with unbelievers:

for what fellowship hath righteousness with unrighteousness? and what communion hath light with darkness?" (2 Corinthians 6:14) The reason, which is confirmed in our experience, is that the "righteous" can behave unrighteously.

Biblical illustrations of the "righteous" behaving out of accord with their being new creatures in Christ are many. To name a few, we think of Moses striking the rock a second time, David taking Bathsheba and murdering her husband, Ananias and Sapphira lying to the Holy Spirit in Acts 5, fornication and litigation in the church in Corinth as recorded in 1 Corinthians 5 and 6, the blasphemy of Hymenaeus and Alexander in 1 Timothy 1, and fornication and eating meat sacrificed to idols in the church in Thyatira as reported in Revelation 2. It seems there is nothing a "righteous" person is not capable of doing, so that over and again the New Testament writers warn their readers not to sin. Paul confirms that the flesh and spirit are at odds: "For the flesh lusteth against the Spirit, and the Spirit against the flesh: and these are contrary the one to the other: so that ye cannot do the things that ye would." (Galatians 5:17) The point of this is that almost everyone would agree that Christians are a new creature in Christ, and yet they do sin. Likewise, an unsaved man can act out of accord with his nature. Although he has a propensity toward sin, he can do good things, including responding favorably to God.

As we have already seen, Paul explains in Romans 2:11-15 that even an unsaved Gentile without any revelation from God has a conscience that can guide him to obey the law. Note especially in 2:14 that Paul does not say that a Gentile, who is without the law, by nature can only sin and reject the gospel. Instead, he says this person can "do by nature the things contained in the law." Even though he has a propensity toward sin, God has written His standards in his heart. When he acts, the conscience God gave him validates whether his actions violate the God's standards or not. Obviously, if he could not do anything good, his conscience could never bear witness "excusing" or validating his actions.

We can also appeal to our own experience at this point. If we apply the Calvinist view that man cannot do anything good to real life, then we must conclude, for example, that unsaved people cannot even love their spouses and children, as many Calvinists expressly teach. At this point, some Calvinists would concede that unsaved men can do some good things, but would insist that they can only do so with bad motives. Some Calvinists create new terminology so that the unsaved man can do "relative good" but not "absolute good." But where is this teaching in the Bible? No verses say that an unsaved man can do nothing good or with good motives. And our experience tells us that lots of unsaved people do good things, just as Christians can do wicked things. The lost man in Jesus' story in Luke 16 begged Abraham to send someone to his five brothers to warn them about the torment. Was this not a lost person expressing genuine love for this brothers as well as spiritual understanding?

So why do people reject God? Is it because that is all they are capable of doing? The Bible confirms that unsaved man can believe: "But God be thanked, that ye were the servants of sin, but ye have obeyed from the heart that form of doctrine which was delivered you." (Romans 6:17) The Bible also teaches that people harden their hearts in sin and that is why they do not respond to God: "after thy hardness and impenitent heart treasurest up unto thyself wrath against the day of wrath and revelation of the righteous judgment of God." (Romans 2:5) People are warned against hardening their hearts as a result of sin: "But exhort one another daily, while it is called To day; lest any of you be hardened through the deceitfulness of sin... 15 While it is said, To day if ye will hear his voice, harden not your hearts, as in the provocation." (Hebrews 3:13, 15) In John's Gospel, we read that sin is the cause of peoples' rejection of Christ: "And this is the condemnation, that light is come into the world, and men loved darkness rather than light, because their deeds were evil." (John 3:19) In Psalm 10:4, the Psalmist says pride is at the core of rebellion, "The wicked, through the pride of his countenance, will not seek after God: God is not in all his thoughts." Over and again, the Bible confirms that people choose to reject God. Consider what God said through the prophet Zechariah concerning the generation God punished with the Babylonians:

> Zechariah 7:9 Thus speaketh the LORD of hosts, saying, Execute true judgment, and shew mercy and compassions every man to his brother: 10 And oppress not the widow, nor the fatherless, the stranger, nor the poor; and let none of you imagine evil against his brother in your heart. 11 But they refused to hearken, and pulled away the shoulder, and stopped their ears, that they should not hear. 12 Yea, they made their hearts as an adamant stone, lest they should hear the law, and the words which the LORD of hosts hath sent in his spirit by the former prophets: therefore came a great wrath from the LORD of hosts. 13 Therefore it is come to pass, that as he cried, and they would not hear; so they cried, and I would not hear, saith the LORD of hosts: 14 But I scattered them with a whirlwind among all the nations whom they knew not. Thus the land was desolate after them, that no man passed through nor returned: for they laid the pleasant land desolate.

Notice that it is the rebellious people that refused to obey God, pulled away their shoulders and stopped their ears. Indeed, they hardened their hearts and refused to respond to God's word through His prophets. God warned Ezekiel when he was called as a prophet that the house of Judah might not listen to him because they are rebellious: "And he said unto me, Son of man, I send thee to the children of Israel, to a rebellious nation that hath rebelled against me: they and their fathers have transgressed against me, even unto this very day. And they, whether they will hear, or whether they will forbear (for they are a rebellious house), yet shall know that there hath been a prophet among them." (Ezekiel 2:4-5) Similarly, in Jeremiah we read:

> Jeremiah 17:21 Thus saith the LORD; Take heed to yourselves, and bear no burden on the sabbath day, nor bring it in by the gates of Jerusalem; 22 Neither carry forth a burden out of your houses on the sabbath day, neither do ye any work, but hallow ye the sabbath day, as I commanded your fathers. 23 But they obeyed not, neither inclined their ear, but made their neck stiff, that they might not hear, nor receive instruction.

Again, we do not read that God made these people unable to obey. They chose not to obey ("made their neck stiff"). Over and again, the Bible speaks to people rebelling against God and disobeying, and it never suggests that God made them do so. And when it comes to the preaching of the good news, we find that some are reported to have believed, others did not believe, but never does the Bible suggests that people are unable to believe. There is not a single historical example of a person in the Bible for which the Bible states the person was unable to believe the gospel. Rather, the testimony of the Scripture is that people are naturally sinful, and if they reject God it is because they prefer sin, not because they are totally unable to comprehend and believe. Lost people cannot save themselves. God does the saving, but they have a choice to respond to the truth of God when it is presented to them.

Concluding Thoughts on Total Depravity

As I stated in chapter 1, it is not a choice between Calvinism and Arminianism that is the issue, but a quest for what the Bible teaches, regardless of whether the Biblical teaching comports with Calvinism, Arminianism, or neither. We have looked at the primary proof texts for TULIP total depravity and seen that none of them support the doctrine. As we saw in the analysis of the proof texts, to force the passages to support total depravity, the passages have to be divorced from their contexts, words have to be defined contrary to their Biblical use (e.g., the word "hear" in John's writings), and unjustified inferences in favor of the doctrine must be made (e.g., that an unsaved person can do no good thing). In fact, we found that many of the proof texts disproved total depravity. In contrast to total depravity, the Biblical concept of depravity is that without exception, we are all sinners in need of a savior. We are slowly drowning in the quicksand of sin and death, and only God can rescue us.

It is important at this point to make an observation about Calvinism and the interrelationship between its teachings. If the Reformed doctrine called the decrees of God were true, then we would know that before creation God decreed some to believe (assuming God intends to save anyone). Assuming that God did not decree to save everyone, then those He did not decree to save cannot possibly believe. In other words, the decrees of God imply total depravity so long as we presume God intended to save some but not all. But since total depravity is false, we can logically conclude that so also is the doctrine of the decrees of God.[91] We will see that all of Calvinism is inextricably linked together with the chain no stronger than its weakest link. It is a house of cards and any card you remove tumbles the house down.

In the chapters that follow, we will press forward and demonstrate that the entire TULIP is unscriptural. Next is the "U" in TULIP, which stands for unconditional election.

---

[91] From basic logic, if the truth of a statement A implies the truth of a statement B, then the statement not B implies not A. In other words, if the truth of the decrees of God necessitates the truth of total depravity, then the falsity of total depravity necessitates the falsity of the decrees of God.

The basic idea is that because of total depravity, the sinner needs God to complete every aspect of salvation for him, including forcing the faith upon him (i.e., irresistible grace). Those whom God will force to believe are the only ones who will be saved, and they are called the elect. In the Calvinists' system, we do not know why the elect were picked for salvation and others were by passed over, only the fact of the selection and that the selection process occurred before the foundation of the world.

Chapter 5

Unconditional Election

Abbott: Strange as it may seem, they give ball
players nowadays very peculiar names.

Costello: Funny names?

Abbott: Nicknames, nicknames. Now, on the
St. Louis team we have Who's on first,
What's on second, I Don't Know is on
third—

Costello: That's what I want to find out. I
want you to tell me the names of the
fellows on the St. Louis team.

Abbott: I'm telling you. Who's on first, What's
on second, I Don't Know is on third—

Costello: You know the fellows' names?

Abbott: Yes.

Costello: Well, then who's playing first?

Abbott: Yes.

Costello: I mean the fellow's name on first base.

Abbott: Who.

Costello: The fellow playin' first base.

Abbott: Who.

Costello: The guy on first base.

Abbott: Who is on first.

Costello: Well, what are you askin' me for?

Abbott: I'm not asking you—I'm telling you. Who is on first.

* * *

As Bud Abbott and Lou Costello's classic "Who's On First?" routine reminds us, sometimes everything hangs on the meaning of a word. And when we do not know what a critical word means in our conversation, we have confusion. This is certainly true in any discussion about theology. The doctrine of unconditional election is unique in the TULIP because the term election, and variations like elect, choose and chosen, occur many times in the Bible. I think that is why I often hear someone say that they are not Calvinist, but they believe in the "Biblical doctrine of election." I often say the same thing because there is a Biblical doctrine of election, but it is not the TULIP doctrine of unconditional election. If we do not know what the term "elect" means, then when we discuss the doctrine of election there will only be confusion.

Let me demonstrate how everything can hang on the meaning of a single word when we talk theology. Jesus told this parable in Matthew to some Pharisees:

<u>Matthew 22:2</u> The kingdom of heaven is like unto a certain king, which made a marriage for his son, 3 And sent forth his servants to call them that were bidden to the wedding: and they would not come. 4 Again, he sent forth other servants, saying, Tell them which are bidden, Behold, I have prepared my dinner: my oxen and *my* fatlings *are* killed, and all things *are* ready: come unto the marriage. 5 But they made light of *it*, and went their ways, one to his farm, another to his merchandise: <u>6</u> And the remnant took his servants, and entreated *them* spitefully, and slew *them*. 7 But when the king heard *thereof,* he was wroth: and he sent forth his armies, and destroyed those murderers, and burned up their city. <u>8</u> Then saith he to his servants, The wedding is ready, but they which were bidden were not worthy. 9 Go ye therefore into the highways, and as many as ye shall find, bid to the marriage. <u>10</u> So those servants went out into the highways, and gathered together all as many as they found, both bad and good: and the wedding was furnished with guests. <u>11</u> And when the king came in to see the guests, he saw there a man which had not on a wedding garment: <u>12</u> And he saith unto him, Friend, how camest thou in hither not having a wedding garment? And he was speechless. 13 Then said the king to the servants, Bind him hand and foot, and take him away, and cast *him* into outer darkness; there shall be weeping and gnashing of teeth.

After he told this parable, Jesus provided this commentary: "For many are called, but few *are* chosen." For many Calvinists, Jesus meant: "For many hear the gospel, but only a few were selected before the foundation of the world for salvation."

Aside from the fact that Jesus said nothing about timing, this interpretation does not do justice to the parable. That "many are called" plainly refers to the invitation to the wedding. The first and second callings were to the Jewish people, who did not come. Then the invitation went to those who were not initially invited, the Gentiles, and they came. But what about the man that came without a wedding garment? We have to keep in mind that those that should have been waiting for the invitation were not prepared and did not come. Those who were not expecting the invitation (those on the highways) dropped what they were doing to attend the wedding. So where did they get proper attire for a royal wedding? Keeping in mind the first century context where clothing was expensive and the average person did not have clothing appropriate for a royal wedding, the answer is that the proper attire for the occasion was given to them by the king for the wedding feast. This pictures salvation by grace. The man that was in attendance without the proper attire was ejected on the king's command. He was speechless because he was caught by surprise that he was not properly attired for the wedding. He is the Pharisee that relied upon his own self-righteousness to qualify him (clothe him) for the wedding, and this ties the parable to Jesus' audience. The only ones that were properly clothed for the wedding were those saved by grace; they were freely given the attire (righteousness) required for the wedding.

Now consider Jesus' statement: "For many are called, but few are chosen." That many are called reflects the universal nature of the invitation to the wedding in the parable. If the Calvinists are correct, those selected by God before the foundation of the world for salvation cannot reject the invitation to the wedding, but this presents a problem. Any elect people should have come irresistibly at the first invitation, but the same group is called twice and refuses both times. In fact, none of these Jewish people come, so are we to conclude that none of the Jewish people are elect? And if they are not elect, whey did God waste time calling them twice. If we let the parable speak for itself, the reason they did not come had nothing to do with being "chosen" or not. The parable says they did not want to come or they were too busy in their worldly affairs to come or that they despised the servants, whom they killed, a clear reference to the prophets.

Moreover, the ones that did come were not specially selected before the foundation of the world, but instead were "as many as they found" on the highways and were only invited after the first group refused. This makes a point Jesus addresses in several places in Matthew, namely the contrast between the unbelieving Jewish people who had significant revelation from God and Gentiles who would believe with virtually no revelation. And then there is the guest without proper attire. If the Calvinists are correct, he obviously is not elect, and therefore must be among the reprobate. He cannot understand the wedding invitation (the gospel); it is foolishness to him. (1 Corinthians 2:14) He has no desire for the things of God and does not seek God. (Romans 3:11) But we must ask, why does he come into the wedding feast? The answer seems to be that he is seeking God, but according to his own terms. As Paul would elsewhere say, "they have a zeal of God, but not according to knowledge." (Romans 10:2)

How we define "chosen" is critical to understanding Jesus' commentary on the parable. Our definition of "chosen" should provide a consistent understanding of the parable rather than just creating new problems. Suppose for a moment that "chosen," which is an adjective in the Greek, had nothing to do with being selected for salvation before the foundation of the world, but instead meant "choice, distinguished or excellent." Then Jesus' commentary would be: "Many are invited, but few are choice/distinguished/excellent." Does this provide a consistent understanding of the parable? Everyone is invited to the wedding, but only those that accept the invitation and come to the wedding are given the proper attire that qualifies them to attend. These invitees were "both bad and good" but when they accept the invitation they are given the proper attire for a royal wedding. They are made choice or distinguished or excellent by the king hosting the wedding. This pictures a mixed bag of people (bad and good) from a human standpoint, and every one of them is made choice, distinguished or excellent because they responded to the invitation. We would understand that they have been clothed with righteousness, and the clothing is a gift from the king. The ejected guest is in the parable to drive home the point. He does not have the proper attire because such attire was not given to him by the king. He showed up in his own clothing, obviously believing it was sufficient, and he was mistaken.

This understanding of "chosen" makes sense of the entire parable and allows it to speak for itself. Moreover, it makes the parable relevant to Jesus' audience. The prideful, self-righteous Pharisees did not need to be told that whether or not they would have salvation depended on whether they were selected for it before the foundation of the world. Had that been the message, they surely would have assumed they were "elect." They needed to be told that their self-righteousness would not be enough. You have to accept the King's invitation, and if you do, He will clothe you properly for the royal wedding. The King and only the King can make you excellent, and this is done only for those that accept the invitation. This is the gospel of grace, not the gospel of unconditional election.

As I indicated in the first chapter, how we define words makes all the difference in our theology. It is apparent what a tremendous difference a definition of a single term can make in a critical Calvinist proof text like Matthew 22. To be sure, the New Testament uses words like elect, election, choose, and chosen over fifty times, but that does not mean there is support for unconditional election. This chapter will not only refute unconditional election, but giving a proper meaning to the Biblical doctrine of election. To do both, we have to arrive at the proper meaning of these key terms. Before we turn to the proof texts and the definitions of the key terms, however, let's look again at how Calvinists define their doctrine of unconditional election.

How the Calvinists Define Unconditional Election

The concept of unconditional election has been formalized for centuries. The Baptist Confession of Faith of 1689 states the Calvinist doctrine of unconditional election:

> Those of mankind who are *predestinated* unto Life, God, before the foundation of the world was laid, according to His eternal and *immutable Purpose*, and the secret *counsel* and good pleasure of His will, hath *chosen* in Christ to everlasting glory, out of His mere free grace and love, without any other thing in the creature as a *condition* or cause moving Him thereunto.

Along the same lines, Steele states the doctrine as follows:

> The doctrine of election declares that God, before the foundation of the world, chose certain individuals from among the fallen members of Adam's race to be the objects of His undeserved favor. These, and these only, He purposed to save.[92]

Other leading Calvinists define the concept of election in relative uniformity:

> Election is an act of God before creation in which he chooses some people to be saved, not on account of any foreseen merit in them, but only because of his sovereign good pleasure.[93]

---

[92] *Supra* note 3, p. 27.
[93] *Supra* note 14, p. 670.

> Election is that eternal act of God, by which in his sovereign pleasure, and on account of no foreseen merit in them, he chooses certain out of the number of sinful men to be the recipients of the special grace of his Spirit, and so to be made voluntary partakers of Christ's salvation.[94]

> It may be defined as *God's* eternal purpose to save some of the human race in and by Jesus Christ.[95]

> By election we mean that sovereign act of God in grace whereby He chose in Christ Jesus for salvation all those whom He foreknew would accept Him.[96]

In addition to the election of people, part of the TULIP includes the election of angels. For this reason, Dabney includes angels in his definition of the doctrine of unconditional election: "By the decree of God, for the manifestation of His own glory, some men and angels are predestinated unto everlasting life, and others foreordained to everlasting death."[97] Dabney's definition recognizes the necessary and logical result of unconditional election, namely that "others [are] foreordained to everlasting death." Whether God foreordained people for the lake of fire as Dabney holds is a point of contention among Calvinists, with many preferring to simply say that God chose to pass over the rest by rather than choosing them for hell. I would submit that whatever distinction can be made here, it does not matter one iota to the people not picked for heaven. This twin concept to unconditional election is called reprobation:

---

94 *Supra* note 30, p. 779.
95 *Supra* note 34, p. 91.
96 *Supra* note 35, p. 344.
97 *Supra* note 36, p. 224.

The doctrine of election naturally implies that some of the human race were not elected. If God purposed to save some, He also purposed not to save others... Reprobation may be defined as *that decree of God whereby He has determined to pass some men by with the operation of His special grace and to punish them for their sin to the manifestation of His justice....*[98]

The Calvinist concepts of *unconditional election* and *reprobation*, taken together, are referred to as the doctrine of *predestination*, a part of the eternal decrees of God that was the subject of chapter 3.[99]

An Analysis of Key Terms

As I have pointed out several times, it matters a great deal how we define the terms we use to discuss theology. Before turning to the Calvinists' proof texts for unconditional election, we should first consider the proper definitions of some Biblical terms that we will find in the proof texts. These words in our English translation include elect, election, choose, and chosen. Calvinists tend to front load their theology into these words,

---

[98] *Supra* note 34, p. 91.

[99] Although beyond the scope of this book to provide a detailed discussion, I would point out that some Calvinists debate the question of "whether in the plan of God the decrees of election and reprobation precede or follow the decrees to create the world and to permit the fall." Berkhof, p. 92. Some Calvinists hold to the *supralapsarian* view. Under this view, God made a decision to save some and damn others, known only in His mind as possibilities at the time, and then subsequently decreed to create both groups of people, then decreed "to permit man to fall" and then decreed a way of salvation for the elect. *Id.*, p. 93. Some Calvinists hold to the infralapsarian view, namely that God first decreed to create man, then decreed to permit the fall, then decreed to elect some and pass over others, and finally decreed a way of salvation for the elect. *Id.*

thereby guaranteeing their interpretation of the proof texts. And by so doing, they find their doctrine taught in nearly every verse where these key words occur. Our goal here is to consider the proper Biblical usage of these words without regard to proving any particular theological conception.

In the New Testament, we find the adjective ἐκλεκτός (eklektos)[100] used twenty-two times and generally translated as chosen or elect. We find the related verb ἐκλέγομαι (eklegomai)[101] used twenty-two times and generally translated as choose. We also find the noun ἐκλογή (ekloge)[102] used seven times. The adjective *eklektos* is used several times in reference to tribulation saints (not all saints) and is also used to describe angels, churches, and Jesus and most often the word is used as an adjective without any further theological explanation (e.g., "for the elect's sake those days will be shortened," "I endure all things for the elect's sake"). Obviously, the word cannot always carry the meaning (assuming it ever does) of having been selected before the foundation of the world for salvation since it refers to angels, churches, and Jesus. Of the twenty-one uses of the verb *eklegomai*, most refer to men's choices, the selection of the apostle or of Israel or the Gentiles, the end-time saints, or Jesus. Indeed, only in Ephesians 1:4 is there a reference to the *eklegomai* of all Christians, a verse I will address in detail. Finally, of the seven uses of the noun *ekloge*, four refer to Israel, one to Paul himself, and two to the believer's "election" without further theological explanation.

With these usages in mind, two preliminary observations are

---

[100] Matthew 20:16, 22:14, 24:22, 24:24, 24:31; Mark 13:20, 13:22, 13:27; Luke 18:7, 23:35; Romans 8:33, 16:13; Colossians 3:12; 1 Timothy 5:21; 2 Timothy 2:10; Titus 1:1; 1 Peter 1:2, 2:4, 2:6, 2:9; 2 John 1, 13; and Revelation 17:14.

[101] Mark 13:20; Luke 6:13, 10:42, 14:7; John 6:70, 13:18, 15;16, 19; Acts 1:2, 24, 6:5, 13:17, 15:7, 22, 25; 1 Corinthians 1:27-28; Ephesians 1:4; James 2:5. The Strong number is 1586.

[102] Acts 9:15; Romans 9:11, 11:5, 7, 28; 1 Thessalonians 1:4; 2 Peter 1:10. The Strong number is 1589.

critical. First, the volume of occurrences of the word "elect" and related terms, standing alone, does not mean there is support for TULIP unconditional election. Second, many of the verses that use these words do not answer the critical questions of when, how and why. For us to get our hands around what the Bible actually teaches about election, we need to know what the key words mean and then isolate the verses that say something about when people become elect, how people become elect, or why people become elect. We start with trying to understand what the key words mean.

The Old Testament makes use of the words "choose" and "chosen" without ever suggesting that anyone was chosen for salvation. Sometimes the term "chosen" (Hebrew בָּחִיר or bachiyr) is in reference to Israel. (e.g., 1 Chronicles 16:13; Psalm 105:6; Isaiah 43:20) But note that the same terminology can carry the meaning of choice, distinguished or excellent as the context may indicate. Instead of being translated "chosen," we find the root of the same Hebrew term translated as "excellent" in reference to Solomon's countenance in Song 5:15, "acceptable" in Proverbs 21:3, "choice silver" in Proverbs 8:19 and 10:20, "choice gold" in Proverbs 8:10, "choice men" in 2 Chronicles 25:5, and "chosen [excellent or the best] chariots" in Exodus 14:7. David is referred to as "my chosen" in Psalm 89:3, Moses is referred to as "chosen" in Psalm 106:23, and Jesus is referred to as "elect" in Isaiah 42:1: "Behold my servant, whom I uphold; mine elect, in whom my soul delighteth; I have put my spirit upon him: he shall bring forth judgment to the Gentiles." In the cases of David, Moses, and Jesus, the idea is that they are choice, distinguished or excellent, and the context involves their role as servants. To see this, consider the quotation of Isaiah 42:1 found in Matthew 12:18: "Behold my servant, whom I have chosen; my beloved, in whom my soul is well pleased: I will put my spirit upon him, and he shall shew judgment to the Gentiles." Matthew replaces "uphold" with "chosen," which equates God's upholding, support, and approval with "chosen." Similarly, Matthew replaces "elect" with "beloved," which equates Jesus being beloved by God with being "elect." Jesus is again referred to by God as "beloved" in Matthew 17:5, Mark 9:7, and Luke 9:35 on the Mount of Transfiguration, a Messianic reference to passages in Isaiah, and I would point out that the Luke passage in some Greek manuscripts uses the term "elect" instead of "beloved" (Greek *agapatos*). Jesus is "the chosen one" in 1 Peter 2:4, 6, and in both verses "chosen" is in close association with "precious."

With this brief look at the Hebrew usage in the Old Testament, we turn to the Greek adjective *eklektos*. A place to start is with the leading Greek lexicon (often referred to as BDAG for short), which defines it as "pertaining to being selected," but with secondary meanings "pertaining to being especially distinguished" (referencing as an example the "elect angels" or "distinguished angels" of 1 Timothy 5:21) and "pertaining to being considered best in the course of a selection, choice, excellent." For the latter definition, BDAG cites numerous examples in the Bible and other Greek literature. Liddell and Scott's lexicon provides a secondary definition of "choice, pure." Since *eklektos* has more than one lexical definition, context must drive our determination of which usage applies in a particular verse. We will see that the meaning of "choice," "distinguished," or "excellent" is most common and best fits most of the New Testament usages. We will start by looking at the occurrences of this term in the Septuagint (the Greek translation of the Old Testament), Apocrypha, and Pseudepigrapha.

To list some of the examples, the term *eklektos* is used as follows: "choice" sepulchres (Genesis 23:6), "well favoured" animals (Genesis 41:2, 4, 18, 20), "rank" corn (Genesis 41:5, 7), "chosen [i.e., the best] chariots" (Exodus 14:7), "pure myrrh" (Exodus 30:23), "young men" (Numbers 11:28; 2 Kings 8:12; Isaiah 40:30; Lamentations 1:15, 5:13-14), "choice vows" (Deuteronomy 12:11), "chosen [i.e., the best] men" (Judges 20:15, 34; 1 Samuel 24:2, 26:2; Judith 2:15; 1 Maccabees 9:5, 15:26; Psalm

78:31), "pure" (2 Samuel 22:27; Psalm 18:26), "fat oxen" and "fatted fowl" (1 Kings 4:23), "choice fir trees" (2 Kings 19:23), "choice...men" (1 Chronicles 7:40), "great stones" (Ezra 5:8), "choice sheep" (Nehemiah 5:18), "best horseman" (1 Maccabees 4:1), the finest foods (Psalm 141:4), "choice silver" (Proverbs 8:19), choice hearts (Proverbs 17:3), "excellent... cedars" (Song of Solomon 5:15), "choice" child (Song of Solomon 6:9), "best myrrh" (Sirach 46:1), "plenteous" meat (Habakkuk 1:16), the "pleasant land" (Zechariah 7:14; Jeremiah 3:10), "choicest valleys" (Isaiah 22:7), "precious cornerstone" (Isaiah 28:16), "polished shaft" (Isaiah 49:2), "pleasant stones" (Isaiah 54:12), "valiant men" (Jeremiah 46:15), "pleasant vessel" (Jeremiah 25:34), "precious clothes" (Ezekiel 27:20), "costly stones" (Enoch 8:1), and "choice portions" (Testament of Levi 14:5).

The Greek writings of Philo are also helpful. His life spanned from approximately 20 B.C. to 50 A.D. He lived in Alexandria, Egypt, and applied an allegorical approach to the Jewish scriptures. Philo referred to Abraham as the "great father of sounds" in Cherubim 7 (with "great" translating *eklektos*), and the "elect father of sounds" in several places. Philo explained his description of Abraham: "The word 'elect' belongs to the mind of the wise man, **for whatever is most excellent** is found in him." (Names 69) And in another place: "And by the addition of the word **elect** his goodness is intimated. For the evil disposition is a random and confused one, but that which is **elect** is good, having been selected from all others by reason of its excellence." (Abraham 83)

As these examples demonstrate, the adjective *eklektos* was commonly used with a derived meaning of choice, distinguished or excellent. The related verb and noun form can also have a similar derived meaning. According to BDAG, the verb *eklegomai* can have the meaning "to pick out someone or something, choose" but has a secondary meaning of "to make choice in accordance with significant preference." As Gordon Olson observes, "[t]he secular and Septuagint Greek predominantly shows a derived meaning of the best or the choice, such as 'the most beautiful of what is to be praised' or 'something good from literary treasures,' 'that which is choice or excellent,' 'what is desired, or costly,' 'what is costly in the concept of the pure,' 'emphasizes the choice or excellent element...'"[103] The noun *ekloge* is defined by BDAG as "a special choice, selection, choice, election." Olson observes that the "meaning of the noun *ekloge* in secular Greek is predominantly 'selection', also having a qualitative meaning, and in Jewish writings, human free choice."[104]

It should come as no surprise that the predominant meaning of these terms in the Septuagint and other Greek literature is also employed in the New Testament. For example, in Acts 15:22, in reference to the circulation of the decision of the Jerusalem Council, we read: "Then pleased it the apostles and elders, with the whole church, to send **chosen** men of their own company to Antioch with Paul and Barnabas; *namely*, Judas surnamed Barsabas, and Silas, chief men among the brethren." The term "chosen" (*eklektos*) means proven or excellent on the basis of the church's experience with these "men that have hazarded their lives for the name of our Lord Jesus Christ." (Acts 15:26) The usage in Acts 15 has nothing to do with the selection of Judas and Silas for salvation. And as already demonstrated, Jesus is often referred to as the chosen one. In Luke 23:35, we read: "And the people stood beholding. And the rulers also with them derided him, saying, He saved others; let him save himself, if he be Christ, the **chosen** of God." The point is that Jesus is the choice or excellent one of Isaiah 42:1, the Messiah. This is consistent with what we read in 1 Peter 2:4, 6 where Jesus is the "chosen of God" and "elect, precious": "To whom coming, as unto a living stone, disallowed indeed of men, but **chosen** of God, and precious...

[103] C. Gordon Olson, *Getting the Gospel Right* (Cedar Knolls: Global Gospel Publishers, 2005), p. 276.
[104] *Supra* note 103, p. 276.

Wherefore also it is contained in the scripture, Behold, I lay in Sion a chief corner stone, **elect**, precious: and he that believeth on him shall not be confounded." And as I demonstrated in the introduction to this chapter, the meaning of "choice, distinguished or excellent" makes the best sense of the wedding parable in Matthew 22:1-14, and so we have Jesus explaining that believers are "chosen" in the sense of being made excellent *after* their accepting the calling or invitation of God. Based upon this usage, the New Testament reference to Christians as "elect" or "chosen" makes perfect sense as a positional truth. Just as Paul referred to Christians as "saints" (literally, holy ones), the references to Christians as choice, distinguished or excellent fits our position in Christ. As Jesus explained in the parable of the wedding feast, the King has given us our attire for the royal wedding, clothing us in righteousness and making us excellent.

Seeing above that our key words unquestionably do not always in the New Testament (or the Old) have anything to do with being selected for salvation, we need to be especially attuned to the verses that use elect or chosen and also answer the critical questions of when, how and why since the answers to those question determine whether TULIP unconditional election is Biblical. For instance, Paul wrote in Romans 16:13: "Salute Rufus **chosen** in the Lord, and his mother and mine." Here, "chosen" (*eklektos*) is further described as being true of Rufus "in the Lord." As we will discuss in detail below in reference to Ephesians 1:4, Paul frequently employed similar phraseology to indicate positional truths about believers. Romans 16:13 thus provides theological content as to the "when" and "how," that is, it suggests Rufus became "chosen" or elect when he became "in the Lord," which occurred when he trusted Christ, and not before the foundation of the world. As another example, Peter wrote his first epistle to the "elect according to the foreknowledge of God the Father, through sanctification of the Spirit, unto obedience and sprinkling of the blood of Jesus Christ." (1 Peter 1:2) We will address this verse in more detail below, but would briefly remark here that the verse helps with the questions of "how" and "why." The "how" is "through the sanctification" or setting apart "of the Spirit," which means that if we are sanctified or set aside by the Spirit at the moment of believing the gospel, then our becoming elect occurs at that moment. The "why" is not said to be for salvation or justification, but instead, for "obedience and the sprinkling of the blood of Jesus."

These examples point away from TULIP unconditional election, not to it. With this background in mind, we will proceed to the Calvinists' proof texts.

Pillar Proof Text: Romans 9

There are two primary Calvinist pillars for unconditional election and then myriad other passages that frequently fill out a cite list without any extended exegesis. If a person accepts that the pillar passages teach unconditional election, there is a danger of writing the doctrine over almost any verse that uses terms like elect or chosen even though those verses provide no answers to the when, how and why questions alluded to earlier. For this reason, I will first address the pillar passages, then move on to some of the more popular (but certainly not all) of the remaining New Testament proof texts. Probably no passage of the Bible is more used (and exegetically abused!) than Romans 9 to support unconditional election and other parts of the TULIP. Some Calvinists appeal to verses like these from Romans 9:

> For *the children* being not yet born, neither
> having done any good or evil, that the purpose
> of God according to election might stand, not
> of works, but of him that calleth. (9:11)

> As it is written, Jacob have I loved, but Esau
> have I hated. (9:13)

> For he saith to Moses, I will have mercy on whom
> I will have mercy, and I will have compassion on
> whom I will have compassion. (9:15)

> Hath not the potter power over the clay, of the
> same lump to make one vessel unto honour, and
> another unto dishonour? (9:21)

Some Calvinists point to 9:11-13 and claim it as an explicit example of God's unconditional election of Jacob for salvation and Esau for eternity in the lake of fire (or at least passing him over). And some would say that God did likewise as between Moses and Pharaoh. And in general, from 9:21, God the potter made some pots for honour (salvation) and some for dishonour (damnation). A typical reaction to this interpretation is that God seems unfair. To this, the Calvinists explain that Paul anticipated that argument and addressed it in 9:19-20: "Thou wilt say then unto me, Why doth he yet find fault? For who hath resisted his will? Nay but, O man, who art thou that repliest against God? Shall the thing formed say to him that formed *it*, Why hast thou made me thus?" God, as the creator of all people, has the right to create them for whatever destiny He desires.

The problem for the Calvinists' position is that, just as Romans 3 (their stronghold for total depravity) had nothing at all to do with total depravity, Romans 9 has nothing to do with election of individuals to salvation from the death penalty of sin. Because this chapter of Romans is central to the entire Calvinist philosophy, it is worth our time to study it in detail. Paul had much to say about Israel prior to chapter 9, so we will begin with a brief overview of the preceding material in Romans about Israel as context for the issues Paul addresses in Romans 9.

In Romans 1, Paul explains how God's wrath is poured out on unrighteousness. Paul writes in Romans 2:11-12: "For there is no respect of persons with God. For as many as have sinned without the law shall also perish without law: and as many as have sinned in the law shall be judged by the law." It is easy for

Gentile believers today to gloss over a truth claim like this, but Paul's statement was controversial in his time. Paul confirms that no one is automatically right before God and that God will judge both Jews and Gentiles. Paul then moves to the problem of hypocrisy among Jews in his day (Romans 2:17-23) that Jesus so often addressed in the gospels and concludes: "For the name of God is blasphemed among the Gentiles through you, as it is written. For circumcision verily profiteth, if thou keep the law: but if thou be a breaker of the law, thy circumcision is made uncircumcision." (Romans 2:24-25) The Jew is not secure before God because of being Jewish or because they have the law, but because of their failure to keep the law, they are no different before God than the Gentiles that were not recipients of the law. Moreover, just as a Jewish hypocrite is like a Gentile, the Gentile that keeps the law is like a Jew. (Romans 2:26) This leads Paul to explain what a true Jew is: "For he is not a Jew, which is one outwardly; neither is that circumcision, which is outward in the flesh. But he is a Jew, which is one inwardly; and circumcision is that of the heart, in the spirit, and not in the letter; whose praise is not of men, but of God." (Romans 2:28-29) Being Jewish in the flesh is not enough to give one standing before God. Whether Jewish or Gentile, what matters is whether one is circumcised of the heart and in the spirit.

This teaching leads to the natural question of whether there is any value at all in being Jewish. (Romans 3:1) The answer is that being Jewish did entail special blessings, especially the "oracles of God." (Romans 3:2; see also Romans 9:4-5) Paul's statement was all-inclusive, but he surely had the covenant with Abraham at the front of his mind. Israel was assured tremendous blessings in God's covenant with Abraham. But the problem was that most Jews had not followed Abraham's example of faith. Paul asks whether their lack of faith somehow cancels God's faithfulness to His promises. (Romans 3:3) In a typical Pauline response: "God forbid: yea, let God be true, but every man a liar...." (Romans 3:4) Paul then quotes

Psalm 51:4, wherein David extols God's justice and faithfulness despite his own failings: "That thou mightest be justified in thy sayings, and mightest overcome when thou art judged." So in fact, the faithlessness of the Jewish people highlights the righteousness of God, a point Paul returns to and explains in detail in chapter 9. Paul then echoes Romans 2:11-12 and states that Jews are not better than Gentiles because both are under sin. (Romans 3:9) Later in chapter 3, Paul reaffirms that "all have sinned, and come short of the glory of God," but also affirms that the righteousness of God by faith is equally available to all. (Romans 3:22-23) Indeed, God is not God of the Jews only, but also of the Gentiles, and He "shall justify the circumcision by faith, and the uncircumcision through faith." (Romans 3:29-30)

In Romans 4, Paul defends his position that the righteousness of God is available by faith to everyone by use of Abraham as an example, who trusted God and was justified before being circumcised. (Romans 4:9-10) Abraham's circumcision did not save him, but was a sign of what had already been completed based on his faith, and the result is that he is the father of all those that come to God by faith: "that he might be the father of all them that believe, though they be not circumcised; that righteousness might be imputed unto them also. And the father of circumcision to them who are not of the circumcisions only, but who also walk in the steps of that faith of our father Abraham, which he had being yet uncircumcised." (Romans 4:11-12) The unfortunate reality of Paul's time was that most of the Jews rejected Christ despite their receipt of the oracles of God.

Romans 8 culminates with Paul's exclamation that nothing can separate Christians from the love of God. (Romans 8:38-39) But one might argue that Israel has been separated from God. This leads Paul to expound upon what he already said about Israel in earlier chapters and address in detail in Romans 9-11 the question of the effectiveness of God's word in regard to Israel.

> Romans 9:1 I say the truth in Christ, I lie not, my conscience also bearing me witness in the Holy Ghost, 2 That I have great heaviness and continual sorrow in my heart. 3 For I could wish that myself were accursed from Christ for my brethren, my kinsmen according to the flesh: 4 Who are Israelites; to whom *pertaineth* the adoption, and the glory, and the covenants, and the giving of the law, and the service *of God,* and the promises; 5 Whose *are* the fathers, and of whom as concerning the flesh Christ *came,* who is over all, God blessed for ever. Amen.

Of course, Paul was himself Jewish, and although he was an "apostle of the Gentiles" (Romans 11:13), he was experiencing great sorrow over national Israel. He even says that he wishes he could be "accursed from Christ" if somehow that would draw to Christ his "kinsmen according to the flesh." Paul explicitly states in 9:4 that he is talking about Israel, the nation that received the covenants and the law and promises in the Old Testament. And in 9:5, Paul speaks of the fathers (i.e., Abraham, Isaac, Jacob) who were Jewish, and that in the flesh Jesus himself was Jewish. Paul's heart is heavy because, despite all of the revelation of God toward Israel, characteristically the Jewish people in Paul's time had rejected Jesus as Messiah.

> Romans 9:6 Not as though the word of God hath taken none effect. For they *are* not all Israel, which are of Israel: 7 Neither, because they are the seed of Abraham, *are they* all children: but, In Isaac shall thy seed be called. 8 That is, They which are the children of the flesh, these *are* not the children of God: but the children of the promise are counted for the seed.

Notwithstanding Israel's characteristic rejection of Jesus, Paul states that God's Word has been effective. Even Israel's unbelief has been consistent with God's Word and God worked through that unbelief to carry out His redemptive plan for humanity. Critically, Paul says, "They are not all Israel, which are of Israel." Paul will argue that not everyone who is physically Jewish is also spiritually Jewish, but God's Word has been effective because there is now a true Israel, which includes both believing Jews and believing Gentiles. Paul builds this argument around the concept of God's selective choices, but Paul never addresses God picking individuals to save from sin's penalty and passing over others.

That selection process began before there was a nation of Israel. Paul especially has in mind the promises made to Abraham, as recorded in the book of Genesis. In Genesis 12:1-3, for example, we read: "Now the LORD had said unto Abram, Get thee out of thy country, and from thy kindred, and from thy father's house, unto a land that I will shew thee: And I will make of thee a great nation, and I will bless thee, and make thy name great; and thou shalt be a blessing: And I will bless them that bless thee, and curse him that curseth thee: and in thee shall all families of the earth be blessed." God promised Abraham (1) land, (2) that He would bless Abraham and make a great nation from him, and (3) that He would bless all the families of the earth through Abraham. Paul says in 9:6 that not everyone that is "of Israel" is "Israel." This is what Paul said back in Romans 2:28-29, that not everyone who is physically a Jew is inwardly (or spiritually) a Jew. And so there is being Jewish physically and being Jewish spiritually, which Paul now illustrates by analogy through Abraham and Isaac. (cf. Galatians 4:28) There are two groups of Abraham's descendants, those who are only physical descendants, and those who are also descendants by promise. This is seen in Abraham's children Ishmael and Isaac.

Paul says: "Neither, because they are the seed of Abraham, are they all children: but, In Isaac shall thy seed be called." (Romans 9:7 quoting Genesis 21:12) Thus, Isaac was designated by God as the seed of Abraham ("In Isaac shall they seed be called"). Ishmael was physically Abraham's descendant, but lacked God's divine designation of the line of descent by promise. God made that choice. We can see how this is an analogy for a spiritual truth, namely that the true sons of Abraham are those that trust Christ, so that there are merely physical Jews (pictured by Ishmael) and there are the true Jews (pictured by Isaac). Thus, Paul explains, "They which are the children of the flesh" like Ishmael "are not the children of God: but the children of the promise" like Isaac "are counted for the seed." (Romans 9:8)

> Romans 9:9 For this *is* the word of promise, At this time will I come, and Sara shall have a son. 10 And not only *this*; but when Rebecca also had conceived by one, *even* by our father Isaac; 11 (For *the children* being not yet born, neither having done any good or evil, that the purpose of God according to election might stand, not of works, but of him that calleth); 12 It was said unto her, The elder shall serve the younger. 13 As it is written, Jacob have I loved, but Esau have I hated.

Paul set out to show the Word of God had not been ineffective, and now he quotes from Genesis 18:10, 14: "At this time will I come, and Sarah shall have a son." (Romans 9:9) Paul argues that Genesis distinguished between the children of the flesh and children of the promise. Isaac, of course, is the child of promise that God selected to fulfill His purposes for Israel. God did not pick Ishmael for this purpose, which has nothing to say about whether Ishmael was saved or not. The analogy regarding physical and spiritual descent from Abraham carries over to the experience of Isaac. Paul is careful to say that Isaac's wife Rebecca "also had conceived by one, even by our father Isaac." (Romans 9:10) With Ishmael and Isaac there were two mothers involved, but here the parentage is identical.

Notwithstanding, God chose who would be in the true line of descent. Those descended from Esau are not Jewish, even though Esau had the same parents as Jacob.

God's choice was made before the twins were born and before they had "done any good or evil." (Romans 9:11) Paul emphasizes that it was God's choice and did not hang on anything about the relative merits of the children. And note that Paul's words say nothing about whether Esau would be a believer (i.e., about his eternal destiny), for that is not even in the picture here. God chose the line of descent from Abraham through whom He would work out His redemptive plan. Both Ishmael and Esau were the physical lineage of Abraham, but not of the divinely designated seed that God would use to build the nation Israel. Paul quotes the prophecy given to Rebecca before the children were born: "The elder shall serve the younger." (Romans 9:12) This prophecy leaves no question, since it preceded their births, that the decision of God was not tied to anything of the relative merits of Esau's or Jacob's lives.

Finally, Paul quotes in Romans 9:13 from Malachi 1:2-3. "Love" and "hate" here do not have to do with the emotions of love and hostility, but a choice to bestow special blessings, and again Paul does not comment on anyone's eternal destiny. Rather, the descendants of Jacob were given by God a set of promises not given to Esau and his descendants. At the time Malachi was written, its recipients knew that to be the case, for they were restored to the blessings of Jacob but the lineage of Esau received no such blessing. As with Ishmael and Isaac, Paul uses the example of Esau and Jacob for an analogy. The Jewish people in Paul's day could be divided between those that were simply physical descendants of Jacob and those God had justified through their faith.

> Romans 9:14 What shall we say then? *Is there*
> unrighteousness with God? God forbid. 15 For
> he saith to Moses, I will have mercy on whom
> I will have mercy, and I will have compassion

> on whom I will have compassion. 16 So then *it*
> *is* not of him that willeth, nor of him that
> runneth, but of God that sheweth mercy.

It is in the context of God's choices between Ishmael and Isaac, and then between Esau and Jacob, neither of which had anything to do with their eternal destiny, that the hypothetical objection is raised: "What shall we say then? Is there unrighteousness with God?" Paul says (my paraphrase), "of course not!" It is God's prerogative to make such choices. Indeed, God always has and exercises the right to show mercy or withhold mercy, as Paul will show.

Paul now draws from the historical exodus from Egypt. After the Israelites leave Egypt under Moses' leadership and while Moses is on the mountain, the golden calf incident occurs. God threatens to destroy the nation and start anew with Moses (Exodus 32:10), but Moses intercedes for them and God did not destroy them. Specifically, Moses successfully intercedes on the basis of God's promises to the fathers: "Remember Abraham, Isaac, and Israel, thy servants, to whom thou swarest by thine own self, and saidst unto them, I will multiply your seed as the stars of heaven, and all this land that I have spoken of will I give unto your seed, and they shall inherit it for ever." (Exodus 32:13) Moses proves faithful and God speaks to him "face to face" (Exodus 33:11) and Moses makes the special request that God would reveal His glory to him. God's response: "And he said, I will make all my goodness pass before thee, and I will proclaim the name of the LORD before thee; and will be gracious to whom I will be gracious, and will shew mercy on whom I will shew mercy." (Exodus 33:19) God extended mercy to Israel by not destroying them, and He extended grace to Moses in honoring his request to see God's glory.

Keeping in mind that Paul is ultimately addressing how God's Word was effective despite Israel's disobedience, Paul's appeal to Exodus 33:19 is fitting. God, for His purposes, may give or withhold mercy, not only in the days of Moses, but in Paul's time as well. And while the incident just discussed demonstrated God giving mercy, another incident from Exodus shows God, for His purposes, withholding mercy.

> Romans 9:17 For the scripture saith unto Pharaoh, Even for this same purpose have I raised thee up, that I might shew my power in thee, and that my name might be declared throughout all the earth. 18 Therefore hath he mercy on whom he will *have mercy*, and whom he will he hardeneth.

Calvinists sometimes wrench 9:17-18 from all the preceding verses and teach that suddenly the subject matter has changed to salvation from the death penalty of sin. Some would say that 9:17 teaches that God created Pharaoh for His own purposes and hardened Pharaoh's heart so that it was not possible for Pharaoh to respond in faith to God. However, basic hermeneutics tells us that Paul's introduction in 9:17, "For the scripture saith ...", is setting up the rest of the verse as an illustration or support for what preceded it. God has the prerogative to show or withhold mercy.

In Romans 9:17, Paul quotes from Exodus 9:16: "And in very deed for this *cause* have I raised thee up, for to shew *in* thee my power; and that my name may be declared throughout all the earth." In view is Pharaoh's rise to political power. God chose to "raise him up," that is, to make him Pharaoh. As with the selection of Isaac over Ishmael and Jacob over Esau, the selection of Pharaoh over his siblings and political rivals was for God's own purposes. While it is evident that salvation is not at all in this picture, Calvinists often argue that the hardening of the heart in 9:18 refers to God's making Pharaoh unable to respond in faith. A few comments are in order here. First, if Pharaoh was reprobate, then he did not need his heart hardened to keep him from believing. Second, the hardening of Pharaoh's heart in the context of the history of Exodus does not refer to salvation or a response to the gospel, but to Pharaoh's refusal to release his Jewish slaves at God's command. Third, Calvinists typically assume that the hardening is something God does to a person's heart/ mind so that they are unable (lack capacity) to make a free will choice. But we see from Romans 1 that God only "gave [people] up" (Romans 1:24) in response to their choice to leave God out of the equation (Romans 1:21-23). The internal hardening of Romans 1 always occurs in response to a personal choice, and so it was with Pharaoh.

God told Moses before he returned to Egypt that He would harden Pharaoh's heart so "that he shall not let the people go." (Exodus 4:21) The point of contention about which Pharaoh's heart would be hardened was not the gospel, but the command to let the people go: "Thus saith the Lord God of Israel, Let my people go that they may hold a feast unto me in the wilderness." (Exodus 5:1; see also 7:16, 8:1, 20, 9:1, 13, 10:3) The purpose of the hardening was to glorify God, "that [his] name may be declared throughout all the earth." (Exodus 9:16) But as we read the historical narrative, we read that Pharaoh first hardened his own heart, and he always did so in conjunction with his own determination to defy God. (e.g., Exodus 8:15, 32, 9:34) The first time we read that God hardened Pharaoh's heart is in Exodus 9:12. As Zane Hodges comments, "But it is unmistakable that all that God really does is to confirm and extend a process of hardening that Pharaoh himself had initiated."[105]

Moreover, we understand that when Pharaoh hardened his heart, this speaks of his sinful defiance of God's command to the let His people go. Pharaoh heard God's command and, as the saying goes, "dug in his heels." It is not as if Pharaoh altered his intellectual capacity to understand or respond to the very simple command. Yet, many Calvinists insist that is meant when the text says that God hardened Pharaoh's heart.

---

[105] Hodges, Zane C., *Romans: Deliverance from Wrath* (Grace Evangelical Society 2013), 273.

But God only hardened Pharaoh's heart in response to his own hardening, which illustrates the progression Paul outlined in Romans 1:20-32. God exercised His prerogative to withhold mercy to Pharaoh, thus hardening Pharaoh by giving him over to his own depravity. And where this is going is that in Paul's day, God was showing mercy on believing Jews and Gentiles while hardening unbelieving Jews in response to their unbelief.

> <u>Romans 9:19</u> Thou wilt say then unto me, Why doth he yet find fault? For who hath resisted his will? <u>20</u> Nay but, O man, who art thou that repliest against God? Shall the thing formed say to him that formed *it*, Why hast thou made me thus? <u>21</u> Hath not the potter power over the clay, of the same lump to make one vessel unto honour, and another unto dishonour? <u>22</u> *What* if God, willing to shew *his* wrath, and to make his power known, endured with much longsuffering the vessels of wrath fitted to destruction: <u>23</u> And that he might make known the riches of his glory on the vessels of mercy, which he had afore prepared unto glory, <u>24</u> Even us, whom he hath called, not of the Jews only, but also of the Gentiles?

Here, Paul anticipates and addresses a predictable objection, namely that if God hardens whom He wills, then how can God find fault in the one that resists Him? Paul's response is that God as creator should not be questioned by the created. Borrowing imagery from Jeremiah 18:3-11, Paul likens this to the absurd notion of a vessel (pottery) questioning the potter why the vessel was made a certain way. Just as the potter has power over the clay, so also God has the right to extend or withhold mercy, and to harden whom He pleases, as He did with Pharaoh.

Paul further argues that God has the right to "shew his wrath, and to make his power known." Critically, we need to remember that "wrath" does not mean eternal damnation, but refers to God's temporal judgment or anger, as it did in Romans 1:18-32. As Paul explains there, God's wrath is presently "revealed from heaven against all ungodliness and unrighteousness of men." (Romans 1:18) Paul speaks in Romans 9:22 of "the vessels of wrath fitted to destruction" as he extends what he had to say about Pharaoh (a vessel of wrath that faced temporal judgment) to unbelieving Israel. And Paul argues that God "endured with longsuffering the vessels of wrath," meaning that for His own purposes, God showed mercy to them just as He had done with Pharaoh in relenting of several of the plagues. But just as with Pharaoh, God will eventually "make his power known" with regard to unbelieving Israel as it experiences His wrath. As Paul says in 1 Thessalonians 2:16, "for the wrath is come upon them to the uttermost." Therefore, God is now extending mercy to unbelieving Israel but in the future will make known his wrath, which likely refers to the coming defeat by the Romans in 70 A.D.

Note further that Paul says the "vessels of wrath" are "fitted to destruction," but the "vessels of mercy" will know "the riches of his glory." (Romans 9:22-23) What many Calvinists see in this passage is God as the potter forming individuals for heaven or hell, although the passage never says anything about this occurring before the foundation of the world as they need to prove for TULIP unconditional election. We should first observe that two different verbs are used in 9:22-23 translated as "fitted" and "prepared": *katērtismena* and *proētoimasen*. These verbs are in different tenses and voices. The word "prepared" has the Greek prefix *pro* and is therefore translated "afore prepared" (i.e., prepared beforehand). The word "prepared" is the third person singular, aorist active, indicative, showing God actively involved in the past preparation of the vessels of mercy. But "fitted" is a plural, middle / passive, perfect participle that agrees with the term "vessels." The perfect tense shows a current state that began in the past. There is debate whether the verb is intended as middle or passive, both of which have the same ending so that context determines which applies. The context here is Paul's contrast between the vessels of wrath and the vessels of mercy, and the middle voice is the better fit, so that Paul is saying that the vessels of wrath fitted themselves out for destruction, which means Paul is unquestionably not talking about TULIP election but building on the concepts addressed in Romans 1. This fits the example already given of Pharaoh defying God and hardening his heart (to which God later responded both with mercy and hardening) and the fact that Paul does not make any reference to God acting beforehand on the vessels of wrath as he does with the vessels of mercy. To these, God will eventually withhold mercy and show His wrath. Second, observe that the word "destruction" can encompass a person's eternal destiny but often speaks of physical destruction or ruin, which is consistent with the notion of wrath taught in Romans 1 and the context here. The Bible does not say about Pharaoh's eternal destiny, but he faced temporal ruin as a vessel of wrath.

So pulling this all together, God can show mercy or withhold it, and harden whom He pleases. And in Paul's time God was "longsuffering," meaning He showed mercy on the vessels of wrath fitted for God's wrath, an obvious reference to unbelieving Israel. God also showed mercy in that he "afore prepared" the vessels of mercy for "glory." These vessels are expressly identified in Romans 9:24 as believing Jews and believing Gentiles together. But how did God prepare them beforehand for glory. Was it by unconditional election? Paul certainly does not say that. Instead he says of the vessels of mercy that they are "us, whom he hath called." God prepared us ahead of time for glory through his calling. God calls us by the gospel. (2 Thessalonians 2:14) As Paul explains in Romans 4 in the context of the true children of Abraham who follow his example of faith: "Now it was not written for his sake alone, that it was imputed to him; But for us also, to whom it shall be imputed, if we believe on him that raised up Jesus our Lord from the dead; Who was delivered for our offences, and was raised again for our justification." (Romans 4:23-25) Paul will later explain in Romans 10:14: "How then shall they call on him in whom they have not believed? And how shall they believe in him of whom they have not heard? And how shall they hear without a preacher?"

> Romans 9:25 As he saith also in Osee, I will call them my people, which were not my people; and her beloved, which was not beloved. 26 And it shall come to pass, *that* in the place where it was said unto them, Ye *are* not my people; there shall they be called the children of the living God.

The prophet Hosea prophesied to the Northern Kingdom of a future restoration, and Paul relates the fulfillment of this prophecy back to God's original promise to Abraham. When God said He would bless the families of the world through Abraham, God meant that He would make of all nations those that would constitute His people, the children of the living God. This is the true Israel of Romans 9:6 and the vessels of mercy of Romans 9:23-24 that are the recipients of God's mercy.

> Romans 9:27 Esaias also crieth concerning Israel, Though the number of the children of Israel be as the sand of the sea, a remnant shall be saved: 28 For he will finish the work, and cut *it* short in righteousness: because a short work will the Lord make upon the earth. 29 And as Esaias said before, Except the Lord of Sabaoth had left us a seed, we had been as Sodoma, and been made like unto Gomorrha.

God's Word is not only effective because Gentiles can follow Abraham's example of faith and become children of God, but also because, despite Israel's characteristic rejection of Christ, there is a remnant of genuine Jewish believers. That unbelieving Israel is comprised of vessels of wrath fitted for destruction does not mean that individuals cannot respond to God's revelation and believe.

> Romans 9:30 What shall we say then? That the
> Gentiles, which followed not after righteousness,
> have attained to righteousness, even the
> righteousness which is of faith. 31 But Israel,
> which followed after the law of righteousness,
> hath not attained to the law of righteousness.
> 32 Wherefore? Because *they sought it* not by
> faith, but as it were by the works of the law. For
> they stumbled at that stumblingstone; 33 As it is
> written, Behold, I lay in Sion a stumblingstone
> and rock of offence: and whosoever believeth on
> him shall not be ashamed.

These final verses draw to a conclusion the first part of Paul's argument about the effectiveness of God's Word. The vessels of wrath (i.e., unbelieving Israel) stumble at Jesus Christ, as foretold in Isaiah 28:16. The vessels of mercy "attained to righteousness, even the righteousness which is of faith." God's prerogative is to show mercy on those that trust Jesus, but wrath awaits those that stumble at Jesus.

The Calvinists do not have support for unconditional election in Romans 9. None of the choices at issue in the chapter have to do with selecting people before the foundation of the world to save or pass over. They can only find support here by extracting verses from their contexts or forcing phrases like "vessels of wrath" and "vessels of mercy" to take on meanings Paul did not intend and that do not fit within the flow of his argument. But consider this. If Paul wanted to teach TULIP election in the extended passage just considered, could not he have been plainspoken? Would it not make more sense that Paul would have simply come right out and explained that God made a choice in eternity past who He would save, and most of national Israel in Paul's day were not picked for saving?

Pillar Proof Text: Ephesians 1:4

Our analysis now moves to Ephesians 1:4. This is also one of the most important, if not the most important, Calvinist proof text because it is the only passage in their "proof text" arsenal that mentions any sort of choosing prior to creation. This is a critical point to understand. Calvinism's unconditional election is not merely that God picked people, but that He picked them prior to creation for the specific purpose of saving them and only them from hell. Their burden is to establish each part of this proposition with Scriptural evidence. And unconditional election cannot be directly established apart from Ephesians 1:4, the linchpin of the whole system.

> Ephesians 1:3 Blessed be the God and Father of our Lord Jesus Christ, who hath blessed us with all spiritual blessings in heavenly *places* in Christ: 4 According as he hath chosen us in him before the foundation of the world, that we should be holy and without blame before him in love: 5 Having predestinated us unto the adoption of children by Jesus Christ to himself, according to the good pleasure of his will, 6 To the praise of the glory of his grace, wherein he hath made us accepted in the beloved.

From this passage, Calvinists teach that God chose the elect for salvation before the foundation of the world. As a preliminary observation, the term "elect" (Greek *eklektos*) is not used in this passage nor in the entire book of Ephesians. Second, the passage does not say that anyone was chosen for salvation, but chosen to "be holy and without blame before him in love." As we will see below, these are not to be equated. Calvinists interpret the passage as if it read as follows: "he hath chosen us [to be] in him before the foundation of the world." But of course, that is not what the passage says. Instead of choosing people to be in Christ, the verse says that the "choosing" occurred "in him." All too often, Calvinists focus on the choosing and ignore the "in him." Before proceeding further with this text, let's take a closer look at some of what Paul teaches about "in him" or "in Christ" since that concept is prevalent in the first two chapters of Ephesians (and, indeed, in much of Paul's writings), beginning with Paul's salutation to the members of the church at Ephesus as "the faithful in Christ Jesus." (Ephesians 1:1)

Jesus remarked in reference to the redemptive work of God: "My Father worketh hitherto, and I work." (John 5:17) For Paul, "in Christ" is the sphere in which God is working to reconcile the world to Himself: "To wit, that God was in Christ, reconciling the world unto himself, not imputing their trespasses unto them..." (2 Corinthians 5:19) The Father's goal is "that in the dispensation of the fullness of times he might gather together in one all things in Christ, both which are in heaven, and which are on earth; even in him." (Ephesians 1:10) This reconciliation includes, of course, people. Paul confirms that "salvation... is in Christ Jesus" (2 Timothy 2:10), for it is in this sphere that we find "grace" (2 Timothy 2:1) and the "love of God" (Romans 8:39). Indeed, those of us who were "baptized into Jesus Christ" were baptized into his death, burial, and resurrection (Romans 6:3-5), are "sanctified in Christ Jesus" (1 Corinthians 1:2), are promised "everlasting life" (Romans 6:22), and have ascended in him, God having "raised us up together, and made us sit together in heavenly places in Christ Jesus" (Ephesians 2:6). As Paul writes: "For as in Adam all die, even so in Christ shall all be made alive." (1 Corinthians 15:22)

For those that have been placed into Jesus Christ, we have "all spiritual blessings in heavenly places in Christ." (Ephesians 1:3) These manifold blessings include the following: "redemption...in Christ Jesus" (Romans 3:24), "no condemnation to them which are in Christ Jesus" (Romans 8:1), God "hath made us accepted in the beloved" (Ephesians 1:6), for we are "the righteousness of God in him" (2 Corinthians 5:21), we are "in Christ... a new creature" (2 Corinthians 5:17), we were "created in Christ Jesus unto good works" (Ephesians 2:10), we have "liberty... in Christ" (Galatians 2:4), we are "all one in Christ Jesus" (Galatians 3:28), and for good reason we "triumph in Christ" (2 Corinthians 2:14). For it is "in him" that Paul says we "walk," are "rooted and built up," and made "complete." (Colossians 2:6-10) As Paul preaches in his Mars Hill sermon, "For in him we live, and move, and have our being." (Acts 17:28)

In Ephesians 1 and 2, Paul particularly emphasizes the spiritual benefits to those "in Christ." Ephesians 1:4 begins with the phrase "According as..." and is a continuation of the thought Paul started in 1:3. Paul says there that the Father "blessed us with all spiritual blessings in heavenly places in Christ." Paul recognizes that Christ is presently before the Father in heaven: "Which he wrought in Christ, when he raised him from the dead, and set him at his own right hand in the heavenly places." (Ephesians 1:20) And from Paul's perspective, we are before the Father and have all spiritual blessings at this moment if we are in Christ: "And hath raised us up together, and made us sit together in heavenly places in Christ Jesus." (Ephesians 2:6) These spiritual blessings are often referred to as positional truths or positional blessings because they are ascribed to us by virtue of our position in Christ even though they may not represent our present condition. For example, the resurrection of believers is a future event (1 Corinthians 15:51-57) in terms of condition, and yet Paul speaks in Ephesians 2:6 of our resurrection in the past tense ("hath raised us up together") in terms of position. Likewise, even though you are presently on the earth reading this book, Paul says you are seated together "in heavenly places in Christ Jesus." Our position as believers is in Christ, not only in his death and resurrection, but his place at the right hand of the Father.

Two critical questions are how do we get "in Christ" and when do we get "in Christ." Christians could not all have been in Christ prior to creation by some decree of God, or even prior to being born, because Paul says other Christians were "in

Christ before me." (Romans 16:7) Paul even speaks of himself as a spiritual father begetting people in Christ with reference to his evangelizing people. He wrote to the Christians in Corinth: "For though ye have ten thousand instructors in Christ, yet have ye not many fathers: for *in Christ Jesus I have begotten you through the gospel.*" (1 Corinthians 4:15) Similarly, Paul called Timothy his son (1 Corinthians 4:17; 2 Timothy 2:1) as well as the runaway slave Onesimus: "I beseech thee for my son Onesimus, whom I have begotten in my bonds." (Philemon 10) So what we have is that people are not placed in Christ before the foundation of the world, but instead, during their lifetime and "through the gospel" when they trust Christ. And no one is "chosen" in the sense of Ephesians 1:4 until they are "in Christ," as reflected in Paul's salutation to Rufus: "Salute Rufus chosen in the Lord, and his mother and mine." (Romans 16:13)

With this background in mind, let's return to the passage at hand: "According as he hath chosen us in him before the foundation of the world, that we should be holy and without blame before him in love." Since we are placed "in him" in time, as we respond to the gospel in faith, the phrase "chosen us in him" cannot mean that all believers were placed "in him" before creation. In the immediate context, Paul explains that his readers "trusted in Christ" "after that ye heard...the gospel of your salvation: in whom also after that ye believed." (Ephesians 1:12-13) There was no salvation or deliverance in eternity past, but in real time as they heard and believed the gospel. And as indicated earlier, the blessing of being "chosen" that we receive once we are "in him" is not justification as the Calvinists need it to be, but that "we should be holy and without blame before" the Father. Both the "chosen" and the positional holiness are only ours "in him" because Jesus is the holy one now seated "at his own right hand in the heavenly places." (Ephesians 1:20)

Someone might try to salvage this verse as a proof text by arguing that the people were not placed in Christ before creation, but were selected before creation to be placed in Christ later or to become holy and blameless later when they come to Christ in faith. This view must be rejected because the verse says "chosen us in him before..." and not "chosen us *to be* in him before...." If Paul were suggesting that individuals were selected for salvation before the foundation of the world, then the "in him" language here would have no meaning. Further, Paul later states in relation to the Christian Gentiles in the church: "Wherefore remember, that ye being in time past Gentiles in the flesh, who are called Uncircumcision by that which is called the Circumcision in the flesh made by hands; That at that time ye were without Christ, being aliens from the commonwealth of Israel, and strangers from the covenants of promise, having no hope, and without God in the world: But now in Christ Jesus ye who sometimes were far off are made nigh by the blood of Christ." (Ephesians 2:11-13) If God had already picked them for salvation before creation, then how could Paul say that "in time past" they were "without Christ...having no hope, and without God in the world"? But what the Bible says is that people become "in Christ" when they become Christians, and so Paul's statement in Ephesians 2:11-13 that before they were Christians they were "without Christ" makes sense.

Jesus is described in Revelation 13:8 as "the Lamb slain from the foundation of the world." God planned then for the reconciliation of lost sinners to himself in Christ, and the benefits and blessings God planned in Christ become ours the moment we respond in faith to the gospel and are placed in Christ. These blessings are ours on the basis of who Christ is, what He accomplished, and His position relative to the Father. The Calvinist view of Ephesians 1:4 that God picked those He would save before creation is unsupportable. Instead, the view that does justice to the context and comports with the large body of positional "in Christ" truths throughout Paul's writings is that God made the decision before creation that all Christians would be positionally holy and blameless before Him in love, just as Jesus is holy and blameless and seated before the Father. We get in on the benefit of this decision the moment we place faith in Christ and are placed "in him." Recall that "chosen" (Greek *ekelgomai*) can have the meaning "to make choice in accordance with significant preference." This definition makes good sense of the context here. The passage does not say God chose individuals before they existed, but that they receive the blessing of His decision in Christ (positional holiness) once they are in Christ, the one who is holy and blameless before the Father. Paul similarly stated in Ephesians 1:11 that in Christ ("in whom") "we have obtained an inheritance." Again, Paul expresses a past-tense reality that becomes our spiritual blessing once we trust Christ and therefore are in him. Paul also wrote in Ephesians 2:6 that God "hath raised us up together" with Christ, but he did not mean that we were resurrected before we were born. Paul speaks of positional truths here—it is the self-existent Jesus that was before the foundation of the world and that we can identify with now by faith to get in on "all spiritual blessings in heavenly places in Christ."

We should note that, in the Greek, verses 3 through 14 constitute a single sentence. We do not have to look far to see how we can appropriate the manifold blessings available in Christ: "In whom ye also *trusted*, after that ye heard the word of truth, the gospel of your salvation: in whom also after that ye believed, ye were sealed with that holy Spirit of promise..." (Ephesians 1:13) The closest Pauline parallel to Ephesians 1:3 elsewhere is 2 Timothy 1:9-10, which also supports this interpretation: "Who hath saved us, and called *us* with an holy calling, not according to our works, but according to his own purpose and grace, which was given us in Christ Jesus before the world began, but is now made manifest by the appearing of our Saviour Jesus Christ, who hath abolished death, and hath brought life and immortality to light through the gospel." As with the Ephesians passage, the sphere of blessing is once again "in Christ Jesus." Paul does not teach that believers were given something before they existed to receive it. Rather, God's redemptive plan, the grace of God toward sinners, was in Christ before time, and later manifested when the God-man died on the cross and was resurrected, conquering death and making eternal life available "through the gospel" (not election).

Many Calvinists also cite 1:5 as a proof text, often with little or no exegesis, solely because it uses the term "predestinated." The verse states, "Having predestinated us unto the adoption of children by Jesus Christ to himself, according to the good pleasure of his will." The translation "predestinated" should be something like "pre-appointed" since the Greek term does not in itself say anything about one's eternal destiny.[106] BDAG defines the term as "decide upon beforehand, predetermine." Obviously, this verse does not say appointed to salvation, but appointed "unto the adoption of children." Like being before the Father, holy and blameless, this is another positional truth that looks forward to a complete realization in the future: "And not only they, but ourselves also, which have the firstfruits of the Spirit, even we ourselves groan within ourselves, waiting for the adoption, to wit, the redemption of our body." (Romans 8:23) The point is that for those that have placed their faith in Christ (see Ephesians 1:12-13), future benefits have been appointed by God (see also Ephesians 1:11).

Sundry Other Verses for Unconditional Election

Another very commonly cited passage for unconditional election is the following:

> John 12:37 But though he had done so many
> miracles before them, yet they believed not on
> him: 38 That the saying of Esaias the prophet
> might be fulfilled, which he spake, Lord, who
> hath believed our report? and to whom hath

---

[106] *Supra* note 105, p. 267.

the arm of the Lord been revealed? 39
Therefore they could not believe, because that
Esaias said again, 40 He hath blinded their
eyes, and hardened their heart; that they
should not see with *their* eyes, nor understand
with *their* heart, and be converted, and I
should heal them. 41 These things said Esaias,
when he saw his glory, and spake of him.

Calvinists take this passage to mean that God has made certain
people unable to believe or even understand the message of the
gospel, and they cite it as evidence for both total depravity and
unconditional election. Their use of this proof text illustrates a
fundamental analytical flaw within Calvinism. Calvinists are so
eager to utilize any verse that speaks of an inability that they
overlook whether, on its face, it actually lends support to what
they are trying to prove. We have to remember that the claim
of unconditional election is that the elect will certainly believe
and the reprobate (non-elect) are born unable to believe, and all
of this was determined in eternity past. That being the case, it
makes no sense to appeal to a passage allegedly teaching that
God blinds people in time and says nothing about His choosing
people in eternity past for salvation. Also, in the many quotes I
have provided of Calvinists defining total depravity and
unconditional election, there was no mention of God making
people unable to believe (would this not be God authoring sin?).

First, the passage speaks of a blinding or hardening that occurs
in time, which of course, would not be necessary if TULIP
unconditional election were true. In the TULIP framework,
the non-elect are born unable to understand or believe, i.e.,
they are born blind and need no additional blinding to ensure
their eternal destiny. Second, the blinding and hardening are
in response to their having witnessed "many miracles before
them" yet persisting in unbelief. Jesus is alluding to Isaiah 6:9-
10, which is also paraphrased or quoted in other verses relied
upon by Calvinists with the same faulty reasoning, namely

Matthew 13:14-15, Mark 4:10-12, Luke 8:9-10, and Acts 28:25-27. The analysis of this verse applies to the others.

Isaiah 6:9-10 states: "And he said, Go, and tell this people, Hear ye indeed, but understand not; and see ye indeed, but perceive not. Make the heart of this people fat, and make their ears heavy, and shut their eyes; lest they see with their eyes, and hear with their ears, and understand with their heart, and convert, and be healed." In the context of Isaiah 6, the passage is speaking about the judicial hardening of Israel, their being given over to their own sinful desires in response to their own initiating rebellion as Paul explained in Romans 1. It is not that God made them initially unable to understand and believe. "In other words, verses 9-10 are a very stark statement of the preacher's dilemma: those who resist the truth can be changed only by telling them the truth, but to do this exposes them to the danger of rejecting the truth yet once again—and maybe this further rejection will push them beyond the point of no return and they will become irretrievably hardened in mind and heart (Heb. 6:4-8)."[107] Similarly, Donald Mills writes:

> Why would God instruct Isaiah to do this? In the divine council (6:8), the sovereign King has determined that the preaching of the Word would make the people's hearts harder and harder because they are ripe for judgment and eventual exile. Judgment occurs because God's grace has been exhausted. Israel has been delivered up to the wrath of God through its continued obstinancy in sinning (Isa 1:5-6), and now the Lord proceeds to shut the door of repentance against His people. In order to fulfill this purpose, Isaiah's preaching ministry would *cause them* to become more blind and

---

[107] J. Alec Motyer, *Isaiah: An Introduction and Commentary*, vol. 20, Tyndale Old Testament Commentaries (Downers Grove, IL: InterVarsity Press, 1999), 84.

deaf.... Because they absolutely refused to see, hear, understand, and obey, but rather turned their backs on the LORD (Isa 1:2-5), He ratified their decision and gave them over to their hardened condition. This is a Scriptural principle, exemplified in Pharaoh (Exod 4:21; 8:15) and others (1 Kgs 22:20 ff; 1 Sam 15:26; 16:1), and explained by Paul (2 Thess 2:11-12).[108]

Accordingly, John 12:37 speaks of the fact that Israel characteristically rejected Jesus' message and his works that validated his message. Because of their repeated disbelief of the greatest revelation of all (that of Jesus), God blinded or hardened them by giving them over to their depravity, just like what happened in Isaiah 6:9-10. As we saw earlier in relation to Romans 9, God hardens whom He pleases, but always in response to their initiating rebellion. But since God does the blinding in time and not eternity past, and in response to their initiating rebellion, this passage expressly refutes unconditional election, which teaches that this group was born blind.

> 2 Thessalonians 2:13 But we are bound to give thanks alway to God for you, brethren beloved of the Lord, because God hath from the beginning chosen you to salvation through sanctification of the Spirit and belief of the truth.

This verse is usually the follow-up verse to Ephesians 1:4. The standard Calvinist interpretation is that "from the beginning" means before creation, but the verse does not say that and in other verses "from the beginning" without additional verbiage is used to indicate the beginning of Jesus' earthly ministry

---

108 Donald W. Mills, "The Use of Isaiah 6:9-10 in the New Testament with Special Attention to the Gospel of John," *Journal of Ministry and Theology Volume 4*, no. 2 (2000): 21.

(1 John 1:1) and the beginning of John's ministry to his readers (1 John 2:7). If Paul had wanted to say before the beginning of the world, he would have done so, just as he did in Ephesians 1:4. What he is calling to mind is that he had not originally intended to go into Macedonia, but Paul was given a vision that directed him to Macedonia, and thus Thessalonica. (Acts 16:7-10) The beginning speaks of that time period, just as in 1 John "the beginning" is used to indicate the time of the planting of the church that John was writing to.

Moreover, the verse does not end with "God hath from the beginning chosen you to salvation." Instead, what they were chosen for was "salvation through sanctification of the Spirit and belief of the truth." And in the verse that follows, Paul writes that his audience was called by the gospel. (2 Thessalonians 2:14) In this context, God's choosing in Acts 16 guaranteed that Paul took the message of the gospel into Macedonia, not that his audience would believe or be saved. This verse has nothing to do with unconditional election before creation.

> Acts 13:48 And when the Gentiles heard this, they were glad, and glorified the word of the Lord: and as many as were ordained to eternal life believed.

This proof text is a Calvinist favorite as they take "ordained" to mean predestined for eternal life before creation. However, this verse says nothing of a decree in eternity past, nor does it say that all Gentiles (or all people) who are ever saved were selected before creation for eternal life. The Greek term *tasso* translated "ordained" is Strong No. 5021, which is defined in Strong's dictionary to mean "to arrange in an orderly manner, i.e., to assign or dispose." BDAG gives the following primary definition: "to bring about an order of things by arranging, arrange, put in place." These definitions say nothing about predestination or even salvation. Also, the word is used only 7 other times in the New Testament and is translated as set

(Luke 7:8), ordained (Romans 13:1), determined (Acts 15:2), appointed (Matthew 28:16; Acts 22:10, 28:23), and addicted (1 Corinthians 16:15). In each case, the word has the idea of arranging, appointing or preparing and in none of these seven verses is it related to eternal life. If Luke intended to say certain people were decreed before creation to be saved, he could easily have explicitly said so rather than utilizing a military word associated with arranging troops or ships in preparation for battle, and that in other contexts simply means to appoint, arrange or prepare.

If we look at Acts 13:48 as a contrast to 13:46, we can understand the proper meaning of *tasso* in this context. In Acts 13:46, Luke writes: "Then Paul and Barnabas waxed bold, and said, It was necessary that the word of God should first have been spoken to you: but seeing ye put it from you, and judge yourselves unworthy of everlasting life, lo, we turn to the Gentiles." The Jewish people in 13:46 rejected the Word, and in so doing, rejected eternal life. In contrast to their rejection, the Gentiles rejoiced that God sent Paul and Barnabas to bring the word of salvation to them. (Acts 13:47) The contrast concerns the two groups' receptivity to the Word. And what we read in 13:48 is the Gentiles' welcoming reception of Paul's words, the apparent result of their being prepared. Before putting a finer edge on this, we can benefit from looking ahead a few chapters in Acts.

A parallel and nearly identical event is recorded in Acts 17 where Paul and Silas preached in a synagogue in Thessalonica. (Acts 17:1) Many Jewish people and proselytes there believed (Acts 17:4), but those Jewish people that did not believe were jealous and caused an uproar in the city. (Acts 17:5-9, compare to Acts 13:45) Paul and Silas left there to Berea, again preaching in a synagogue. (Acts 17:10) And in contrast to the synagogue in Thessalonica, the Jewish people in the synagogue in Berea "were more noble than those in Thessalonica, in that they received the word with all readiness of mind, and searched the

DECONSTRUCTING CALVINISM

scriptures daily, whether those things were so. Therefore, many of them believed." (Acts 17:11-12) The word "noble" (Greek *eugenes*) means noble-minded or open-minded. BDAG states the primary definition of "being of high status, well-born, high-born," as in a literal noble, but a secondary meaning of "having the type of attitude ordinarily associated with well-bred persons, noble-minded, open-minded." The latter captures Luke's point here. Even though many in Thessalonica believed, the Berean Jews were nevertheless more open-minded and thus "received the word with all readiness of mind" with the result that "many of them believed."

The sense in which the Gentiles in Acts 13:48 were arranged or prepared for eternal life was in their receptivity or open-mindedness to God's Word, just like the Bereans. Of course, if everyone who believes was decreed to do so, then Luke could have plainly said so both in Acts 13 and 17. But in that event, the contrast between those in Thessalonica (many of whom believed) and those more noble-minded in Berea would not make sense. By God's decree, those that believed in both cities would have been equally noble-minded. Moreover, Paul's comment in Acts 13:46 that the unbelieving Jews judged themselves unworthy of eternal life would be a ludicrous statement for Paul to make if he believed God had simply passed them over in eternity past. We should understand both passages to simply state that those receptive to God's Word, when they were provided additional revelation, believed it. This does not mean God had no role in preparing their hearts, as other passages teach He does through the ministry of the Holy Spirit. (e.g., John 16:7-11) But it leaves no room for forcing unconditional election over the passages.

> 1 Peter 1:1 Peter, an apostle of Jesus Christ, to the strangers scattered throughout Pontus, Galatia, Cappadocia, Asia, and Bithynia, 2 Elect according to the foreknowledge of God the Father, through sanctification of the Spirit,

unto obedience and sprinkling of the blood of
Jesus Christ: Grace unto you, and peace, be
multiplied.

This passage is important because both Calvinists and non-
Calvinists find support for their relative positions. Many non-
Calvinists suggest that God foreknew those would place faith
in Christ and elected or chose them in eternity past based on
that foreknowledge. Recall that many Calvinists equate
foreknowledge to foreordination, and so for them, this verse
teaches that God decreed in eternity past those He would save.

Despite what some newer translations do with this verse, there
is no verb here about anyone being picked. Instead, Peter is
teaching about the basis upon which those he is writing to
(Jewish believers) have been made elect (i.e., excellent,
distinguished, pure). Recall from the parable in Matthew 22
that this chapter opened with, the king (God the Father) made
those who accepted his wedding invitation (the gospel)
excellent on that basis. The point here is the same except that
Peter brings in the role of the Holy Spirit in the transaction.
Peter expressly states that they are "elect [excellent,
distinguished, pure]...through sanctification of the Spirit, unto
obedience and sprinkling of the blood of Jesus Christ." This
use of the Greek adjective *eklektois* (plural of *eklektos*) to
describe their excellence is consistent with Peter's use of *the*
term "elect" in 1 Peter 2:4, 6 to speak of Jesus, who clearly did
not need to be selected before creation for salvation.

Moreover, in the Greek text, the adjective "elect" does not
occur in verse 2, but in the first verse immediately before
strangers. While in Greek the words of the sentence do not
require the standard ordering of our English sentences, it helps
to see that in the literal word ordering of the first verse, Peter
wrote to the "[elect] strangers scattered... according to the
foreknowledge of God...." The preposition according to
(Greek *kata*) does not denote purpose, but has the sense of
being in harmony with the foreknowledge of God. It is not

that people were "elected" based on God's foreknowledge that they would in their lives trust Christ, but that their excellence in Christ was foreknown of God. For the Calvinistic view of election these verses should say that God selected people prior to creation for salvation. Instead, Peter wrote that the means by which his audience became elect was through or by sanctification of the Spirit. The word sanctification (Greek *hagiasmo*) is a noun and means a setting aside or holiness. The point then is that the basis of their being elect is that they were set aside by the Holy Spirit, and that happens when a person places faith in Christ in response to the gospel. (Romans 15:16; 1 Corinthians 1:2, 6:11)

Thus, in Peter's thinking, believers become elect, distinguished, excellent or pure by their being set aside by the Holy Spirit when they trust Christ. And indeed, what Peter added further confirmed this view, when he wrote "unto obedience and sprinkling of the blood of Jesus Christ." The word unto is the common Greek preposition *eis* and is the first of several uses by Peter of "to" or "unto" to mean something like "with a view to" or "for the purpose of." Here, Peter wrote that his readers were set aside by the Spirit with a view to their obedience and sparkling of the blood of Jesus Christ (this latter phrase likely indicating covenant faithfulness).

> 1 Peter 2:7 Unto you therefore which believe he is precious: but unto them which be disobedient, the stone which the builders disallowed, the same is made the head of the corner, 8 And a stone of stumbling, and a rock of offence, *even to them* which stumble at the word, being disobedient: whereunto also they were appointed. 9 But ye *are* a chosen generation, a royal priesthood, an holy nation, a peculiar people; that ye should shew forth the praises of him who hath called you out of darkness into his marvellous light:

I addressed the proper interpretation of 1 Peter 2:7-8 in the prior chapter. They are quoted again here for the context of 2:9, a verse Calvinists cite in support of unconditional election. We should immediately note that the verse does not say that the "elect" were "chosen" to salvation or anything about a decree before the foundation of the world. Peter speaks of Christians (contextually, Jewish believers) collectively as "a chosen generation, a royal priesthood, an holy nation, a peculiar people." The adjectives "chosen" (or "elect", Greek *eklektos* again), "royal," "holy," and "peculiar" all speak of their positional worth, distinctness, and excellence. These descriptions come from Old Testament descriptions of Israel in Exodus 19:6 and Deuteronomy 14:2 where national Israel is in view and not individuals. The mere use of the adjective "chosen" in this verse cannot be stretched to support the doctrine of unconditional election. Peter already explained the basis of their being "chosen" or "elect" (excellent) in 1 Peter 1:2 as being "through sanctification of the Spirit, unto obedience and sprinkling of the blood of Jesus Christ." This also fits the immediate context as a description of those that believe. (1 Peter 2:7) Peter does not say that they were picked to believe, but that they believed and, on that basis, he can use adjectives to describe them like elect, royal, holy and peculiar.

> 1 Thessalonians 5:9 For God hath not appointed us to wrath, but to obtain salvation by our Lord Jesus Christ,

This passage sometimes finds itself in a list of proof texts for unconditional election on the mistaken view that "us" means "the elect" and "salvation" refers to deliverance from the death penalty of sin. Both of these conclusions are incorrect. The preceding eight verses in 1 Thessalonians 5 clarify the context of this passage, which is the future day of the Lord. (see 1 Thessalonians 5:2) It is the wrath of the day of the Lord that is in view, and the salvation in view is deliverance from that day. It is helpful to note that "wrath" indicates temporal judgment, hence Paul's statement in Romans 1:18 that God's wrath is presently being revealed: "For the wrath of God is revealed from heaven against all ungodliness and unrighteousness of men, who hold the truth in unrighteousness." In Romans 1:19-32, Paul explained God's wrath as His giving people over (e.g., Romans 1:28) to their depravity. There and here in 1 Thessalonians 5, it is temporal judgment and not eternal damnation in view.

Accordingly, this verse says nothing about unconditional election to salvation from the death penalty of sin. Further, Paul plainly states in 1 Thessalonians 1:5-6 ("For our gospel came not unto you in word only, but also in power, and in the Holy Ghost, and in much assurance; as ye know what manner of men we were among you for your sake. And ye became followers of us, and of the Lord, having received the word in much affliction, with joy of the Holy Ghost.") that the believers in Thessalonica were saved by receiving the word, not by unconditional election.

> John 15:16 Ye have not chosen me, but I have chosen you, and ordained you, that ye should go and bring forth fruit, and *that* your fruit should remain: that whatsoever ye shall ask of the Father in my name, he may give it you.

This and several other verses in John's Gospel are often offered to prove various parts of the TULIP. In John 15:16, Jesus is not talking about choosing people to salvation, nor is he speaking generally of believers. Rather, he is talking specifically of picking his apostles and preparing them for their ministry, all of which Jesus accomplished during his earthly ministry. There is nothing here about selecting people for salvation before creation.

> Philippians 1:29 For unto you it is given in the behalf of Christ, not only to believe on him, but also to suffer for his sake.

Calvinists sometimes argue that this verse teaches that God gives the elect their faith. The Greek term translated as "given" is *charizomai*, the verbal form of the word grace. If this verse teaches that all believers are given their belief or faith in Christ, then it also teaches that all believers are given suffering for Christ's sake. But it is readily observable that that not all Christians suffer for Jesus' sake. Rather than making a sweeping theological statement about all Christians for all time, Paul is making a much more narrow statement about the experience of the members of the Philippian church at the time of his writing the letter. Paul is not saying that their faith was given to them, but that the opportunity to believe was given to them by God's grace as God sent Paul there to present the gospel and plant the church:

> Acts 16:9 And a vision appeared to Paul in the night; There stood a man of Macedonia, and prayed him, saying, Come over into Macedonia, and help us. 10 And after he had seen the vision, immediately we endeavoured to go into Macedonia, assuredly gathering that the Lord had called us for to preach the gospel unto them. 11 Therefore loosing from Troas, we came with a straight course to Samothracia, and the next *day* to Neapolis; 12 **And from thence to Philippi**, which is the chief city of that part of Macedonia, *and* a colony: and we were in that city abiding certain days.

By the same grace of God, the Philippians now have the opportunity to suffer for Christ's sake. In our evangelical culture today, few Christians think of the opportunity to suffer for Christ as the grace of God in their lives. Peter says it is God's blessing to suffer: "But even if you do suffer for doing what is right, you are blessed." (1 Peter 3:14)

> Philippians 4:3 And I intreat thee also, true yokefellow, help those women which laboured

with me in the gospel, with Clement also, and *with* other my fellowlabourers, whose names *are* in the book of life.

Revelation 13:8 And all that dwell upon the earth shall worship him, whose names are not written in the book of life of the Lamb slain from the foundation of the world.

Revelation 17:8 The beast that thou sawest was, and is not; and shall ascend out of the bottomless pit, and go into perdition: and they that dwell on the earth shall wonder, whose names were not written in the book of life from the foundation of the world, when they behold the beast that was, and is not, and yet is.

Revelation 20:15 And whosoever was not found written in the book of life was cast into the lake of fire.

Revelation 21:27 And there shall in no wise enter into it any thing that defileth, neither *whatsoever* worketh abomination, or *maketh* a lie: but they which are written in the Lamb's book of life.

Some Calvinists equate unconditional election with names being placed in the book of life, but Philippians 4:3, Revelation 20:15 and 21:27 say nothing about when the names were placed in the book of life, and 13:8 and 17:8 say "from the foundation of the world," i.e., post-creation, not "from before" as Calvinists need for unconditional election. (cf. Matthew 13:35; Luke 11:50; John 17:24; Ephesians 1:4). What these verses tell us is that since creation those whose names were not added were disobedient. The clear implication is that after creation other names were added to the book of life, thus refuting unconditional election.

> Romans 8:28 And we know that all things work
> together for good to them that love God, to
> them who are the called according to *his*
> purpose. 29 For whom he did foreknow, he
> also did predestinate *to be* conformed to the
> image of his Son, that he might be the
> firstborn among many brethren.

Sometimes Calvinists cite this passage to support
unconditional election, and then they wrangle over the order
of the verbiage since calling precedes foreknowledge, which
itself is listed separate from, and prior to, predestination. They
also have to tool other words so that "conformed to the image
of his Son" is the same as salvation from the death penalty of
sin. Noticeably missing is any mention of the elect or of a
decree in eternity past of those God would save. Instead, the
verse identifies "them that love God" with "them who are
called." This group was foreknown and subsequently
"predestinated" to be conformed to the image of Jesus. Part of
the confusion that sometimes arises with this verse is the word
"predestinate" that suggest establishing one's destiny
beforehand. However, this word translates the Greek *proorizo*
that simply means to "pre-appoint." BDAG provides primary
definition: "decide upon beforehand, predetermine." The
concept of one's eternal destiny is not inherent in the term.
God appointed those who love Him, who are "the called" (i.e.,
those that responded to the gospel, 2 Thessalonians 2:14; see
the treatment of this aspect of the verse in the irresistible
grace chapter), to be conformed to the image of His Son. No
one here is being selected before creation to be saved.

> 1 Timothy 5:21 I charge *thee* before God, and
> the Lord Jesus Christ, and the elect angels, that
> thou observe these things without preferring
> one before another, doing nothing by partiality.

This verse is a Calvinist favorite, for from this one verse they
teach a parallel unconditional election doctrine that applies to

angels. This entire doctrine is based on the phrase "elect angels." There is nothing in 1 Timothy 5:21 that would prompt anyone to draw conclusions about a selection process of angels before creation. The verse says nothing of timing, nor of angels being selected to or for anything. Nor is there anywhere in the Bible that speaks of a redemptive program for angels. The term elect is the familiar adjective *eklektos,* not a verb, and is used here to describe certain angels as distinguished, excellent or proven, just as the men sent abroad with the decision of the Jerusalem Council were "chosen men" (Acts 15:22, 25). The distinguished, excellent or proven angels, in view of revelation elsewhere, refers to the non-fallen angels, i.e., those that did not rebel with Satan, but one cannot build an entire TULIP angel house from this one board.

> Romans 11:5 Even so then at this present time also there is a remnant according to the election of grace.

> Romans 11:7 What then? Israel hath not obtained that which he seeketh for; but the election hath obtained it, and the rest were blinded.

Calvinists also find support for unconditional election in Romans 11:5 and 7. Calvinists key in on the "election of grace" language and argue that these verses stand for the proposition that certain people (the "remnant" of Israel) were decreed before the foundation of the world for salvation. It is helpful to first look at the immediate context of these verses:

> Romans 11:1 I say then, Hath God cast away his people? God forbid. For I also am an Israelite, of the seed of Abraham, of the tribe of Benjamin. 2 God hath not cast away his people which he foreknew. Wot ye not what the scripture saith of Elias? how he maketh intercession to God against Israel, saying, 3 Lord, they have killed

thy prophets, and digged down thine altars; and
I am left alone, and they seek my life. 4 But
what saith the answer of God unto him? I have
reserved to myself seven thousand men, who
have not bowed the knee to the image of Baal.
5 Even so then at this present time also there is
a remnant according to the election of grace.
6 And if by grace, then is it no more of works:
otherwise grace is no more grace. But if it be of
works, then is it no more grace: otherwise work
is no more work. 7 What then? Israel hath not
obtained that which he seeketh for; but the
election hath obtained it, and the rest were
blinded.

Keep in mind, the overarching subject matter of Romans 9-11
is that God's Word has been effective, both because there are
Jewish people who have trusted Christ and because God has
bestowed mercy on believing Jews and Gentiles. Paul begins
here by affirming that God is not finished with national Israel.
To support his declaration that God has not cast away national
Israel, Paul appeals to the episode in 1 Kings 19. Elijah was on
the run from Jezebel and, in his exhaustion, came to the belief
that he was the only faithful person left. God quickly cured his
"Elijah Complex" by telling him that He had 7,000 people that
had not bowed the knee to Baal. These faithful people were a
"remnant" of true Jewish believers in that time.

In verse 5, Paul begins with "even so," looking back at the
prior four verses, and stating that in his present time there was
also a Jewish remnant corresponding to the remnant in Elijah's
day. That ancient remnant were not elected to salvation, but
reserved by God because they did not bow the knee to Baal.
So also the new remnant has nothing to do with unconditional
election, but instead, God reserved a remnant on the basis of
their faith. Although the Jewish people characteristically
rejected Jesus, they had not all done so. But many Jewish

people "followed after the law of righteousness" (Romans 9:31) "being ignorant of God's righteousness, and going about to establish their own righteousness, have not submitted themselves unto the righteousness of God" (Romans 10:3). Likewise, Paul writes in 11:7 of the same issue: "What then? Israel hath not obtained that which he seeketh for; but the election hath obtained it, and the rest were blinded." Paul's point is that to be saved from the death penalty of sin, the Jewish people need to be partakers of the "election of grace," which is by faith and not works. As Paul wrote in Romans 4:16: "it is of faith, that it might be by grace." Those that exercised faith are the "election" of 11:7. The rest were temporarily blinded as a result of their stumbling (rejection) at Jesus. (Romans 11:25)

For many Jewish people, merely being Jewish and having the law of Moses equated to being right with God and in this sense their national election guaranteed salvation. Paul corrects this mistaken notion of election and says that it is the "election of grace" that saves. Because Calvinists are too eager to write into every Biblical use of "election" they miss the point. This is just like in Romans 3 where Paul says it is not the works of the law that save, but the law of faith: "Where is boasting then? It is excluded. By what law? of works? Nay: but by the law of faith. Therefore we conclude that a man is justified by faith without the deeds of the law." (Romans 3:27-28) Paul builds from familiar terminology as a literary device to make a point. The "law of faith" is simply an expression Paul uses to teach that salvation is available by faith and not by the works of the law. Paul uses the phrase "election of grace" to make exactly the same point, but this time builds from the notion of Israel's national election (chapter 9). As Paul stated in Romans 5:2: "By whom also we have access by faith into this grace wherein we stand, and rejoice in hope of the glory of God." The election of grace is the blessing of salvation that comes by grace through faith, which is exactly how the remnant was saved.

> Matthew 24:22 And except those days should
> be shortened, there should no flesh be saved:
> but for the elect's sake those days shall be
> shortened.

> Matthew 24:24 For there shall arise false
> Christs, and false prophets, and shall shew
> great signs and wonders; insomuch that, if *it*
> *were* possible, they shall deceive the very elect.

> Matthew 24:31 And he shall send his angels
> with a great sound of a trumpet, and they shall
> gather together his elect from the four winds,
> from one end of heaven to the other.

These verses further illustrate the common practice of citing as a proof text for unconditional election any verse that uses the word "elect." All of these come from the famous Olivet Discourse, and each use of "elect" is the Greek adjective *eklektos*, which as discussed earlier carries the idea of being distinguished, excellent or pure. The context concerns the coming tribulation and the "elect" refers to the Jewish remnant at that time. Jesus speaks to his disciples of the coming affliction and persecution (e.g., Matthew 24:9) and how people in Judea must flee (Matthew 24:16-20). This passage has nothing to do with unconditional election. Many other commonly cited proof texts similarly say nothing about TULIP election but end up in a list because they refer to "elect" or "chosen." There is little benefit in addressing all of these, but we address one more below to illustrate.

> 2 Timothy 2:10 Therefore I endure all things
> for the elect's sakes, that they may also obtain
> the salvation which is in Christ Jesus with
> eternal glory.

Obviously, if God selected before the foundation of the world those He would save, and if those persons are the "elect" of this verse, then they are getting saved with or without Paul. So why does Paul need to "endure all things...that they may also obtain the salvation which is in Christ Jesus with eternal glory"? Certainly God can use Paul, but Paul's choices cannot affect the eternal destiny of the elect in the TULIP world. Most likely, Paul refers here to national Israel, his "brethren" and "kinsmen according to the flesh" (Romans 9:3) that he longed to reach with the gospel. Remember, it was non-believing Jews that were usually the ones persecuting Paul. Again, this verse illustrates that just because a word like elect or chosen is in a verse does not mean that TULIP unconditional election is that verse.

An Alternative View

What we have seen is that the unconditional election proof texts rely on most any verse that mentions certain words, but what about those verses that use those key words and explicitly refute unconditional election. I previously argued that the parable of Matthew 22:1-14 does exactly that, teaching that people who respond in faith become elect and are clothed with the Son's righteousness. Another obvious problem passage that actually refers to "election" is the following:

> 2 Peter 1:10 Wherefore the rather, brethren, give diligence to make your calling and election sure: for if ye do these things, ye shall never fall.

Incredibly, this verse also finds itself in proof-text lists since it mentions "election." As Charlie Bing points out: "The [Calvinist] interpretation has a problem on the face of it. If, as some understand it, calling and election are sovereignly determined by God, then how can anything we do influence that determination in the sense of making it more sure?"[109] The TULIP cruise liner runs aground on this verse not only because no person can affect God's decree concerning election and

---

[109] Bing, *Grace, Salvation, and Discipleship: How to Understand Some Difficult Bible Passages*, 222.

those passed over, but as we will see with the "P" of TULIP, all believers are by God's decree going to live a life of obedience to the end. This verse shows Peter saying something a TULIP proponent would never say.

In any event, the "wherefore" looks back to the preceding material where Peter affirms that his audience is composed of believers for whom God provided "exceeding great and precious promises: that by these ye might be partakers of the divine nature, having escaped the corruption that is in the world through lust." (2 Peter 1:3-4) Peter thus exhorts his readers to give "all diligence" to add to their "faith virtue... knowledge... temperance... patience... godliness... kindness... [and] charity." (2 Peter 1:5-7) These things, Peter says, will make them fruitful (2 Peter 1:8), but he that lacks these things is "blind...and hath forgotten that he was purged from his old sins." (2 Peter 1:9) This background brings Peter to the "wherefore" of 1:10 and a second exhortation to "diligence," this time that these believers would making their "calling and election sure." Again, Charlie Bing's commentary is helpful:

> The adjective translated "sure" (bebaios) means to be certified, confirmed, validated by evidence. But to whom is their calling and election to be confirmed? Surely it is not the reader, because Peter has repeatedly confirmed that in the preceding verses. There is no evidence that the readers were struggling with any doubts about their salvation. Peter must have in mind their visible testimony to others as their works confirm to those people their faith in Christ, which the readers claim to have (cf. Rom. 4:2, John 13:35; Jas. 2:21-25).[110]

In short, Peter did not want his readers to be like those he described in 1:9, but he wanted their walk to evidence their salvation and blessings in Christ.

---

[110] *Supra* note 109, p. 223.

Calvinism teaches that God will only save a specific group of people—the elect—who will hear the gospel and believe at a point in time that God decreed. The rest will never believe, neither can they even understand the gospel. We have seen that the critical words Calvinists rely upon do not have the meanings they force upon the terms to derive their theology. We have consequently seen that the Bible does not teach unconditional election, but in contrast to this doctrine, the Bible teaches unconditional grace, the "U" in NULIF. The concept of unconditional grace is that anyone (not just some select group) that hears the gospel can believe, and after they believe they will be elect, that is, distinguished, excellent, and pure in Christ. We will consider below four arguments against unconditional election and in favor of unconditional grace: (1) presentations of the gospel in the Bible are presented for the purpose of convincing people who Jesus is, and by this means some are convinced and others are not; (2) Paul acknowledges that wicked men prevented people from being saved; (3) over and again, the Bible emphasizes that salvation is to "whosoever" believes and that people are saved by believing, without any reference to election or regeneration; and (4) if the Bible teaches election as the Calvinists understand the term, that election is certainly not unconditional.

A Convincing Gospel

What utility is there in the gospel being presented to different people in different ways? Why try to be convincing in the presentation of the gospel? Why preach the gospel at the end of a sermon? Why not present only the historical facts of the gospel (1 Corinthians 15) without more? After all, in the Calvinist system, no one is ever convinced on his own of who Jesus is, but is simply regenerated so that he will certainly believe at a moment in time decreed by God as He gives the regenerated person his faith. If Paul and Peter were Calvinists who believed in unconditional election, surely they understood that all they needed to do was present the facts of the gospel and waste no time on anything else. God would regenerate the elect, or at least those elect in the audience decreed to be regenerated at that moment. God's regeneration rested solely on His decree and not on any human effort including their persuasiveness in their sermon and gospel presentation. Yet, unaware of this, Paul writes:

> 1 Corinthians 9:19 For though I be free from all men, yet have I made myself servant unto all, that I might gain the more. 20 And unto the Jews I became as a Jew, that I might gain the Jews; to them that are under the law, as under the law, that I might gain them that are under the law; 21 To them that are without law, as without law, (being not without law to God, but under the law to Christ), that I might gain them that are without law. 22 To the weak became I as weak, that I might gain the weak: I am made all things to all men, that I might by all means save some. 23 And this I do for the gospel's sake, that I might be partaker thereof with you.

Paul does not sound much like a Calvinist when he says he makes himself a "servant unto all" in order to win more souls. Paul was "made all things to all men, that [he] might save some." If Paul were a Calvinist, then he surely knew that God would save a fixed number of people and nothing he could do would result in more or less salvations than God decreed. But Paul does not say that. Instead, he went to great efforts to be "all things to all men" in order to reach more people for Christ.

In the Acts, Luke records that Paul did everything he could to convince people about Jesus: "And he reasoned in the synagogue every sabbath, and persuaded the Jews and the Greeks." (Acts 18:4) The term translated "persuaded" is the Greek *peitho* (Strong no. 3982) and means according to Strong's "to convince (by argument, true or false)." BDAG gives primary definition: "to cause to come to a particular point of view or course of action." Luke also records that Paul successfully persuaded some: "And some of them believed, and consorted with Paul and Silas; and of the devout Greeks a great multitude, and of the chief women not a few." (Acts 17:4) The term "believed" here is not the usual *pisteuo* (believe), but is the same word translated "persuaded" in Acts 18:4. In other words, what Luke records in Acts 17:4 is that some were convinced or persuaded by Paul's argumentation. Likewise, we read of Paul preaching in Rome, again trying to persuade people of the truth about Jesus: "And when they had appointed him a day, there came many to him into his lodging; to whom he expounded and testified the kingdom of God, persuading them concerning Jesus, both out of the law of Moses, and out of the prophets, from morning till evening. And some believed the things which were spoken, and some believed not." (Acts 28:23-24) Here again, Paul was "persuading [convincing, *peitho*] them concerning Jesus" and "some believed [were convinced, *peitho*]" but others "believed [*pisteuo*] not."

Consistent with God's report that Paul persuaded people to become Christians, Paul (and Peter and Stephen) preached with passion, not merely setting forth the bare historical facts of the gospel, but tailoring their messages to their audience. In Acts 2, Peter preached to a group of people about the recent crucifixion of Jesus, tailoring his sermon to his specific audience. Peter used the recent events leading to the crucifixion of our Lord to convict them. (Acts 2:37) In Acts 7, Stephen tailored his sermon to his Jewish audience. In Acts 17, Paul preached to Gentiles in Athens a carefully constructed message based on their altar inscribed to the unknown god and quoted one of their famous poets. This practice of preaching convincingly and tailoring the sermon and gospel presentation to the audience was also Jesus' practice. Our Lord always met people where they were at in life. Jesus' presentation to

Nicodemus is quite different from his presentation to the Samaritan woman at the well, and rightly so since Nicodemus was an educated Pharisee and the Samaritan woman was at the opposite end of the social and educational spectrum. We have to ask why Jesus would present his message to different people differently rather than making the same speech to everyone. If Jesus or Peter or Paul were Calvinists, they would never have made the presentations of truth that they did in the ways that they did.

People Blocking Others from Believing

The opposite side of this issue is that if God elected before the foundation of the world those that will be saved and decreed their salvation, then surely no man can stand in the way of God's decreed will in this matter. That is, no man can prevent people from getting saved. And yet we find Paul reminding the Thessalonians of Jewish persecutors: "Forbidding us to speak to the Gentiles that they might be saved, to fill up their sins alway: for the wrath is come upon them to the uttermost." (1 Thessalonians 2:16) If Paul held to unconditional election, then he would not have had any concern about Jewish persecutors blocking the spread of the gospel through him and thereby preventing Gentiles from being saved. Paul's statement to the church at Thessalonica reveals his belief that anyone he could present the gospel to could believe, and likewise, that they might never be saved if he were prevented from presenting the gospel. Similarly, Jesus said: "Those by the way side are they that hear; then cometh the devil, and taketh away the word out of their hearts, lest they should believe and be saved." (Luke 8:12) Jesus indicates that Satan—implicitly, through people and circumstances—acts to prevent people from believing and being saved. Obviously, if unconditional election is Biblical, Satan cannot prevent anyone from being saved.

<u>Whosever</u>

Finally, the Bible says that salvation is available to *whosoever* believes. "And as Moses lifted up the serpent in the wilderness, even so must the Son of man be lifted up: That whosoever believeth in him should not perish, but have eternal life. For God so loved the world, that he gave his only begotten Son, that whosoever believeth in him should not perish, but have everlasting life." (John 3:14-16) To the woman at the well, Jesus said whosoever: "But whosoever drinketh of the water that I shall give him shall never thirst; but the water that I shall give him shall be in him a well of water springing up into everlasting life." (John 4:14) To groups of people, Jesus said whosoever: "I am come a light into the world, that whosoever believeth on me should not abide in darkness." Indeed, the Bible comes to a close with an appeal to whosoever: "And whosoever will, let him take the water of life freely." (Revelation 22:17) And in response to the invitations, we read again and again of people believing, without any reference to being elect.

> <u>John 2:11</u> This beginning of miracles did Jesus in Cana of Galilee, and manifested forth his glory; and his disciples believed on him.

> <u>John 2:22</u> When therefore he was risen from the dead, his disciples remembered that he had said this unto them; and they believed the scripture, and the word which Jesus had said.

> <u>John 2:23</u> Now when he was in Jerusalem at the passover, in the feast *day*, many believed in his name, when they saw the miracles which he did.

> <u>John 4:39</u> And many of the Samaritans of that city believed on him for the saying of the woman, which testified, He told me all that ever I did.

John 4:41 And many more believed because of his own word;

John 4:53 So the father knew that *it was* at the same hour, in the which Jesus said unto him, Thy son liveth: and himself believed, and his whole house.

John 8:30 As he spake these words, many believed on him.

John 10:42 And many believed on him there.

John 11:45 Then many of the Jews which came to Mary, and had seen the things which Jesus did, believed on him.

John 12:11 Because that by reason of him many of the Jews went away, and believed on Jesus.

John 12:42 Nevertheless among the chief rulers also many believed on him; but because of the Pharisees they did not confess *him*, lest they should be put out of the synagogue:

John 20:8 Then went in also that other disciple, which came first to the sepulchre, and he saw, and believed.

John 20:29 Jesus saith unto him, Thomas, because thou hast seen me, thou hast believed: blessed *are* they that have not seen, and *yet* have believed.

Over and again, people believe in Jesus in response to his word or his miracles, and there is not one instance in John where there is any suggestion that they were made to believe. If we take John's Gospel at face value, rather than trying to write Calvinism into it, people believed because they heard Jesus' message (e.g., John 4:41) and because they witnessed his works (e.g., John 11:45). One passage of particular interest is John 10. Although Calvinists rely on John 10 for support for unconditional election, the passage disproves their case. In John 10, Jesus claims that he and the Father are one, and in response the crowd is going to stone him:

> John 10:30 I and my Father are one. 31 Then the Jews took up stones again to stone him. 32 Jesus answered them, Many good works have I shewed you from my Father; for which of those works do ye stone me?

At this point, they accuse Jesus of blasphemy. To this accusation, Jesus says that if they will not believe his words (see also John 10:25), they should at least believe his works: "If I do not the works of my Father, believe me not. But if I do, though ye believe not me, believe the works: that ye may know, and believe, that the Father is in me, and I in him." (John 10:37-38) This is a curious statement. According to the Calvinists, at the time chosen by God the elect person is regenerated so that he will believe. So we must ask why Jesus would speak to a crowd that has already rejected his message and invite them to instead believe based the works they witnessed. Since they rejected the message, they were either not elect, or if they were elect, this was not the decreed time they would be regenerated to believe. In either case, Jesus' admonition to believe because of the works after they already rejected the message is absurd if Jesus believed in unconditional election, but his appeal makes perfect sense if they in fact were able to believe.

Elsewhere in the Bible, we find that people believed based on works. Luke records: "Then the deputy, when he saw what was done, believed, being astonished at the doctrine of the Lord." (Acts 13:12) Others believed because they compared Paul's words to the Old Testament: "These were more noble than those in Thessalonica, in that they received the word with all readiness of mind, and searched the scriptures daily, whether

those things were so. Therefore many of them believed...."
(Acts 17:10-11) And for Israel, we are told that the present
blessings to the Gentiles are to provoke Israel to jealousy.
(Romans 11:11) They were not cut off because of election or a
decree, but because of unbelief. (Romans 11:20) And yet Paul
sought to persuade them so that some might be saved: "For I
speak to you Gentiles, inasmuch as I am the apostle of the
Gentiles, I magnify mine office; If by any means I may
provoke to emulation them which are my flesh, and might save
some of them." (Romans 11:13-14) If God had to give faith to
these people to believe, regenerating them so that they would
choose to respond favorably to the gospel, then why does the
Bible record people believing because of works or careful study
of the Old Testament or jealousy? The Biblical record bears
out that people are convinced, not programmed.

Conditional Election

Another observation to make is that if the Bible teaches
election as the Calvinists understand the term, it is
conditional, which destroys their whole system. For the
TULIP to stand, election must not be based in any way on
personal merit. Yet, we find Jesus stating that wealthy people
more often reject God: "It is easier for a camel to go through
the eye of a needle, than for a rich man to enter into the
kingdom of God." (Mark 10:25) We also find instances where a
person is saved and then his or her entire household gets
saved. (see, e.g., John 4:53; Acts 16:15, 16:34, 18:8) And Jesus
seemed to have anticipated entire cities rejecting the good
news: "And whosoever shall not receive you, nor hear your
words, when ye depart out of that house or city, shake off the
dust of your feet. Verily I say unto you, It shall be more
tolerable for the land of Sodom and Gomorrha in the day of
judgment, than for that city." (Matthew 10:14-15; see also
Matthew 11:21) If we accept the Biblical record, it seems that
God elects more poor and middle-class people than rich

people, skips over entire cities, and often if God elects a person He elects the entire household, which apparently includes both family and servants. So if people are saved based on their election, it is certainly not unconditional.

Rather than teaching unconditional election, we see that the Bible actually teaches unconditional grace. God did not divide the world before creation into those enabled to believe and those unable to believe. This has significant implications for our Christian walk. It means that our evangelism matters and how we present the gospel matters. We cannot console ourselves that our efforts are unimportant since, if God elected a certain individual, He will bring that individual to salvation no matter what we do. Our efforts, or lack of efforts, really have eternal consequences. In addition, when we preach the gospel we can do it with integrity. How genuine would the message be if some could not believe, and others had no choice? Would our gospel presentation tell them we have only contingent good news? But like Jesus and the apostles, we can share the message and persuade sinners, knowing that they can believe if they choose. In this way, God's grace is unconditional—it is available to everyone.

Concluding Thoughts on Unconditional Election

Calvinists boast much scriptural support (evidence for the jury) for unconditional election, but the reality is that the doctrine has two pillar passages, namely Romans 9 and Ephesians 1:4. We have seen that Romans 9 addressed God's choices to extend or withhold mercy, but said nothing about decreeing whom He would save. And the election is Ephesians 1 is a positional truth about all believers' positional excellence and holiness, not about justification. The remaining proof texts are even further removed from having anything to do with people being selected for salvation before the foundation of the world. Unfortunately, what often happens is that a person accepts the

Calvinists' definitions of key terms like elect with little or no study of the word, and then accepts their interpretation of the pillar passages with at least some measure of consideration. But the remaining proof texts are accepted with far less attention. All of these verses, and others that Calvinists cite for unconditional election, need to be scrutinized carefully and without reliance on the pillar passages or the bogus definitions. After all, if Ephesians 1:4 does not support unconditional election, then no other proof text cited by the Calvinists says anything about a selection process being made before creation. And if Romans 9 is not about God making certain people unable to believe the gospel, then where else in the Bible do they find proof for such a notion?

What this means for us is that when we evangelize, we need not worry about whether our audience is selected for salvation before the foundation of the world. Since the people we interact with are not totally unable to believe and their eternal destinies were not predetermined by God, we need to focus on clearly presenting the gospel message and providing a defense for the hope that we have. We need to evangelize like their souls depend on it. We cannot back away from our responsibility and console ourselves with the idea that God is going to save the elect and damn the rest apart from anything we say or do. Without unconditional election, we have a heavy personal responsibility. "And Jesus came and spake unto them, saying, All power is given unto me in heaven and in earth. Go ye therefore, and teach all nations, baptizing them in the name of the Father, and of the Son, and of the Holy Ghost: Teaching them to observe all things whatsoever I have commanded you: and, lo, I am with you alway, even unto the end of the world. Amen." (Matthew 28:18-20)

The "T" and "U" have been clipped from the TULIP. It has been demonstrated that the Calvinists' proof texts for total depravity and unconditional election do not prove the doctrines. Rather than teaching that God has selected only a subset of humanity to believe, in fact, the Bible teaches unconditional grace, namely that all can believe. And without the "TU" the TULIP is dead. The "L" goes away because it makes no sense to speak of Jesus only going to the cross for a subset of humanity (the elect) when the Bible does not teach that salvation is exclusively theirs. Nor does irresistible grace survive since the Bible does not teach that people are incapable of believing (total depravity) and thus require irresistible grace to impose faith on them. And finally, the perseverance of the saints also falls away because God has not given people their faith. Nonetheless, it is worthwhile to press on and analyze in more detail the remaining doctrines of Calvinism and tackle the proof texts independent of whether or not total depravity and unconditional election are themselves supportable since our primary goal is to find out whether any of the doctrines are Biblical.

Chapter 6

Limited Atonement

Under the Mosaic Law, the nation of Israel was commanded to keep seven feasts. These were, in this order, the Passover, the Feast of Unleavened Bread, the Feast of the Sheaf of First Fruits, the Feast of Weeks (Pentecost), the Feast of Trumpets, the Feast Day of Atonement (Yom Kippur), and the Feast of Tabernacles. All of these feasts find ultimate fulfillment in Jesus Christ. The Feast Day of Atonement provided an especially fascinating and illuminating picture of the grace of God.

On this special day, the 10th day of the 7th month (Tishri), and only on this day, the High Priest could enter the Holy of Holies within the Temple and make atonement for the children of Israel. On this day, the High Priest would take a ritual bath and put on special clothing for the occasion. In addition to the offering of a bull for his own personal sins, two goats were selected for use in the feast. Lots were cast to determine which goat was for God and which was to be the scapegoat. Then the High Priest would place his hand on the head of the goat for God and confess the sins of Israel: "Then shall he kill the goat of the sin offering, that *is* for the people, and bring his blood within the vail, and do with that blood as he did with the blood of the bullock, and sprinkle it upon the mercy seat, and before the mercy seat: And he shall make an atonement for the holy *place*, because of the uncleanness of the children of Israel, and because of their transgressions in all their sins: and so shall he do for the tabernacle of the congregation, that remaineth among them in the midst of their uncleanness." (Leviticus 16:15-16) The Bible is clear that the sacrificed goat was for the sins of all Israel: "And he shall sprinkle of the blood upon it with his finger seven times, and cleanse it, and hallow it from the uncleanness of the children of Israel." (Leviticus 16:19)

Not only was the sacrificed goat representative of the shedding of blood for all Israel, the azazel was representative of the removal of the sins of all Israel: "And when he hath made an end of reconciling the holy *place*, and the tabernacle of the congregation, and the altar, he shall bring the live goat: And Aaron shall lay both his hands upon the head of the live goat, and confess over him all the iniquities of the children of Israel, and all their transgressions in all their sins, putting them upon the head of the goat, and shall send *him* away by the hand of a fit man into the wilderness. And the goat shall bear upon him all their iniquities unto a land not inhabited: and he shall let go the goat in the wilderness." (Leviticus 16:20-22) The purpose of the Feast Day of Atonement is indisputable: "And this shall be an everlasting statute unto you, to make an atonement for the children of Israel for all their sins once a year." (Leviticus 16:34)

In the Feast, we see the High Priest make atonement by the goats for all Israel for the year. The priestly work was for all

Israel, not part. In addition to the work of the High Priest, the people were obligated to afflict their souls. (Leviticus 16:31) They were not just passive onlookers but had to participate in the feast in a time of self-denial when they fasted and focused on what God had done for them. What is pictured is the death of Jesus for the sins of the world. (Hebrews 9:7-12) Commenting on the Day of Atonement, Timothy Pierce explains the profound significance of Christ's fulfillment of this Old Testament feast:

> The Day of Atonement represented the centerpiece of the Levitical law. For the writer of the book of Hebrews, the importance of recognizing that Jesus perfectly and completely fulfilled the purposes of this day is that Jesus did not come to destroy but to fulfill the old covenant. In Christ the law found perfection, whereas previously it was incomplete. So perfect was Christ's sacrifice that a new covenant was formed, which was written on human hearts... Much has been made of comparisons between Jesus and the elements of the Day of Atonement... While exegetically speaking some of these points are questionable (such as Jesus' descent into hell), the point is that of all of the sacred events of Scripture, none found expression as fully in the NT as the Day of Atonement—because Christ's death and resurrection was the ultimate Day of Atonement.[111]

Calvinists, however, teach that Jesus did not die for the sins of all the world, but only for the elect. If Jesus only died for some, then the Feast Day of Atonement fails to meaningfully foreshadow Christ's redemptive work. The error in many

---

[111] Timothy M. Pierce, *Enthroned on Our Praise, An Old Testament Theology of Worship* (Nashville: B&H Academic, 2008), p. 107.

Calvinists' soteriology is that they view salvation of the elect as a completed event at the cross, which guarantees but is in no way dependent upon a subsequent appropriation by faith. On this basis, the reality that many people reject Christ proves that Christ did not die for them. To say Jesus died for all is equated with universalism. The Old Testament feasts and Levitical laws are helpful here because they were no doubt intended to foreshadow and ultimately be fulfilled in Christ. It was never good enough to simply have the priest slay an animal—what we might call the provision—but there had to be a personal appropriation. We see this in the requirements of participation in the Feast Day of Atonement and elsewhere. For instance, we read in Leviticus 1:4 with regard to the burnt offerings: "And he shall put his hand upon the head of the burnt offering; and it shall be accepted for him to make atonement for him."

As we shall see, in addition to the inconsistency with the Old Testament blueprint of God's redemptive plan, the Calvinists' teaching called limited or particular atonement lacks any scriptural support and is expressly rejected by numerous New Testament passages. The teaching is less a conclusion based on the Bible than it is a philosophical conclusion flowing from total depravity and unconditional election.

How the Calvinists Define Limited Atonement

Grudem succinctly states the issue: "...when Christ died on the cross, did he pay for the sins of the entire human race or only for the sins of those who he knew would ultimately be saved?"[112] Steele, Thomas and Quinn relate the historical Calvinist answer:

> Historical or mainline Calvinism has consistently
> maintained that Christ's redeeming work was
> definite in *design* and *accomplishment*—that it

---

[112] *Supra* note 14, p. 594.

was intended to render complete satisfaction for certain specified sinners, and that it actually secured salvation for these individuals and for no one else.[113]

It is important to note that the historical Calvinist view is not merely that Jesus died for the elect, but that his death actually saved them. For this reason, Sproul states the question thus: "Is Christ a real Savior or merely a 'potential' Savior?"[114] Other Calvinists are in agreement:

> God decreed to create the race, to permit the fall, and then, in His infinite compassion, He elected out of the fallen an innumerable multitude, chosen in Christ, to be delivered from this ruin; and for them Christ was sent, to make full penal satisfaction for their unrighteousness, and purchase for them all graces of effectual calling and spiritual life and bodily resurrection, which make up a complete redemption, by His righteousness and intercession founded thereon.[115]

> It is generally admitted that the satisfaction rendered by Christ was in itself sufficient for the salvation of all men, though they do not attain unto salvation... In distinction from them [non-Reformed] the Reformed churches believe in a limited atonement. They maintain that it was the intention of both the Father and the Son to save only the elect, a purpose that is actually accomplished... The advocates of a limited atonement, on the other hand, maintain that Christ actually saves to the uttermost

---

[113] *Supra* note 3, pp. 39-40.
[114] *Supra* note 18, p. 164.
[115] *Supra* note 36, p. 520.

every one of those for whom He has laid down His life. Not one of those for whom the price is paid finally falls short of salvation.[116]

When we speak of the meritorious work of Christ on the cross, do we rightfully say the He died for all men equally and alike (as say the Arminians), or do we more accurately state (with the Calvinists) that Christ died for the elect only?[117]

The Calvinists' arguments to support limited atonement are threefold: (1) that limited atonement necessarily follows from total depravity and unconditional election; (2) that several verses indicate that Jesus died for the sins of a discrete group of people; and (3) that certain verses expressly teach that Jesus died only for the elect. We shall address these in this order. First, the philosophical argument:

You see, if you believe that the Bible teaches that God is sovereign, His plan immutable, and His election unconditional, you *must* conclude that the atonement is limited to those whom He freely willed to make the objects of grace. (Actually *grace* means unmerited favor. It is an act that is wholly undeserved, so that the term, by its very nature of definition, denies *conditional* election.) The Arminian view insists that it is man's act of faith that merits his being elected according to the foreknowledge of God. If such be the case man is saved by works and not by the grace of God, because he has done at least one thing pleasing to God, and all on his own![118]

---

[116] *Supra* note 34, p. 216.
[117] *Supra* note 13, p. 45.
[118] *Supra* note 13, p. 47.

What is inherent in this argument is that if Christ died for someone they will be saved, and if faith had anything to do with it, then salvation is by works since faith is a work. Dabney also offers the philosophical argument in favor of unlimited atonement:

> The Scriptures tell us that those who are to be saved in Christ are a number definitely elected and given to Him from eternity, to be redeemed by His mediation. How can anything be plainer from this than that there was a purpose in God's atonement, as to them, other than that it had as to the rest of mankind? ...If God ever intended to save any soul in Christ ... that soul will certainly be saved. Hence, all whom God ever intended to save in Christ will be saved. But some souls will never be saved; therefore some souls God never intended to be saved by Christ's atonement. The strength of this argument can scarcely be overrated.[119]

Again, the premise underpinning the philosophical argument is that Jesus' death secured (rather than made available) salvation, and since not all are saved (or for the Calvinist, only the elect will be saved), it naturally follows that Jesus only died for some (the elect). Based on this premise, Sproul concludes that unlimited atonement necessarily implies universalism (all will be saved):

> The atonement of Christ was clearly limited or unlimited. There is no alternative, no *tertium quid*. If it is unlimited in an absolute sense, then an atonement has been made for every person's sins. Christ has then made propitiation for all persons' sins and expiated them as well.[120]

---

[119] *Supra* note 36, p. 521 (citations omitted).
[120] *Supra* note 18, pp. 164-65.

Building on this argument, Sproul concludes that the unlimited atonement view implies that "faith is not only a condition for redemption, but also one of the very grounds for redemption" and thus "faith becomes a work."[121] He elaborates further and concludes that if Christ died for all then He died for none at all:

> This means that if Christ really, objectively satisfied the demands of God's justice for everyone, then everyone will be saved. It is one thing to agree that faith is a necessary condition for the appropriation of the benefits of Christ's atoning work, for justification and its fruits. It is quite another to say that faith is a necessary condition for the satisfaction of divine justice. If faith is a condition for God's justice to be satisfied, then the atonement, in itself, is not sufficient to satisfy the demands of God's justice. In itself the atonement is not "sufficient" for anyone, let alone for all. Full satisfaction is not rendered until or unless a person adds to the atonement his faith.[122]

For the Calvinists, the only way Jesus could have paid for the sins of the world is if the entire world were saved! This view is neither logical nor scriptural. If Christ's death secured salvation for the elect, then why the gospel at all? Why the emphasis on believing that permeates John's Gospel if salvation were already a completed past event for the elect? The better view is simply that Jesus paid the price for everyone but to obtain the benefits of Christ's payment a person must respond to the gospel. Calvinists will not accept this view because they insist that believing is a work, and since you cannot be saved by works, you cannot be saved by

---

121 *Supra* note 18, p. 165.
122 *Supra* note 18, p. 166.

believing! What would you answer in response to the Roman jailor? The jailor "brought them out, and said, Sirs, what must I do to be saved? And they said, Believe on the Lord Jesus Christ, and thou shalt be saved, and thy house." (Acts 16:30-31)

The Bible Expressly Teaches Unlimited Atonement

Limited atonement is the Calvinists' attempt to reconcile with the Bible the illogical conclusions that necessarily follow from total depravity and unconditional election. Since they have concluded that people have no role whatsoever in obtaining salvation (even their believing or faith is itself given to them by God) and that God picked only a subset of humanity (the elect) for salvation, they must teach that Jesus completed the salvation of the elect on the cross. That being the case, Jesus could only die for the elect because if he died for a non-elect person that person would also be saved. One of the many problems with this logic is that we know that atonement can be universal provisionally, but not universally effective, from the Feast Day of Atonement. The goat for God died for the sins of all Israel and the azazel carried the sins away, a picture of universal atonement. But the benefits of the two goats were effective only for those that participated in the Feast and afflicted their souls.

Before turning to the Calvinists proof texts, we do well to first consider the many verses that expressly teach unlimited atonement. Calvinists generally offer little direct support for limited atonement but instead give more attention to refuting verses like the ones below. First, there are the "world" verses (these are not all of them):

> John 1:29 The next day John seeth Jesus coming unto him, and saith, Behold the Lamb of God, which taketh away the sin of the world.

John 3:16 For God so loved the world, that he gave his only begotten Son, that whosoever believeth in him should not perish, but have everlasting life.

John 3:17 For God sent not his Son into the world to condemn the world; but that the world through him might be saved.

John 4:42 And said unto the woman, Now we believe, not because of thy saying: for we have heard *him* ourselves, and know that this is indeed the Christ, the Saviour of the world.

1 Corinthians 5:19 To wit, that God was in Christ, reconciling the world unto himself, not imputing their trespasses unto them; and hath committed unto us the word of reconciliation.

1 John 2:2 And he is the propitiation for our sins: and not for ours only, but also for *the sins of* the whole world.

1 John 4:14 And we have seen and do testify that the Father sent the Son *to be* the Saviour of the world.

The Calvinists' solution to these verses is to argue that the term "world" does not mean all people in the world, but means the elect or, generally, all kinds of people. They would say that John uses the term to emphasize that the elect come from every tribe, tongue and nation, or consists of both Jews and Gentiles. Although they do not have any verses where world unambiguously means the elect, they latch on to John 12:19 where the term "world" does not mean all individuals without exception: "The Pharisees therefore said among themselves, Perceive ye how ye prevail nothing? behold, the world is gone after him." Calvinists would say that this verse proves that world does not always mean all people and therefore the context must determine the meaning of world. There are four problems with this logic. First, world almost always means world, especially in John and 1 John; citing a single counter-example is hardly conclusive of anything. Second, if God wanted to say elect, He certainly knows how, and surely if God wanted to communicate with clarity He would have said elect if that is what He meant. Third, John 12:19 is an example of the Greek term *kosmos* ("world") being as hyperbole for effect. None of the unlimited atonement verses quoted above give any indication of the term *kosmos* being used as hyperbole. Fourth, the Calvinists cannot effectively argue that the context of verses like John 3:16 merit limiting world to the elect. Instead, they argue that in view of the truths of total depravity and unconditional election, to take "world" in John 3:16 to meaning anything except "elect" (or Jews and Gentiles) would contradict these other Biblical teachings and thus it must mean only the "elect." This, of course, is circular logic since it has already been demonstrated that neither of those two doctrines are Biblical.

It will suffice to consider John 3:16-18 with "world" replaced by "the elect" as the Calvinists insist:

> For God so loved the [elect], that he gave his only begotten Son, that whosoever [of the elect] believeth in him should not perish, but have everlasting life. For God sent not his Son into the world [to the elect?] to condemn the [elect]; but that the [elect] through him might be saved. He [of the elect?] that believeth on him is not condemned: but he [of the elect?] that believeth not is condemned already, because he [of the elect?] hath not believed in the name of the only begotten Son of God.

If we apply the Calvinists definition all the way through the passage, we have that God loved only the elect so that those of the elect that believe in Jesus would be saved. We also must face the fact that those elect persons that do not believe remain condemned, an obvious contradiction to the TULIP philosophy. In short, it makes nonsense of many of these passages to substitute "the elect" for "world," and even if that were appropriate in some of the passages, it stretches credulity to assert that the same is appropriate for all of them. Without anything more, the selected "world" verses quoted above should be sufficient to reject limited atonement, but there is a great deal more.

There is also a category of verses that contain the word "whosoever" (these are not all):

> John 3:16 For God so loved the world, that he gave his only begotten Son, that whosoever believeth in him should not perish, but have everlasting life.

> Acts 2:21 And it shall come to pass, *that* whosoever shall call on the name of the Lord shall be saved.

> Acts 10:43 To him give all the prophets witness, that through his name whosoever believeth in him shall receive remission of sins.

> Romans 10:13 For whosoever shall call upon the name of the Lord shall be saved.

> Revelation 22:17 And the Spirit and the bride say, Come. And let him that heareth say, Come. And let him that is athirst come. And whosoever will, let him take the water of life freely.

You may have already guessed how Calvinists deal with the "whosoever" verses. When God says "whosoever" He does not mean "whosoever," but rather, "whosoever that is elect." There is nothing contextually to suggest overwriting the Text in this manner. Rather, Calvinists redefine these words because they are inconvenient and irreconcilable with their doctrines of total depravity and unconditional election. This is blatant *eisogesis* of these passages, and without context clues that "whosoever" should be read restrictively, these verses should be taken at face value. If God wanted to say "whosoever that is elect" He would have done so.

In addition to the "world" and "whosoever" verses that squarely refute limited atonement, there are also the "all" verses and their equivalents (e.g., where "all" is implicit), and you have probably guessed that "all" does not mean "all" but "some." Selected "all" verses and their equivalents are below:

> Luke 19:10 For the Son of man is come to seek and to save that which was lost.

> Romans 5:6 For when we were yet without strength, in due time Christ died for the ungodly.

> 2 Corinthians 5:14 For the love of Christ constraineth us; because we thus judge, that if one died for all, then were all dead.

> 2 Corinthians 5:15 And *that* he died for all, that they which live should not henceforth live unto themselves, but unto him which died for them, and rose again.

> 1 Timothy 2:6 Who gave himself a ransom for all, to be testified in due time.

> 1 Timothy 4:10 For therefore we both labour and suffer reproach, because we trust in the living God, who is the Saviour of all men, specially of those that believe.

> Titus 2:11 For the grace of God that bringeth salvation hath appeared to all men,

> Hebrews 2:9 But we see Jesus, who was made a little lower than the angels for the suffering of death, crowned with glory and honour; that he by the grace of God should taste death for every man.

> 1 Peter 3:9 The Lord is not slack concerning his promise, as some men count slackness; but is long-suffering to us-ward, not willing that any should perish, but that all should come to repentance.

Consider 2 Corinthians 5:14-15 and suppose "all" means "the elect": "For the love of Christ constraineth us; because we thus judge, that if one died for [the elect], then were [the elect] dead: And that he died for [the elect] that they which live should not henceforth live unto themselves, but unto him which died for them, and rose again." The phrase "that they which live" clearly implies a subset of the larger group. So we must ask, what of "they which [don't] live"? Is "they which live" better understood as a subset of "all" or a subset of "the elect"? Making "all" mean "the elect" leads to the conclusion that only a subset of the elect people will live, a problem for the Calvinists. As with John 3:16-18, the Humpty Dumpty approach of redefining common terms with uncommon meanings pushes them over the wall and they fall apart.

To consider another example (not listed above), we have in Romans 5:18: "Therefore as by the offence of one *judgment came* upon all men to condemnation; even so by the righteousness of one *the free gift came* upon all men unto justification of life." This verse leaves no dispute that "all" can only mean "all persons without exception." The first clause tells us that by Adam's sin ("the offence of one") judgment came upon all men, and the Calvinists would agree that "all men" in this instance means everyone. The second clause beginning with "even so" is a contrast to the first. By the offence of one person, namely Adam, all men were condemned. In contrast, by the righteousness of one man, Jesus, salvation was made available "upon all men." The contrast here mandates that "upon all men" means all men without exception and not "upon some men" as some Calvinists insist.

Proof Texts for Limited Atonement

In addition to refuting verses like the "world," "whosoever," and "all" verses, Calvinists also claim support in Bible verses that speak of Jesus' death on behalf of less than everyone:

> Isaiah 53:5 But he *was* wounded for our transgressions, *he was* bruised for our iniquities: the chastisement of our peace *was* upon him; and with his stripes we are healed.

> Matthew 1:21 And she shall bring forth a son, and thou shalt call his name JESUS: for he shall save his people from their sins.

> Matthew 20:28 Even as the Son of man came not to be ministered unto, but to minister, and to give his life a ransom for many.

> Matthew 26:28 For this is my blood of the new testament, which is shed for many for the remission of sins.

> John 10:15 As the Father knoweth me, even so know I the Father: and I lay down my life for the sheep.

> Galatians 3:13 Christ hath redeemed us from the curse of the law, being made a curse for us: for it is written, Cursed *is* every one that hangeth on a tree:

> Ephesians 5:25 Husbands, love your wives, even as Christ also loved the church, and gave himself for it;

> Hebrews 9:28 So Christ was once offered to bear the sins of many; and unto them that look for him shall he appear the second time without sin unto salvation.

> Acts 20:28 Take heed therefore unto yourselves, and to all the flock, over the which the Holy Ghost hath made you overseers, to feed the church of God, which he hath purchased with his own blood.

The reason none of these verses prove limited atonement is simple. It is obvious that if Jesus died for all, then it can be said without contradiction that he died for Israel (e.g., Isaiah 53:5, Matthew 1:21) or for many (e.g., Matthew 20:28). But simply because there are verses that focus on Jesus' death for the sins of a sub-group of humanity does not imply that he did not die for anyone else, or for everyone. If these "limited" verses were all that we had in the Bible, the Calvinists might have an argument to make, but in view of the substantial number of verses indicating unlimited atonement, these "limited" verses provide no support for limited atonement. In addition, I would point out that the verses that speak of Jesus' death for "many" actually support unlimited atonement because "many" is being used as an idiom for "all." Consider the following excerpt from Romans 5:

> Romans 5:12 Wherefore, as by one man sin entered into the world, and death by sin; and so death passed upon all men, for that all have sinned: 13 (For until the law sin was in the world: but sin is not imputed when there is no law. 14 Nevertheless death reigned from Adam to Moses, even over them that had not sinned after the similitude of Adam's transgression, who is the figure of him that was to come. 15 But not as the offence, so also is the free gift. For if through the offence of one many be dead, much more the grace of God, and the gift by

grace, which is by one man, Jesus Christ, hath abounded unto many. <u>16</u> And not as it was by one that sinned, so is the gift: for the judgment was by one to condemnation, but the free gift is of many offences unto justification. <u>17</u> For if by one man's offence death reigned by one; much more they which receive abundance of grace and of the gift of righteousness shall reign in life by one, Jesus Christ.) <u>18</u> Therefore as by the offence of one judgment came upon all men to condemnation; even so by the righteousness of one the free gift came upon all men unto justification of life. <u>19</u> For as by one man's disobedience many were made sinners, so by the obedience of one shall many be made righteous.

This passage is particularly interesting because in the fifteenth and nineteenth verses, Paul writes that Jesus died for many, but in the eighteenth verse, Paul writes that Jesus died for all. As we have already seen, the word "all" in verse eighteen means everyone and not simply the elect or some other subset of humanity. Paul is paralleling the fact that Adam's sin brought condemnation to everyone (the same thought conveyed also in verse twelve) with the fact that the free gift provided by Jesus is available to everyone. Since Paul is using "all" to mean everyone and he makes similar declarations in verses fifteen and nineteen using the term "many" as he does in twelve and eighteen using the term "all," we conclude that Paul uses "many" in this passage as an expression to indicate everyone.

Pillar Proof Text: John 10

There is only one passage that Calvinists consistently point to as direct explicit support for limited atonement, and that is John 10, particularly the eleventh and fifteenth verses. We will consider some additional verses because Calvinists find much of the TULIP here.

> John 10:11 I am the good shepherd: the good shepherd giveth his life for the sheep. * * * 15 As the Father knoweth me, even so know I the Father: and I lay down my life for the sheep. * * * 24 Then came the Jews round about him, and said unto him, How long dost thou make us to doubt? If thou be the Christ, tell us plainly. 25 Jesus answered them, I told you, and ye believed not: the works that I do in my Father's name, they bear witness of me. 26 But ye believe not, because ye are not of my sheep, as I said unto you. 27 My sheep hear my voice, and I know them, and they follow me: 28 And I give unto them eternal life; and they shall never perish, neither shall any *man* pluck them out of my hand. 29 My Father, which gave *them* me, is greater than all; and no *man* is able to pluck *them* out of my Father's hand.

When Jesus rebukes the Pharisees in 10:26, Calvinists understand Jesus to mean that the Pharisees have rejected him because they were not elect ("of my sheep"). And since Jesus tells them in 10:26 that they are not his sheep, then his statements in 10:11 and 10:15 are explicit statements that he will not give his life for them. Preliminarily, I would point out that nowhere in this passage do we find the adjective "elect" or any variation of it, and for that matter we do not find it in John's Gospel at all, even though he clearly knew how to use the term. (see 2 John 1) The verb "chosen" is used several times but never in relation to salvation.

To properly understand the passage, we must first keep in mind that Jesus' earthly ministry was primarily focused on the Jewish nation. Many Jewish people were believers prior to Jesus' earthly ministry. We might think of them as Old Testament believers who were looking forward to the coming Messiah. John the Baptist's ministry included announcing that

Messiah's coming was imminent, and then as recorded in John 1, identifying the Messiah when he arrived. Jewish believers accepted the witness of the Old Testament prophesies and the witness of John the Baptist, and when Jesus was formally presented as Messiah by John and as Jesus presented his message and works during his earthly ministry, Jewish believers accepted the additional revelation that Jesus is the Christ. Obviously, there were unsaved Jews who also accepted Jesus during his earthly ministry. What is helpful as we look at a passage like John 10 is distinguishing the two. Let's begin with John 10:1-5:

> John 10:1 Verily, verily, I say unto you, He that entereth not by the door into the sheepfold, but climbeth up some other way, the same is a thief and a robber. 2 But he that entereth in by the door is the shepherd of the sheep. 3 To him the porter openeth; and the sheep hear his voice: and he calleth his own sheep by name, and leadeth them out. 4 And when he putteth forth his own sheep, he goeth before them, and the sheep follow him: for they know his voice. 5 And a stranger will they not follow, but will flee from him: for they know not the voice of strangers.

John 10 is a continuation of John 9 as Jesus continues addressing the Pharisees he was speaking to in John 9:40-41. It is not surprising then that Jesus addresses false shepherds, which no doubt applied to the Pharisees in Jesus' audience. The true shepherd is known because he enters at the door, that is, after being identified by the porter as the true shepherd. The porter is John the Baptist who prepared a way for the Lord and identified Him as the Messiah in the first chapter of John's Gospel. The Jewish believers immediately accepted John's identification of Jesus as the Christ, and these are the sheep in verse 3 that "hear his voice: and he calleth his own sheep by name, and leadeth them out." These Jewish believers accepted the new revelation concerning Jesus of Nazareth and they followed him and will follow no other. We specifically see how that occurred with some of John the Baptist's disciples: "And the two disciples heard him speak, and they followed Jesus." (John 1:37)

When there is confusion about his parable, Jesus builds on the same sheep and shepherd imagery, but makes a different point. Jesus claims to be the door by which people can enter and become sheep (believers): "I am the door: by me if any man enter in, he shall be saved, and shall go in and out, and find pasture." (John 10:10) This verse is critical because it tells us that the flock is not static. The flock grows as people enter by the door (Jesus). Since the flock grows, the flock cannot possibly represent a fixed group of elect persons that God selected to save before the foundation of the world.

Moreover, Jesus speaks in this passage of other sheep that "are not of this fold: them also I must bring, and they shall hear my voice; and there shall be one fold, *and* one shepherd." (John 10:16) The imagery of the original fold is that the sheep are in a cave or stable with Jesus as the door and John as the porter. In contrast, the other sheep Jesus will bring as they hear his voice, and they will join the fold following one shepherd. The other sheep, of course, represent the Gentiles who would come to Jesus on the other side of the cross. Most importantly for the issue of limited atonement, since the flock will continue to grow even after the cross as sheep enter through the door (Jesus), we know that when Jesus says he lays down his life for the sheep he is not teaching limited atonement because he is not talking about dying for a static group of people.

With this in mind, consider John 10:25-27, which Calvinists often cite in support of total depravity and unconditional election: "Jesus answered them, I told you, and ye believed not: the works that I do in my Father's name, they bear witness of me. But ye believe not, because ye are not of my sheep, as I said unto you. My sheep hear my voice, and I know them, and they follow me." This passage hearkens back to the original flock in the first five verses of the chapter that accepted the testimony of the porter, John the Baptist. (see also John 1:29) We must remember that the unbelieving Jewish people Jesus is addressing in verses 25 through 27 are the same he addressed in the first five verses of the chapter, which itself is a continuation of the episode in chapter 9 with the healing of the blind man and his cross-examination before the Jewish leadership. Unlike the Jewish believers that readily accepted the additional revelation of John the Baptist and later of the Son, these non-regenerate people had not responded to John the Baptist's ministry and were not waiting for Messiah Jesus to arrive on the scene and be identified by the forerunner. They were not within the sheep of the first five verses and when Jesus came identifying himself by words and deeds (e.g., healing the blind man in John 9) as the true shepherd that the porter had announced, these Jews rejected Jesus' testimony. They rejected the message of the porter and they rejected the door, and therewith, membership in the fold.

There is no basis here for the Calvinists to try to squeeze in part of the TULIP. If Jesus wanted to say they did not believe because they were not in "the elect," he would not have wasted time speaking of their rejection of his words and works as he does here and over and again in the Gospel of John. Rather than supporting limited atonement, John 10 explicitly rejects it because Jesus teaches that his fold grows, which means that it is not a static group of elect people predetermined in eternity past.

An Alternative View

We have seen that the Bible teaches emphatically that Jesus died for the sins of every person without exception. Like the other TULIP petals, limited atonement has significant practical implications. The integrity of what we say to lost people is called into question by TULIP. How can I preach the gospel to someone? Maybe they are elect and maybe not. Maybe Jesus died for them and maybe not. The word "gospel" means good news, but if TULIP is true then the gospel is only contingent good news. Most people in the world are not Christians, which apparently means the percentage of people God decreed to save before the foundation of the world was far less than 50%. For the majority of the world, then, there is no good news, and there never will be.

In John 3, Jesus used the Old Testament episode of the raising of the brass serpent by Moses to heal the snake bites as a picture of salvation. All the people in Moses' day had to do to be delivered from the bites was look up at the serpent. What should Moses have told the people? All you have to do is look up at the brass serpent. Some of you are incapable of doing so, indeed you do not even understand my instructions to you, and the serpent will not work for you anyway. The rest of you will look up because you have no choice. God decreed your sin, your judgment and your deliverance!

The fact is that we need not complicate our gospel in order to maintain our integrity in presenting the message. As I touched on in the third chapter, one of the interesting things we read about in the gospels is the healings Jesus did. These healings validated Jesus as Messiah as well as providing a physical object lesson that this Jesus, who could heal any sickness, cast out evil spirits, and even raise the dead, could also heal our sin problem. (1 Peter 2:24) Notably, Jesus healed everyone that came to him. (e.g., Matthew 8:16, 12:15; Luke 6:19) Contrary to the self-proclaimed healers for hire on television, Jesus healed them all. What a wonderful picture we have that Jesus is willing to heal anyone spiritually as well. We really can say "whosoever" because Jesus died for all and all can believe. Just as the serpent was lifted up before the entire nation of Israel so that all had the opportunity to look up at it for deliverance, so also Jesus was lifted up before the world to "draw all men" so that all would have the opportunity to believe. This is *limitless atonement*, the "L" in NULIF. I would also point out that if Jesus died for the sins of the whole world, then what possible reason would God have for predetermining a subset of humanity for salvation and passing over the others? Why not give people free will? To the former question the Calvinists can only say that it was God's good pleasure to do so, and to the latter they say that God is incapable of creating people with an undecreed free will. But what is God's testimony in the matter? "The Lord is not slack concerning his promise, as some men count slackness; but is longsuffering to us-ward, not willing that any should perish, but that all should come to repentance." (2 Peter 3:9)

The Calvinists interpret this verse to mean that God is not willing that any of the elect should perish. They take "willing" to mean decreed, i.e., God has not decreed that any of the elect should perish. But "willing" here is the Greek *bulomai* that does not speak of a decree but of a desire or wish. (see, e.g., Matthew 1:19, Acts 12:4, Acts 27:43) God does not desire that any people perish. This is consistent with the verse that follows and is a contrast verse: "But the day of the Lord will come as a thief in the night; in the which the heavens shall pass away with a great noise, and the elements shall melt with fervent heat, the earth also and the works that are therein shall be burned up." (2 Peter 3:10) In other words, Peter reminds his readers that God is not slack regarding Jesus' return, but because his return involves worldwide judgment on sinners, God is longsuffering. Thus we have God's own testimony that He is longsuffering toward this world so that people will come to the Saviour, which would make no sense if not all people were capable of doing so or if their ransom had not been paid in full at the cross.

Concluding Thoughts on Limited Atonement

I have tried to demonstrate that unlike total depravity and unconditional election, the "T" and "U" in TULIP for which the Calvinists boast much scriptural support, when it comes to limited atonement the Calvinists offer little independent scriptural analysis but instead rely on total depravity and unconditional election as premises upon which to infer limited atonement. On that point, a couple of comments are in order. First, because the evidence for limited atonement is so weak, even many Calvinists reject it. This group is often referred to as "four point Calvinists." Second, Calvinists that hold to limited atonement typically argue that since God selected before creation those He would save, it only makes sense that the Son would die only for those selected, for otherwise His death would in part be for persons God knew would spend eternity in the lake of fire. In other words, the L necessarily follows from the TU. They rarely try to establish it as a stand-alone doctrine because, as we saw, too many verses expressly speak to salvation being made available to the "world," to "all" men, or to "whosoever" believes. But if the L necessarily follows from T and U as they argue, then as a matter of logic, disproving L from the Scriptures as we have done in this chapter conclusively disproves T and U. And without T, U, and L, the rest of TULIP is unnecessary.

Since the Bible explicitly teaches that Jesus died for all. Each person is provided with a choice—a real choice, not a predetermined one. And this means that when we evangelize, we can truly say to our audience that Jesus died for their sins and they will be reconciled to God if they will only appropriate it by faith. Not one person can ever say they were excluded from salvation because God did not make a way for them. As the old hymn goes, Jesus paid it all, and all to Him we owe. Sin had left a crimson stain, but Jesus washed it white as snow.

Chapter 7

Irresistible Grace

For some supposedly Biblical doctrines, there are obvious places in the Bible where they should be explicitly taught if, indeed, they are Biblical. Irresistible grace is one such doctrine. Recall from chapter 2 that irresistible grace is the concept that God regenerates the elect so that when they hear the gospel they can understand it and will certainly believe. Like limited atonement, Calvinists offer almost no direct (alleged) scriptural support for irresistible grace, but rather they argue that it necessarily follows from total depravity and unconditional election and need not have any independent and explicit scriptural support. Since man is totally depraved, they reason, he can do nothing good and pleasing to God, and in fact, he cannot even comprehend the gospel message, much less believe it. Since God is going to save all of the unconditionally elect, God has to address their total depravity at a point in time or else they would never be saved.

Irresistible grace is the doctrine that explains how God overcomes the elect person's depravity by regenerating them and giving them faith so that they will necessarily find the gospel compelling.

But what of those obvious places in the Bible where this doctrine ought to at least be hinted at but the text is silent? Consider, for example, the many places in the Gospel of John where people respond to Jesus' message or miracles and believe without any indication in the text of prior irresistible grace or an "effectual calling" that rendered them spiritually alive so that they would certainly believe:

> John 2:11 This beginning of miracles did Jesus in Cana of Galilee, and manifested forth his glory; and his disciples believed on him.

> John 2:22 When therefore he was risen from the dead, his disciples remembered that he had said this unto them; and they believed the scripture, and the word which Jesus had said.

> John 2:23 Now when he was in Jerusalem at the passover, in the feast *day*, many believed in his name, when they saw the miracles which he did.

> John 4:39 And many of the Samaritans of that city believed on him for the saying of the woman, which testified, He told me all that ever I did.

> John 4:41 And many more believed because of his own word;

> John 4:53 So the father knew that *it was* at the same hour, in the which Jesus said unto him, Thy son liveth: and himself believed, and his whole house.

> John 8:30 As he spake these words, many believed on him.

John 10:42 And many believed on him there.

John 11:45 Then many of the Jews which came to Mary, and had seen the things which Jesus did, believed on him.

John 12:11 Because that by reason of him many of the Jews went away, and believed on Jesus.

John 12:42 Nevertheless among the chief rulers also many believed on him; but because of the Pharisees they did not confess *him*, lest they should be put out of the synagogue:

John 20:8 Then went in also that other disciple, which came first to the sepulchre, and he saw, and believed.

John 20:29 Jesus saith unto him, Thomas, because thou hast seen me, thou hast believed: blessed *are* they that have not seen, and *yet* have believed.

Over and again, people believe in Jesus in response to the word or his miracles, and there is not one instance in John's Gospel where there is any suggestion that they were made to believe or given their faith. Indeed, the consistent picture in the New Testament is a universal invitation. Some people believe and some do not, but the Bible never says that those who reject the gospel could only reject it, nor that those who do believe could not reject it. Indeed, the Bible says God desires the salvation of all people. (e.g., 1 Timothy 2:4)

How do the Calvinists deal with this apparent scriptural obstacle? They must balance these passages with their view that God cannot desire something without it happening, and in particular, God cannot desire the salvation of all men, for otherwise all men would be saved. To deal with this problem, they teach that there are two "calls" in the Bible. There is the external call that occurs when the gospel is preached and there is the internal call that makes the elect respond with the faith God gave them. The external call is made to everyone, but for the non-elect it's like asking a turtle to run a fast hundred-yard dash. In a theoretical sense the call is genuine, but not in a real sense because of the turtle's incapacity to comply. The internal call is made only to the elect (the only ones God wills to be saved), and it's like asking the fish to come to the boat as you reel him in by a hook in its mouth. In a theoretical sense the call is genuine, but not in a real sense because of the fish's incapacity to refuse compliance.

This two-call system deals at the same time with the universal invitations in the New Testament and the seeming contradiction between those universal invitations and the Calvinistic view of the will of God. In their view, God only desires to save the elect, and He saves all of them and no one else. But does this patch one leak and create another? By providing an answer to why the Bible contains general invitations, Calvinists make the gospel of none effect because in the TULIP framework, it is not the gospel that ultimately saves, but the inward or efficacious call. Apart from the inward call, none would be saved no matter what. Yet, Paul writes: "For I am not ashamed of the gospel of Christ: for it is the power of God unto salvation to every one that believeth." (Romans 1:16) Paul says "the gospel...is the power of God unto salvation." TULIP says the inward call is the power of God unto salvation. And again Paul says: "For the **preaching of the cross** is to them that perish foolishness; but unto us which are saved it **is the power of God**." (1 Corinthians 1:18) This is not to take away from the role of the Holy Spirit in convicting a lost person about Jesus, but we need no internal efficacious call to explain away universal invitations when God says there is power in the preaching of the cross. All Christians are a testimony to that power.

How the Calvinists Define Irresistible Grace

Before looking at whether any of this is actually in the Bible, let's look at irresistible grace in the words of Calvinist writers. Steele, Thomas and Quinn explain the difference between the two calls. Of the outward or general call that is made to anyone, they write:

> The *gospel invitation extends a call* to salvation to every one who hears its message. It invites all men without distinction to drink freely of the water of life and live. It promises salvation to all who repent and believe. But this outward general call, extended to the elect and nonelect alike, will not bring sinners to Christ. Why? Because men are by nature dead in sin and under its power. They are of themselves unable and unwilling to forsake their evil ways and to turn to Christ for mercy.[123]

The Calvinists' view of depravity combined with the obvious fact that the gospel is offered universally in the New Testament creates a problem for them. If people could be saved by simply accepting the general call, then the universal call of the gospel could save anyone, even the non-elect. Thus, they conclude that instead people are saved by an inner or efficacious or effective call:

> Although the general outward call of the gospel can be, and often is, rejected, the special inward call of the Spirit never fails to result in the conversion of those to whom it is made. This special call is not made to all sinners, but is issued to the elect only. The Spirit is in no way dependent upon their help or cooperation for success in His work of bringing them to Christ.

---

[123] *Supra* note 3, pp. 52-53.

> It is for this reason that Calvinists speak of the Spirit's call and of God's grace in saving sinners as being "efficacious," "invincible," or "irresistible." The grace which the Holy Spirit extends to the elect cannot be thwarted or refused; it never fails to bring them to true faith in Christ.[124]

Along the same lines, Berkhof distinguishes the Calvinist view of the "internal" versus the "external" call:

> When we speak of calling in general, we have reference to *that gracious act of God whereby He invites sinners to accept the salvation that is offered in Christ Jesus.* It is a work of the triune God... This calling may be either external or internal. God is the author of both; the Holy Spirit operates in both; and in both the Word of God is employed as an instrument. Yet there are important differences: the external calling comes to all those who hear the Word, while the internal calling comes only to the elect; the external calling as such, that is, without the special operation of the Holy Spirit, affects only the natural life, while the internal calling affects the internal or spiritual life. It is the external calling made effective unto salvation.[125]

Similarly, Grudem succinctly defines the effective call as that which saves sinners: "Effective calling is an act of God the Father, speaking through the human proclamation of the gospel, in which he summons people to himself in such a way that they respond in saving faith."[126] The effective call that is accomplished by the Holy Spirit is what the Calvinists term

---

[124] *Supra* note 3, p. 53-54.
[125] *Supra* note 34, p. 231.
[126] *Supra* note 14, p. 693.

regeneration: "Regeneration is a secret act of God in which he imparts new spiritual life to us."[127] "In this sense of the word regeneration may be defined as *that act of God by which the principle of the new life is implanted in man, and the governing disposition of the soul is made holy.*"[128] In other words, God regenerates a person so that they will believe, and this is the effective call made only to the elect. From this brief summary, we can see an immediate issue of concern in the timing of the two calls. It seems that a person is regenerated prior to exercising faith, indeed prior to hearing the gospel at all. Grudem states, "On this definition [of regeneration], it is natural to understand that regeneration comes before saving faith."[129] Indeed, most Calvinists would say that regeneration precedes faith (the effective call precedes the general call) or occurs at the same time. Berkhof explains:

> The order in which calling and regeneration stand to each other may best be indicated as follows: The external call in the preaching of the Word, except in the case of children, precedes or coincides with the operation of the Holy Spirit in the production of the new life. Then by a creative act God generates the new life, changing the inner disposition of the soul. This is regeneration in the restricted sense of the word. In it the spiritual ear is implanted which enables man to hear the call of God to the salvation of his soul. Having received the spiritual ear, the call of God is now brought home effectively to the heart, so that man hears and obeys. This effectual calling, finally, secures the first holy exercises of the new disposition that is born in the soul. The new life begins to manifest itself and issues in the

---

[127] *Supra* note 14, p. 699.
[128] *Supra* note 34, p. 236.
[129] *Supra* note 14, p. 702.

> new birth. This is regeneration in the broader sense and marks the point at which regeneration passes into conversion. [130]

You might be wondering whether they are saying that a person is saved prior to hearing the gospel. Calvinists readily agree that being regenerated is being "born again,"[131] but generally refrain from saying the person is "saved" before hearing the gospel.

In view of the foregoing explanation of irresistible grace, one last consideration is why the doctrine is termed irresistible grace. The Calvinists generally do not favor the term because, in their mind, it suggests that God is forcing salvation on the elect. That, of course, is exactly what they teach, but they attempt to soften the blow. Hodge states, "It is to be lamented that the term irresistible grace has ever been used, since it suggests the idea of a mechanical and coercive influence upon an unwilling subject, while, in truth, it is the transcendent act of the infinite Creator, making the creature spontaneously willing."[132] Sproul explains:

> Irresistible grace is not irresistible in the sense that sinners are incapable of resisting it. Though the sinner is spiritually dead, he remains biologically alive and kicking. As Scripture suggests, the sinner always resists the Holy Spirit. We are so opposed to the grace of God that we do everything in our power to resist it. *Irresistible grace* means that the sinner's resistance to the grace of regeneration cannot thwart the Spirit's purpose. The grace of regeneration is irresistible in the sense that it is invincible.[133]

---

[130] *Supra* note 34, p. 237.
[131] *Supra* note 14, p. 699.
[132] *Supra* note 39, p. 452.
[133] *Supra* note 17, p. 189.

Spencer similarly elaborates on the use of the term irresistible:

> What is meant when the Calvinist speaks of irresistible grace? We answer first in the negative. It does *not* mean that God does violence to man's spirit by forcing him to do something he does not want to do... Judas, without coercion, fulfilled the will of God (cf. Acts 2:22-23). *Irresistible*, when used of the grace of God toward His elect, means that God, of his own free will, gives life to whom He chooses. Since the *living* human spirit, which is "born of God," finds the living God wholly *irresistible*, just as the *dead* human spirit finds the gods of the dead (Satan) wholly irresistible, the Lord "quickens" ("makes alive") all whom He chose in Christ Jesus before the foundation of the world. It is the gift of the new nature that makes us find Jesus Christ absolutely irresistible. The new nature, which is a living human spirit, a new creation in Christ, finds God as irresistible as his formerly "dead" human spirit once found the devil irresistible.[134]

In summary, the Calvinists' doctrine of irresistible grace is that the Bible teaches two types of calls, the outward universal invitation of the gospel to the elect and non-elect, and the inward or effective call to the elect only. This latter call results in the regeneration of the elect person so that when they hear the gospel they find it irresistible and they accept it on the spot. Prior to hearing the gospel, the regenerated elect person is spiritually alive, born again, in union with Christ, and able to understand and respond favorably to God, but not yet saved. With this background information, we can examine whether or not any of this is actually in the Bible.

---

[134] *Supra* note 13, pp. 56-57.

Pillar Proof Text: John 6

A pillar proof text for irresistible grace is John 6:44 and 65. As I have commented before, the entire weight of the TULIP rests on about five or six pillar proof texts. Once these load-bearing members are removed from the Calvinists' arsenal, there is really nothing left to prop it up. Although Calvinists cite dozens of verses and find the TULIP all over the Bible, all the weight is really on these load-bearing verses, for these are the ones actually relied upon to convince people of the TULIP. But when they are removed from the picture, the other verses do not even come close to carrying the load. For this reason, I will begin by addressing these verses in detail.

> John 6:44 No man can come to me, except the Father which hath sent me draw him: and I will raise him up at the last day... 65 And he said, Therefore said I unto you, that no man can come unto me, except it were given unto him of my Father.

Calvinists interpret these verses to say that no one can come to Jesus in faith unless they are part of the elect and first regenerated and irresistibly drawn by the Father at a point in time. To get to a proper understanding of these passages, we need to take a careful look at the overall context of John 6. We also need to carefully consider the meaning of the key term "draw" used in 6:44 and the concept in John's Gospel of those given by the Father to His Son Jesus. The context shows that Jesus is unquestionably dealing with a mixed crowd of Jewish believers and Jewish non-believers. Jesus' teaching is designed to meet the needs of both groups.

In the early part of chapter 6, Jesus feeds the 5,000 by the Sea of Galilee. The crowd would take him by force to make him king, which is not in accord with the Father's will, so Jesus departs. He sends his disciples by boat to Capernaum and walks on the water to join them later. The following day, some of the people that witnessed the feeding of the 5,000 realized

Jesus left (although not by boat) and they pursue by boat, heading toward Capernaum. When these people catch up with Jesus in Capernaum, they ask the question, "Rabbi, when camest thou hither?" (John 6:25) It becomes apparent that their question is more than curiosity. They witnessed a great miracle in the feeding of the 5,000 and they want more. They may even suspect that Jesus' arrival in Capernaum involved some miracle. This is confirmed by Jesus' response to them: "Ye seek me, not because ye saw the miracles, but because ye did eat of the loaves, and were filled." (John 6:26) Remember, Jesus' signs validate his message. Jesus' point here is that they do not seek him because they accepted that the feeding of the 5,000 validated that he is the Christ, but because they filled their bellies and now they want more.

Accordingly, these men are following Jesus as if they were disciples but they really are not. As throughout John's Gospel, there is a contrast between people focusing on purely physical matters and Jesus telling them of spiritual matters. (e.g., physical versus spiritual birth in John 3; physical versus spiritual water in John 4) Here, there is physical meat, which is the extent of their interest in Jesus, and spiritual meat, which is representative of the work of real disciple. (John 6:27) Upon hearing this, this group asks Jesus, "What shall we do, that we might work the works of God?" (John 6:28) Jesus' response: "This is the work of God, that ye believe on him whom he hath sent." (John 6:29) Jesus does not mean that believing is a work. They asked him how to do the "works of God," and because Jesus knew they were not believers, he focuses them on what should be their first priority, namely believing on him. This interaction is key to the rest of the dialogue and Jesus will keep pointing these "would be" disciples to their central need, just as he did in John 4 with the woman at the well and John 3 with Nicodemus.

Rather than responding in belief, they demand a sign from Jesus. (John 6:30) While one might think demanding a sign is a legitimate request for validation of Jesus' claims, the demand of signs reflects non-belief because they already witnessed the feeding of the 5,000. (e.g., John 2:18-19) They even try to manipulate Jesus by referring to God's provision of manna in the wilderness, quoting from Psalm 78:24. (John 6:31) It is ironic they would demand a work from Jesus and then try to support their demand from Psalm 78, which recalls the Jews' complaining and lack of faith when they demanded works from God in the wilderness. But once again, their focus is physical and Jesus wants to convey spiritual realities to them. Thus, Jesus' response is that Moses provided only physical bread, but Jesus is the "true bread from heaven" that "giveth life to the world." (John 6:32-33) Yet again there is disbelief. As the woman at the well misunderstood and asked Jesus to "give me this water, that I thirst not, neither come hither to draw" (John 4:15), this group asks for "this bread." (John 6:34)

In response, Jesus builds on their reference to the manna and explains how he is the true bread that gives life: "I am the bread of life: he that cometh to me shall never hunger; and he that believeth on me shall never thirst." (John 6:35) This is yet another call to these non-believers to believe on him. And then Jesus makes a very strong statement to the crowd demanding a sign about their lost condition: "But I said unto you, That ye also have seen me, and believe not." (John 6:36)

The group Jesus is speaking to are curious (curious enough to follow Jesus to Capernaum), but not convinced. They are certainly not committed, and at the end of the day, John 6 is largely about Jesus separating from his legitimate disciples those that are merely curious and looking for signs and filled bellies and sending them on their way. While Jesus openly shares with them that they must believe in him for eternal life, Jesus is not interested in having a non-regenerate entourage following him around in his ministry as if they were disciples when their only interest is the next meal or miracle. And what unfolds at this point in the dialogue goes to the issue of who Jesus' real disciples are in his earthly ministry.

Jesus states: "All that the Father giveth me shall come to me; and him that cometh to me I will in no wise cast out." (John 6:37) We first need to determine who it is that the Father gave to Jesus to aid our understanding of the overall passage. Calvinists need those that the Father gave Jesus to refer to the "elect," but that is not the case. This phraseology is repeated several times in John 17, all part of Jesus' high priestly prayer, where the context reveals that Jesus has his disciples during his earthly ministry in mind.

> <u>John 17:1</u> These words spake Jesus, and lifted up his eyes to heaven, and said, Father, the hour is come; glorify thy Son, that thy Son also may glorify thee: <u>2</u> As thou hast given him power over all flesh, that he should give eternal life to as many as thou hast given him... <u>6</u> I have manifested thy name unto the men which thou gavest me out of the world: thine they were, and thou gavest them me; and they have kept thy word... <u>9</u> I pray for them: I pray not for the world, but for them which thou hast given me; for they are thine... <u>20</u> Neither pray I for these alone, but for them also which shall believe on me through their word.

In saying the Father gave these people to Jesus, the text is not speaking of salvation. For the text plainly says in 17:6 that these were regenerate people ("thine they were, and thou gavest them me") before they were given to Jesus. Moreover, the group of people given to Jesus is necessarily limited to people alive during his earthly ministry who interacted with Jesus ("I have manifested thy name [to them]"). Of course, by use of "thy name" Jesus is saying he manifested the Father to those regenerate people the Father gave him, just as he said to Philip: "Have I been so long time with you, and yet hast thou not known me, Philip? he that hath seen me hath seen the Father; and how sayest thou then, Shew us the Father?" The group also cannot include future saints since it says, "they have kept thy word." And in John 17:20, Jesus says: "Neither pray I for these alone, but for them also which shall believe on me through their word." Jesus distinguishes in his prayer between those given to him by the Father and those who would believe in the future "through their word." Accordingly, those given to Jesus cannot possibly be the "elect" as Calvinists employ that term.

We have to keep in mind that there were many Jewish believers in Israel prior to the formal beginning of Jesus' earthly ministry. We may think of them as Old Testament believers, looking forward to Messiah, much as we would think of Abraham, Moses, or even John the Baptist. We should also recall that the ministry of John the Baptist was not done in a corner. This was a time of great Messianic expectation and, after John the Baptist formally announced Jesus as "the Lamb of God, which taketh away the sin of the world" and as Jesus traveled about doing signs and miracles, many Jewish believers came to accept the additional revelation that Jesus of Nazareth was the Messiah they had been looking forward to. We see this early in John's Gospel with Philip, Nathanael, Andrew, Peter, and likely the apostle John as well. Many of these believers spent significant time with Jesus, and some even followed him from place to place for a time, and some Jesus picked as apostles. These regenerate Jews were the Father's, but when Jesus began his earthly ministry, the Father gave them to him. (John 10:1-5) There is not one example of a Jewish believer rejecting the revelation of John the Baptist or of Jesus.

Returning to verse 37, the point Jesus is making is that the regenerate Jews that the Father gives him will come to him and he will not cast them out. We sometimes speak of "coming to Jesus" in a figurative/spiritual sense and might also assume that being cast out is also a spiritual reference. But Jesus is speaking to a group of disciple "wannabe's" about literally coming to him and whether they will be sent away, which is exactly what he does as the chapter unfolds. The next

242

three verses further confirm that Jesus has his earthly ministry in focus in this passage:

> John 6:38 For I came down from heaven, not to do mine own will, but the will of him that sent me. 39 And this is the Father's will which hath sent me, that of all which he hath given me I should lose nothing, but should raise it up again at the last day. 40 And this is the will of him that sent me, that every one which seeth the Son, and believeth on him, may have everlasting life: and I will raise him up at the last day.

Jesus is plainly dealing with two groups of people, genuine disciples and the wannabe disciples looking for another meal or sign. Jesus will not lose any of the disciples given to him by the Father, and he will resurrect them at the last day. But what about the lost people in the crowd? They also can be a part of the resurrection, for Jesus will give everlasting life to everyone that "believeth on him."

At this point, there is confusion in his audience and some are murmuring about his earlier statement that he is "the bread which came down from heaven." (John 6:41) In response to this murmuring, Jesus makes the statement that Calvinists use to support total depravity and irresistible grace: "No man can come to me, except the Father which hath sent me draw him: and I will raise him up at the last day." (John 6:44) Calvinists understand the drawing to mean that all people drawn by God get saved. For this reason, they understand the passage to speak of the "elect" even though that term is not used. To get to the proper meaning of the text, we need first to consider the meaning of the word "draw."

As with other key terms, Calvinists front load their doctrine into the word "draw" (Greek *helkuō*) by saying it means to drag, so the picture is of God spiritually dragging the lost person to Jesus by an efficacious or irresistible call. While the term can have the meaning "to drag" when the context shows it is physical exertion or compulsion at issue, the lexicon BDAG says it can also mean "to draw a person in the direction of values for inner life." Liddell and Scott include the definition, "draw to oneself, attract." The sense of the word is to attract or woo someone to oneself. The term is used exactly that way in the Septuagint, the Greek translation of the Old Testament, and other Greek literature. For instance, in Jeremiah 31:3, we read: "The LORD hath appeared of old unto me, saying, Yea, I have loved thee with an everlasting love: therefore with lovingkindness have I drawn thee." This is being drawn by God's love (Hebrew *chesed*), not dragged. Likewise, in Song of Solomon 1:4, we read: "Draw me, we will run after thee: the king hath brought me into his chambers: we will be glad and rejoice in thee, we will remember thy love more than wine: the upright love thee." This is Solomon drawing his wife, obviously not dragging her. Moreover, in John 12:32, we read that Jesus "will draw all men unto me" and we know that not all men are dragged to salvation because that would be universalism. The picture in John 12:32 is that the cross will draw all men to Christ, but that does not guarantee their salvation. When used of physical objects, "draw" means drag, but when where no physical exertion or coercion is involved, that meaning does not work.[135]

Returning to v. 44 then: "No man can come to me, except the Father which hath sent me draw him: and I will raise him up at the last day." The phrase "come to me" mirrors verse 37, where Jesus spoke of the regenerate Jews that the Father gave to him to be true disciples during his earthly ministry. To the wannabe disciples in the crowd, looking for the next meal or miracle, Jesus makes an implicit contrast between being attracted to him based on physical versus spiritual matters. Thus, Jesus says that disciples are drawn by the Father, and not by the fleshly

---

[135] C. Gordon Olson, *Getting the Gospel Right* (Cedar Knolls: Global Gospel Publishers, 2005), p. 311.

desire to see another sign or get another meal. So the question becomes, how does the Father draw people to Jesus? What is obvious is that physical compulsion is not in view, so the notion of anyone being dragged does not fit here. At this point, many Calvinists try to conflate the different definitions of *helkuō* and argue for a spiritual dragging, but that is foreign to the context here as well as the lexical meaning of the word. As already addressed, the term *helkuō* in the context where physical compulsion or coercion is not at issue has the sense of attracting or wooing people. And it should not surprise us that the Father attracts or woos people by His word.

To the would be disciples who just quoted from Psalm 78 to demand another sign, Jesus quotes from the Old Testament to support his statement that those who would come to him as true disciples must be drawn by the word of God: "It is written in the prophets, And they shall be all taught of God. Every man therefore that hath heard, and hath learned of the Father, cometh unto me. Not that any man hath seen the Father, save he which is of God, he hath seen the Father. Verily, verily, I say unto you, He that believeth on me hath everlasting life." (John 6:45-47) Jesus is quoting from Isaiah 54:13: "And all thy children *shall be* taught of the LORD; and great *shall be* the peace of thy children." This passage from Isaiah speaks of the redeemed Jewish people in the Millennium who are attracted or drawn to Messiah as the Lord teaches them. So also in Jesus' earthly ministry, Jesus' true disciples had accepted the Old Testament teaching concerning Messiah and responded to Jesus when he presented himself as Messiah. But making application to the non-regenerate wannabe disciples in the crowd, Jesus said, "every man therefore that hath heard, and hath learned of the Father, cometh unto me."

This raises the question, how is it that one may hear and learn from the Father? This relates John 6 back to John 5 where Jesus addressed exactly that issue, arguing that there are various witnesses that he is the Christ: (1) John the Baptist (5:32-35); (2) "the works which the Father hath given me to finish...bear witness of me, that the Father hath sent me" (John 5:36); (3) the Father (5:37); and (4) the Scriptures (John 5:38-40, 46-47). Note Jesus' comment to that audience that "ye have not his word abiding in you: for whom he hath sent, him ye believe not." (John 5:38) In other words, if they had believed God's word, they would have also believed Jesus. He tells them, "Search the scriptures...they are they which testify of me... For had ye believed Moses, ye would have believed me: for he wrote of me. But if ye believe not his writings, how shall ye believe my words?" (John 5:39, 46-47)

Bringing this back to John 6:44, then, what we have is that people have been drawn to Jesus as Messiah through the testimony of the Old Testament, the word of God, and in Jesus' day by the last Old Testament prophet, John the Baptist, just as we see in John 1. But if the wannabe disciples reject the Father's teaching, then they are not welcome as disciples and will be cast out. Thus, Jesus returns to the issue of his being the true bread from heaven. By today's standards, this is not a seeker friendly sermon. Jesus preaches the "hard saying" that to have eternal life, a person must eat his flesh and drink his blood, figurative language for believing. Although he makes clear that he is speaking figuratively (John 6:63), the result of his teaching is that many of his followers murmur against him (John 6:61) and many abandon him (John 6:66). Jesus returns in John 6:64-65 to the point he made in John 6:44, directing his words to the pretenders: "But there are some of you that believe not. For Jesus knew from the beginning who they were that believed not, and who should betray him. And he said, Therefore said I unto you, that no man can come unto me, except it were given unto him of my Father." Incredibly, there were people that had been with Jesus for a long time and sat under his teaching that acted the part of disciples and yet had not believed. They arguably had more revelation than any people in any other time, yet rejected it. Because of their rejection, they are not given the privilege of being Jesus' disciples and they are sent away (or cast out).

For various reasons, many people would flock to Jesus during his earthly ministry, especially the curious who came for utilitarian reasons (e.g., after all, Jesus could feed 5,000 from 5 barley loaves and 2 small fishes). They would even try to take him by force to make him king. This was contrary to God's will and these were not true disciples seeking Jesus as the spiritual bread. Jesus was not interested in being followed by an entourage of unregenerate people. What we have seen unfold in John 6 is a dividing out of the followers that are no more than the curious or hungry. Of real disciples, Jesus says they must be drawn by the Father through the Old Testament testimony regarding Messiah, and that he will not send them away, and will raise them at the last day.

Although the Father only drew some people to Jesus to be disciples during his earthly ministry, Jesus explains that when it comes to salvation, he personally draws all men to himself by the cross: "And I, if I be lifted up from the earth, will draw all men unto me." (John 12:32) This passage, like John 6:44, obviously does not involve physical compulsion, and so the meaning of attract or woo is what is intended by "draw" and is why the KJV says "draw" and not "drag." Moreover, although Jesus does not reference here the ministry of the Holy Spirit, his words later in the Gospel indicate that the Holy Spirit is involved in convicting people: "Nevertheless I tell you the truth; It is expedient for you that I go away: for if I go not away, the Comforter will not come unto you; but if I depart, I will send him unto you. And when he is come, he will reprove the world of sin, and of righteousness, and of judgment: Of sin, because they believe not on me; Of righteousness, because I go to my Father, and ye see me no more; Of judgment, because the prince of this world is judged." (John 16:7-11) Accordingly, no one will ever be dispatched to the lake of fire simply because the Father chose not to draw him. The Son now draws all men by the cross, and the issue is whether or not they will believe on him.

Pillar Proof Text: Acts 16:14

When pressed for a single verse that explicitly states that God enabled a lost person to believe the gospel, Calvinists offer Acts 16:14. As the argument goes, Lydia was effectually called so that she could respond in faith to the gospel Paul presented to her.

> Acts 16:14 And a certain woman named Lydia, a seller of purple, of the city of Thyatira, which worshipped God, heard *us*: whose heart the Lord opened, that she attended unto the things which were spoken of Paul.

There are two critical issues to address in order to properly exegete the verse. First, we cannot assume from the bare description of Lydia as one who "worshipped God" that she is lost. If anything, that description suggests the opposite. And second, we cannot assume that God opened Lydia's heart so she could get saved.

Turning to the first issue, there is insufficient basis in the inspired Text for assuming that Lydia was lost. That she "worshipped God" indicates she is a Gentile proselyte, and indeed, she was gathered with other women at the river to pray to God. (Acts 16:13) Luke uses the Greek term *sebomai* ("worshipped") elsewhere in the Acts to describe Gentiles as God-fearing. In particular, Luke uses the term to refer to "religious" proselytes in Acts 13:43, "devout" Greeks in Acts 17:4, "devout" persons in Acts 17:17, and of an apparent Gentile believer named Justus in Acts 18:7 that "worshipped" God. As I pointed out in the exegesis of John 6 and 10, there were many believers that we would think of as Old Testament believers who, upon hearing Jesus, immediately accepted the additional revelation that he was the Messiah, who had died and rose again. And certainly after the cross, as the gospel was carried beyond Judah by Paul and others, the message was not only carried to the lost but to God-fearing Jews and Gentiles that had not yet heard the additional revelation of God that Jesus was the Christ.

As to the second issue, note that the verse does not say that Lydia was saved after listening to Paul, nor does it tell us what Paul's message was. Consistent with his preaching elsewhere in Acts, Paul presumably brought Lydia the message that the Messiah had already come, that he was Jesus, and that he died and rose again, but the fact that the Lord "opened" her heart need not be assumed to be an efficacious TULIP calling. As already noted, the evidence more likely indicates that Lydia was already a believer, but we can say more. This concept of God opening hearts to understand is used once elsewhere by Luke in the 24th chapter of his Gospel, as well as the related idea of opening eyes to see. But Calvinists usually ignore Luke 24 in exegeting Acts 16:14 because Luke's usage there of God opening eyes and hearts does not support what they want to say about Lydia.

Luke 24 opens with the empty tomb, followed by the story of the two disciples on the Emmaus Road. They understood that the tomb was empty but had failed to grasp the resurrection and the fulfillment of the Old Testament law and prophets. They meet up with the resurrected Jesus on the Emmaus Road but do not recognize him, and after they explain to Jesus what occurred, he admonishes their lack of understanding: "O fools, and slow of heart to believe all that the prophets have spoken: Ought not Christ to have suffered these things, and to enter into his glory?" (Luke 24:25-26) Jesus then begins with the Torah and explains the Scriptures to them, and in particular, their fulfillment in him: "And beginning at Moses and all the prophets, he expounded unto them in all the scriptures the things concerning himself." (Luke 24:27) Only after the teaching lesson and eating with them Jesus opens their eyes to who he was: "And their eyes were opened, and they knew him; and he vanished out of their sight." (Luke 24:31) Obviously, we are not to understand that the two disciples on the Emmaus

Road were non-believers. They accepted Jesus as the Messiah that would redeem Israel (Luke 24:19-21), but what they had failed to fully comprehend prior to Luke 24 was the additional revelation that Messiah Jesus would die and be resurrected.

After Jesus departed them, the two Emmaus Road disciples joined the eleven apostles and told them about what had happened, and in the midst of that conversation, Jesus appears to all of them. The eleven had also not understood how Jesus' death fit in with what they believed about him, and in the context of this post-resurrection appearance, we read in Luke 24:44-45: "And he said unto them, These are the words which I spake unto you, while I was yet with you, that all things must be fulfilled, which were written in the law of Moses, and in the prophets, and in the psalms, concerning me. Then <u>opened he their understanding, that they might understand the scriptures</u>." The apostles were indisputably genuine believers who eyes were opened to the further revelation of Jesus' resurrection as the fulfillment of the Old Testament law and prophets.

There is no basis in the wording or the context of Acts 16:14 to understand the episode with Lydia differently. All we can take from this verse is that Lydia, who was already a Gentile believer, had her heart affected by the Lord so that she could attend to additional revelation given to her in Paul's teaching in the same way that occurred with disciples on the Emmaus Road and the eleven. The story of Lydia is part of the larger historical record of the establishment of the church at Philippi. She was a Gentile believer who, accepting the additional revelation about Jesus brought to her by Paul, believed that revelation, was baptized, and became a "charter member" of a new church in Philippi. The story about Lydia provides no support whatsoever for irresistible grace.

Proof Texts for Two Calls

As we turn to the remaining Calvinists' proof text for irresistible grace, what we find is that they hang on to almost any verse with the words called or chosen in them. There is nothing particularly extraordinary about these words. The burden for the Calvinists is to show that there are in fact two separate callings in these verses. Calvinists tend to load these terms with special meaning to find support in these verses, but this is inappropriate. The Bible speaks of people being called in many senses. For a few examples, consider that God called Jesus (Matthew 2:15), Simon was called Peter (Matthew 4:21), Paul was called as an apostle (Romans 1:1), believers are called to peace (1 Corinthians 7:15), believers are called to holiness (1 Thessalonians 4:7), Aaron was called to be high priest (Hebrews 5:4), Jesus was called as a high priest after the order of Melchisedec (Hebrews 5:10), Abraham was called to leave Ur of the Chaldees (Hebrews 11:8), and people are called to the marriage supper of the Lamb (Revelation 19:9). The fact that the term "called" is used over and again in the Bible is undisputed, but this alone proves nothing regarding irresistible grace. We must look to these purported proof texts to see if two types of calls related to salvation are taught, and in particular, whether any verse teaches the so-called "effectual call."

<u>Matthew 22:14</u> For many are called, but few *are* chosen.

This verse is the conclusion of the parable of the wedding banquet, which was discussed in the opening of the unconditional election chapter, but will be addressed in more detail here. Jesus' audience includes the chief priests and Pharisees who want to kill him but fear the multitudes. The parable is squarely directed at them. In the parable, the king's son is to be married and a group of people were invited to the wedding banquet. This group not only refuses to come despite multiple invitations, but their refusal is shocking because they are presumably the nobles and leaders we would expect to attend a royal wedding. They knew well in advance about the wedding and surely should have planned to attend. Some merely refused, while others used their business as an excuse, and others killed the king's servants. The point, of course, is that Israel was first invited and it characteristically rejected Jesus. Indeed, Israel slew God's servants the prophets, including John the Baptist. In response, the King sent his troops to destroy them, which was fulfilled when the Romans quashed the Jewish rebellion and destroyed Jerusalem in 70 A.D.

When they refused to come to the wedding, the king sent his servants to invite everyone else—to basically just grab anyone they can find. These people came, and of course, they represent the Gentiles. The focus in the parable on the one guest that showed up without proper attire is critical. We would expect the first group to have obtained the proper attire having been invited by the king well in advance of the wedding, but of course they did not come. With regard to the second group, however, they were not expecting to come to a wedding. So where did they get clothes befitting a royal wedding? The answer is that the king provided the clothes required for attendance to those that accepted the invitation to come. We are to understand that the king has clothed them with righteousness in response to their faith. The king is shocked to see a guest without a proper wedding garment. The man is speechless when accused of not having proper attire and is ejected from the wedding. The contrast is between those that accepted the king's invitation and then received proper garments from the king and those who would try to attend in their own clothes, or in other words, between those clothed with righteousness by the king and those clothed only in their self-righteousness. The man ejected from the wedding is a warning to the priests and Pharisees that have rejected Jesus.

Jesus' commentary on his parable is that "many are called, but few are chosen." To understand his commentary, we must rely on the parable that the commentary is based on. The calling in view is the general invitation in the parable. Since there is only one type of calling in the parable, namely the invitation to the wedding, it cannot be the Calvinists' "effectual calling" because, if it were, everyone invited would have come. Further, the people that came to the wedding did not do so because they were chosen, but were chosen because they accepted the invitation and came. Recall that this term "chosen" has a common derived meaning of choice, distinguished, excellent or pure. In the parable, everyone gets invited, both good and bad. Those that accepted the invitation and came to the wedding were made choice/distinguished/excellent by the king who gave them their proper wedding attire, i.e., clothed them in righteousness. This verse provides no evidence for irresistible grace.

> Matthew 20:16 So the last shall be first, and the first last: for many be called, but few chosen.

This verse relates to another parable in Matthew and uses the same phrase as the wedding banquet parable just analyzed, "for many be called, but few chosen." The phrase has the same meaning here as it does in Matthew 22:1-14. Nevertheless, Calvinists argue that the meaning of this verse is that many are called (i.e., the general call of the gospel to the elect and non-elect alike) but only few are chosen (i.e., the elect effectually called). First of all, it should be pointed out that there is some debate about whether the phrase "for many be called, but few chosen" should be in the verse since there is evidence that it does not appear in some of the older manuscripts. But putting aside the potential textual issue, the focus of the parable is rewards. At the end of Matthew 19, Peter asked Jesus: "Behold, we have forsaken all, and followed thee; what shall we have therefore?" (Matthew 19:27) And then Matthew records Jesus' response: "Verily I say unto you, That ye which have followed me, in the regeneration when the Son of man shall sit in the throne of his glory, ye also shall sit upon twelve thrones, judging the twelve tribes of Israel. And every one that hath forsaken houses, or brethren, or sisters, or father, or mother, or wife, or children, or lands, for my name's sake, shall receive an hundredfold, and shall inherit everlasting life. But many *that are* first shall be last; and the last *shall be* first." (Matthew 19:28-30) The latter phrase should look familiar, for together with Matthew 20:16 it forms bookends on the parable, and that parable responds to Peter's question. In short, Jesus says to serve faithfully and leave the distribution of any reward to him.

In the parable, a landowner hires day laborers in the morning and at several points throughout the day, even an hour before the end of the workday. At the end of the day, he instructs his steward to distribute the wages beginning with those he hired last: "So when even was come, the lord of the vineyard saith unto his steward, Call the labourers, and give them *their* hire, beginning from the last unto the first." (Matthew 20:8) When those hired at the end of the day receive a full days' wage, those hired earlier assume they should be paid more. The landowner had told them when he hired them that "whatsoever is right I will give you." It was up to the landowner to pay them as he saw fit and in accordance with their agreement. Of course, the landowner is Jesus, and the day during which the work is done is the span of time until Jesus' return, at which point he will reward those that served. Jesus' commentary is that "the last shall be first, and the first last." (Matthew 20:16)

Keeping in mind that the day is the span of time until Jesus' return when he will distribute rewards, the teaching is that believers ought to serve faithfully until the Lord returns. Believers at all points in time who serve faithfully will be rewarded, and the distribution of the reward is wholly the Lord's prerogative. Thus, Peter and the other disciples were to learn that they should focus on their service and not be concerned about who would get the most reward. They should trust Jesus to be just and do what is right, and understand that the reward will be based on faithfulness and not necessarily the task or length of service.

Notwithstanding the obvious context of this parable, Calvinists often cite Matthew 20:16 in support of both unconditional election and irresistible grace because of the phrase, "many be called, but few chosen." As with the first half of this verse, we have to relate it back to the parable. In the parable, the householder hired laborers for his vineyard "early in the morning" (Matthew 20:1), then hired more laborers "about the third hour" (20:3), then hired more laborers "about the sixth and ninth hour" (20:5), and still more laborers "about the eleventh hour" (20:6). Each time he hired whoever would come and sent them to his vineyard with a promise to pay them for their labor. This pictures a general invitation to come work in the vineyard, but only those that agree enter the householder's employ. The "many be called" is the invitation extended to anyone "standing idle in the marketplace," and the "few chosen" reflects their status as laborers for the householder due to be rewarded. As in the wedding parable of Matthew 22, they are chosen because they came to work the vineyard; they did not come to work because they were chosen.

Accordingly, there are not two calls in the parable, but one. Whereas the wedding banquet parable was directed as the priests and Pharisees, this parable is directed at Jesus' disciples, which is why the focus is on service and rewards. Jesus reminds them not to get tangled up in pride with regard to their service. What really matters is the privilege of being one of Jesus' laborers, and they should serve faithfully.

> Romans 8:28 And we know that all things work together for good to them that love God, to them who are the called according to *his* purpose. 29 For whom he did foreknow, he also did predestinate *to be* conformed to the image of his Son, that he might be the firstborn among many brethren. 30 Moreover whom he did predestinate, them he also called: and whom he called, them he also justified: and whom he justified, them he also glorified.

Calvinists often rely on this verse even though it overturns their entire *ordo salutis* (order of salvation). They teach that God elected people to save before the foundation of the world, then "foreknew" them based on that election (or decree), then effectually called them, then called them with the gospel, and then justified them. But the text says God foreknew them, then predestinated them (note the verse does not say "to salvation"), and then called them. It makes no sense to suggest that God predestinated people to do exactly what they were going to do anyway. Instead, God predestinated (i.e., pre-appointed; see the treatment of this passage in unconditional election chapter) them to be conformed to the image of his Son, and this explains how "all things work together for good to them that love God."

The passage then says God "called" the people He pre-appointed. Paul does not say how they are called, nor does he say that God only called them. Calvinists must insist on an effectual calling and that no one else is called, but the text does not say it. Elsewhere, Paul would clarify that God calls the lost by the gospel: "Whereunto he called you by our gospel, to the obtaining of the glory of our Lord Jesus Christ." (2 Thessalonians 2:14) In his letter to the Galatians, Paul similarly taught that they were called by the gospel: "I marvel that ye are so soon removed from him that called you into the grace of Christ unto another gospel: Which is not another; but there be some that trouble you, and would pervert the gospel of Christ." (Galatians 1:6-7) It is also evident in Romans how they were called in relation to their salvation: "So, as much as in me is, I am ready to preach the gospel to you that are at Rome also. For I am not ashamed of the gospel of Christ: for it is the power of God unto salvation to every one that believeth; to the Jew first, and also to the Greek." (Romans 1:15-16) Paul would also say that faith comes by hearing the word of God without any reference to a supposed effectual calling: "So then faith *cometh* by hearing, and hearing by the word of God." (Romans 10:17) With all the evidence that calling to salvation simply refers to preaching of the gospel, and no evidence to the contrary in Romans 8:28-30, there are no grounds for taking the term in Romans 8:28-30 to mean the effectual calling of TULIP irresistible grace.

> 1 Corinthians 1:22 For the Jews require a sign, and the Greeks seek after wisdom: 23 But we preach Christ crucified, unto the Jews a stumblingblock, and unto the Greeks foolishness; 24 But unto them which are called, both Jews and Greeks, Christ the power of God, and the wisdom of God.

Calvinists argue that the calling in verse 24 is the effectual calling of the Holy Spirit. The text does not say, "called by the Holy Spirit." Moreover, we do well to start in verse 21: "For after that in the wisdom of God the world by wisdom knew not God, it pleased God by the foolishness of preaching to save them that believe." The verse does not say God saved the ones He regenerated or effectually called, but instead that these people were saved when they believed the preaching they heard. This is an express statement in God's Word about how people are called to salvation, and yet when Calvinists find the term "called" just a few verses later they give it special meaning not found in the passage. Verses 22 and 23 describe those that, in contrast to the believers in verse 21, rejected the preaching. The reference in verse 24 to "called" is not suggesting a second or different route to salvation than what Paul just stated in verse 21 (Calvinists write in the term *effectually*), but instead Paul refers to those that believed as "called." They accepted the gospel and for them it was the power and wisdom of God, not a stumbling block. This is further confirmed by verse 26: "For ye see your calling, brethren, how that not many wise men after the flesh, not many mighty, not many noble, *are called.*" They could "see" their calling in the sense of observing the word preached and the response of the audience. Characteristically, those in the audience that had pride, prominence or position rejected the preaching. They certainly could not reject an "effectual calling," but they could reject a calling through the gospel, the very subject Paul is discussing throughout this passage. If the Calvinists were correct about the meaning of called, then Paul is confirming in verse 26 that (contrary to the Calvinists' insistence that the effectual calling is not merits based) most people of wealth, power, or prominence are not effectually called. In other words, election is conditional, which flies in the face of the Calvinists' own teaching.

We should take particular note of a passage in 1 Corinthians 15 since Paul obviously would not teach something there contrary to 1 Corinthians 1:

> 1 Corinthians 15:11 Therefore whether *it were* I or they, so we preach, and so ye believed. 12 Now if Christ be preached that he rose from the dead, how say some among you that there is no resurrection of the dead? 13 But if there be no resurrection of the dead, then is Christ not risen: 14 And if Christ be not risen, then *is* our preaching vain, and your faith *is* also vain. 15 Yea, and we are found false witnesses of God; because we have testified of God that he raised up Christ: whom he raised not up, if so be that the dead rise not. 16 For if the dead rise not, then is not Christ raised: 17 And if Christ be not raised, your faith *is* vain; ye are yet in your sins.

Paul notes in verse 11 that they believed his preaching, which is a reference to the gospel by which they were saved as Paul explained at the beginning of chapter 15. The Corinthians were facing questions about the resurrection. Paul says that if Christ was not resurrected, then his preaching of the gospel (the death, burial and resurrection of Christ) was in vain, as was their response of faith. The same thought is stated in verses 14 and 17. Paul explicitly relates their faith, and whether or not it is efficacious (not in vain), to the veracity of the facts of the gospel. If Paul believed in an effectual calling, nothing about this argument makes any sense because the Holy Spirit would have regenerated them apart from the gospel. But if he believed that people were saved through a faith response to the gospel, then his words make perfect sense.

There is no basis in 1 Corinthians to amend the text to understand "called" to mean "effectually called." Instead, Paul describes those that believed the gospel with the adjective "called." Paul will do the same elsewhere and these verses provide no support for irresistible grace.

> <u>Romans 1:6</u> Among whom are ye also the called of Jesus Christ: <u>7</u> To all that be in Rome, beloved of God, called *to be* saints: Grace to you and peace from God our Father, and the Lord Jesus Christ.

This is another passage that refers to Christians as "called" or "the called," and for that reason alone is cited by Calvinists as support for irresistible grace. (see e.g., 1 Corinthians 1:1-2, 9; Hebrews 9:15; 2 Peter 1:3) It is evident from the analysis of Pauline verses above that the calling he refers to is the gospel, and that those that respond in faith may be described as "called" or referred to as "the called." The only way to find irresistible grace in verses like Romans 1:6-7 is to assume it to be so because the text does not say it. Such a reading is inconsistent with other statements in Romans and other Pauline writings. Without any evidence in the passage for irresistible grace beyond the mere use of the term "called," there is no basis for reading Romans 1:6-7 to refer to an effectual calling.

> <u>Galatians 1:15</u> But when it pleased God, who separated me from my mother's womb, and called *me* by his grace, <u>16</u> To reveal his Son in

me, that I might preach him among the
heathen; immediately I conferred not with
flesh and blood:

Calvinists sometimes cite this verse and others that speak of
the calling of a prophet or apostle. Note that this verse does
not say "effectually called," but just called. We know Paul was
called on the Damascus Road, but like all Christians, Paul was
saved upon placing faith in Christ (he says in 2 Timothy 1:12
that "I know whom I have believed"). Moreover, his unique
experience on the Damascus Road is certainly not normative
for all Christians and verses like these should not be relied
upon to draw universal conclusions about the salvation of all
Christians. There is nothing in the Biblical account of Paul's
calling suggesting that he had no choice but to believe when
Jesus spoke to him on the Damascus Road or that an effectual
calling preceded Christ's words to Paul that day.

General Proof Texts

Ezekiel 37:1 The hand of the LORD was upon
me, and carried me out in the spirit of the
LORD, and set me down in the midst of the
valley which *was* full of bones, 2 And caused
me to pass by them round about: and, behold,
there were very many in the open valley; and,
lo, *they were* very dry. 3 And he said unto me,
Son of man, can these bones live? And I
answered, O Lord GOD, thou knowest. 4
Again he said unto me, Prophesy upon these
bones, and say unto them, O ye dry bones, hear
the word of the LORD. 5 Thus saith the Lord
GOD unto these bones; Behold, I will cause
breath to enter into you, and ye shall live: 6
And I will lay sinews upon you, and will bring
up flesh upon you, and cover you with skin, and

put breath in you, and ye shall live; and ye shall
know that I *am* the LORD.

Calvinists inexplicably cite the "valley of dry bones" passage as
support for irresistible grace. These verses have nothing to do
with irresistible grace. They instead speak of a future bodily
resurrection and restoration of the "whole house of Israel."
(see Ezekiel 37:11-12) Other Old Testament verses that are
often cited similarly have nothing to do with irresistible grace.

> Jeremiah 31:3 The LORD hath appeared of old
> unto me, *saying*, Yea, I have loved thee with an
> everlasting love: therefore with lovingkindness
> have I drawn thee.

Because the prophet writes, "have I drawn thee," Calvinists
argue that the drawing is irresistible grace. First, the people
drawn are not the elect, but Israel. (See Jeremiah 31:1) And
second, the context is the future of Israel and not the salvation
of believers generally. The drawing is the future regathering of
the Jewish people to the land of Israel as the subsequent verses
confirm. (see Jeremiah 31:7-8)

> Psalm 65:4 Blessed *is the man whom* thou
> choosest, and causest to approach *unto thee,*
> *that* he may dwell in thy courts: we shall be
> satisfied with the goodness of thy house, *even*
> of thy holy temple.

This verse is obviously not dealing with God irresistibly
drawing people to salvation from sin's penalty. Instead, David
speaks of God causing people to come and dwell in His courts,
likely the courts of the temple.

> John 5:21 For as the Father raiseth up the dead,
> and quickeneth *them*, even so the Son
> quickeneth whom he will.

This verse sometimes finds itself in the irresistible grace list.
The reference to Jesus quickening those "whom he will" is

understood by Calvinists to mean regeneration. But the immediate context says otherwise. Jesus is saying that just as the Father raises the dead, so also does he. The prior verse helps here: "For the Father loveth the Son, and sheweth him all things that himself doeth: and he will shew him greater works than these, that ye may marvel." Jesus is talking about observable works that people will see and respond to by marveling. Clearly, this is not about an effectual calling that no one can observe, but a resurrection like that of Lazarus in John 11.

An Alternative View

Calvinists teach that at a moment in time God regenerates a person (the new birth) so that when they subsequently hear the gospel they will believe. To make their point, they must argue that faith is itself a work, and since people are not saved by works (lest they boast) then faith itself must be given to some people (the elect).

Calvinists find much support in Romans 3 for total depravity but ignore the latter part of the chapter because it undermines their whole system. Paul writes:

> Romans 3:27 Where is boasting then? It is excluded. By what law? of works? Nay: but by the law of faith. 28 Therefore we conclude that a man is justified by faith without the deeds of the law. 29 Is he the God of the Jews only? is he not also of the Gentiles? Yes, of the Gentiles also: 30 Seeing it is one God, which shall justify the circumcision by faith, and uncircumcision through faith. 31 Do we then make void the law through faith? God forbid: yea, we establish the law. * * * 4:3 For what saith the scripture? Abraham believed God, and it was counted unto him for righteousness.

4 Now to him that worketh is the reward not reckoned of grace, but of debt. 5 But to him that worketh not, but believeth on him that justifieth the ungodly, his faith is counted for righteousness.

Paul could not be more clear that in his theology, believing or faith is not a work ("man is justified by faith without the deeds of the law" and "to him that worketh not, but believeth"). This passage needs to be read in conjunction with Ephesians 2, the Calvinist stronghold for the idea that faith is a work and therefore must be given to someone by God. Paul is contrasting the law and works with the "law of faith." It is the law of faith that justifies sinners, both Jew and Gentile. Paul could have simply stated that Abraham was unconditionally elected, but instead uses him as an example of the law of faith ("Abraham believed God, and it was counted unto him for righteousness."). Like Abraham, the person "that worketh not, but believeth" on Jesus is the one that is saved. Our believing or faith is not a work.

Accordingly, we need not impose a theological construct on the Bible like irresistible grace to try to make consistent those many verses that speak of people being saved by believing with those that say people cannot be saved by works. Paul writes: "So then, faith cometh by hearing, and hearing by the word of God." (Romans 10:17) Paul could have simply written that faith comes as a gift from God, but he didn't. He said that faith cometh by hearing. Jesus also made statements contrary to irresistible grace. We know that some people came to believe in Jesus as a result of the signs he did. (see, e.g., John 1:50, 4:39, 53) Jesus made this statement in John 10:38, "...though ye believe not me, believe the works: that ye may know, and believe, that the Father is in me, and I in him." Similarly, in John 14:11: "Believe me that I am in the Father, and the Father in me: or else believe me for the very works' sake." If people were effectually called to salvation, they would never reject

Jesus' testimony and then believe based on the works. Having been regenerated, they would have found Jesus' testimony compelling. The regenerated person would never require convincing signs.

If we accept irresistible grace, we have to grapple with the fact that the Biblical record has a multitude of instances of the good news being presented to a group, with some believing and others not believing, and no mention of the believing group having previously been regenerated to believe. When we put the record together with the fact that the Bible **does not teach** that believing is a work and the Bible **does teach** that "whosoever" believes will be saved, the natural conclusion is that people are not made to believe but invited to believe. Hence, in contrast to irresistible grace, the Bible presents an invitation to all sinners alike. This is the "I" in NULIF, the invitation to accept the free gift of eternal life.

Concluding Thoughts on Irresistible Grace

Although they cite a substantial number of verses that happen to mention terms like "called" or "the called," none of these verses specify two separate callings or an effectual calling. It is plain from numerous passages in the New Testament that people are called by the gospel. The notion of an effectual calling is a philosophical concept concocted for the TULIP paradigm but foreign to the Scriptures. When we set aside those verses that are cited by Calvinists simply because they use these terms, they have only two actual direct proof texts, namely John 6 and Acts 16 (the episode with Lydia), both of which we have seen do not teach irresistible grace. The reality is that Calvinists do not hold to irresistible grace because they find it taught explicitly in the Bible, but because they accept total depravity and unconditional election. If those doctrines are accepted then irresistible grace must be true even if the Bible refutes it. We have already examined those doctrines and demonstrated that they are without Biblical evidence, and accordingly, irresistible grace is likewise unsupported.

As a practical matter, this means that how we deliver the gospel message really does matter. We cannot make people believe, but we should strive to speak with clarity and conviction. We do not just throw out the facts of the gospel and rely on God to turn on the light so that the elect must believe. Instead, like Jesus with the woman at the well, we should strive as best we can to meet people where they are and explain the truth of the gospel so that they can understand it. At that point, the choice is theirs to make. Those that believe should follow their profession with a life lived for Jesus Christ, and this brings us to the final petal of the withered TULIP, namely the "P" or perseverance of the saints.

Chapter 8

Perseverance of the Saints

Some like to quote "half verses," which always leaves me wondering if they know the other half, or the context for the half they quote. One of those is, "ye shall know them by their fruits." This half verse is frequently used to express the idea that someone cannot possibly be a Christian because of some bad act they committed. But as we saw earlier in this book, Jesus' words from Matthew 7:15-20 are directed to his disciples about how to identify "false prophets" based on their words (their "fruits") because being evil ("inwardly they are ravening wolves") they disguise themselves as believers ("in sheep's clothing"). Most unfortunate, however, is that the sentiment reflects a common belief among Christians that certain conduct, other than rejecting the gospel, categorically excludes a person from being a Christian. In short, a real Christian cannot do that.

But this raises an important question. What sin is a Christian incapable of doing?

If a person murders someone else, does that prove he or she is not a Christian? Or what if they are a drunk? Or they struggle with a drug addiction? Or what about a sexual sin issue? Many believers believe that certain sins prove a person is not a believer. Of course, they tend to leave out the ones they know they do—the ones Paul lists in Romans 1:29-30 like "envy... debate... deceit... whisperers [gossips], backbiters... proud, boasters... disobedient to parents." We read or hear about what someone is doing and rush to righteous indignation: "he can't be a Christian."

But think of our heroes of the faith. There was Noah with his drunkenness (and more than that happened when he was drunk), Abraham who on two occasions offered his wife to another man, Jacob who was a swindler, Moses with his anger problem that persisted his entire life and once caused him to murder an Egyptian, David who had multiple wives and had an affair with a married woman and murdered her husband, Solomon who saturated himself with women and permitted rampant idolatry even at the Temple complex, just to name a few. And someone will respond, "well, of course a Christian can sin, but they will never continue in it." Why not? Peter called Lot a "just" man "vexed with the filthy conversation of the wicked" (2 Peter 2:7), but from the history in Genesis his actions are hard to defend at any point in his life. This man stayed in Sodom while its ways consumed his family, and after leaving he impregnated both of his daughters while drunk. It is difficult to isolate what good things he did that we can see, but the divine commentary is clear. What about the judge, Samson? If ever there was a man that always acted to satisfy his flesh, Samson was it. He blatantly violated his Nazarite vow, defied his parents, engaged in sexual sin, was prideful and violent, and persisted in his ways his whole life. Yet we find Samson in the Hall of Fame of Faith in Hebrews 11.

The issue is not whether there are dire consequences for a Christian that persists in a particular sin. There are many, and no one is saying that a person who persists in a particular sin is getting away with it. But no verse in the Bible says that such conduct excludes that person as a Christian. No verse in the Bible says there are certain sins that prove a person is not really a believer.

I would hasten to add at this point that every Christian persists in sin until they die. Let that sink in. This mantle of the Pharisees that many have taken on in our day by happily condemning those they think are too sinful to be believers is a tremendous plague on Christianity. When we engage in the fruit inspecting business, we always set ourselves as the standard. We focus on a perceived persistent sin in someone else like a sexual sin, alcoholism, drug addictions, and other things that we feel we can safely say we are not guilty of. People who know us would never think we do those things. We become that Pharisee that "stood and prayed thus with himself, God, I thank thee, that I am not as other men are, extortioners, unjust, adulterers, or even as this publican." (Luke 18:11)

But what if those around us knew the whole truth about us? What if they knew what we really think? What if they knew that we remain prideful, still enjoy some good gossip, have inner thoughts about others we should not have, fail to properly channel our anger even in basic situations (like when we are cut off in traffic), make unkind responses to our spouse and words of ridicule toward our children when we had a bad day at work? What if they knew how much (or how little) we give at church, how we do not provide food and clothes to the destitute, how outside of church we talk about people in the church with a critical spirit?

When we get in the fruit inspecting business—testing other people's salvation by what we think we know about them or see in their conduct—we take on a role we are not qualified to have and should not desire. We all struggle in various areas and most or all of us will struggle in some area our entire lives, not ever totally overcoming it. And I would venture to say almost all of us struggle with pride our entire lives. And if that is true, then does it not prove we are not truly Christians? That any commitment to obedience to Christ was hollow? The "P" in TULIP, the last petal we will address, basically contends that true Christians will persevere in obedience to the end of their mortal lives. The pernicious flip side to this doctrine, that would require an entire book to address in any detail, is the popular Lordship Salvation doctrine, which transforms the gospel into a commitment to faithful discipleship so that a persistent failure in a person's walk proves the initial commitment was false and they are not a Christian. It preaches well because we like hearing the preacher rail on the guy at the other end of the pew, but works salvation by any other name is still works salvation.

To get our hands around perseverance, we need to start at the beginning, with the issue of what faith means.

What Is Faith?

In plain everyday English the noun "faith" is defined to mean "confidence or trust in a person or thing; belief in the truth of a statement or doctrine."[136] Similarly, the verb "believe" is defined to mean "to have confidence (in); trust; rely through faith (on); be persuaded of the truth or reality of a thing (with in); to have belief in; credit; accept as true."[137] In our New Testaments, the Greek word typically translated "faith" is the noun *pistis.* The word typically translated as "believe" is the related verb *pisteuo.* According to the Greek lexicon BDAG, the verb *pisteuo* has the primary meaning "to consider something to be true and therefore worthy of one's trust, believe." The noun *pistis* has the primary meaning of "that which evokes trust and faith" and a secondary meaning of a "state of believing on the basis of the reliability of the one trusted, trust, confidence, faith."

---

[136] H.G. Emery and K.G. Brewster, *The New Century Dictionary of the English Language Volume One* (New York: D. Appleton-Century Company 1948).

[137] *Supra* note 136.

A bedrock principle of Reformed theology is *sola fide,* that people are saved by faith alone in Christ alone. But modern Reformed theology rejects the notion that we are saved by faith alone in Christ alone if by faith it is meant simply trusting, believing, or having confidence in. Merely trusting in Christ for salvation is dead faith, head faith, and spurious faith, but not genuine faith, heart faith, or living faith. Merely trusting in Christ without more is the essence of a false profession. It is the heresy of easy believism. The reason is that the faith that saves is never alone, that is, it must be accompanied by a whole-hearted commitment to faithfully serve Christ. And since God gives each elect person their faith—a faith that includes the whole-hearted commitment to faithfully serve Christ—it is the faith alone that saves but it will always produce a life of enduring fruitfulness. The person whose life is unfruitful or ends in unfruitfulness necessarily made a false profession because if they had the type of faith that God gives to the elect, their life would have looked different. This life of fruitfulness is the perseverance of the saints. After we look at how the Calvinists define the perseverance of the saints in their own words, we will return this critical issue of defining faith, which is at the root of this doctrine.

How the Calvinists Define Perseverance

Grudem succinctly defines the perseverance of the saints: "The perseverance of the saints means that all those who are truly born again will be kept by God's power and will persevere as Christians until the end of their lives, and that only those who persevere until the end have been truly born again."[138] This author agrees wholeheartedly in the eternal security of the believer, or as Grudem states, "those who are truly born again will be kept by God's power." A saint cannot lose their justification, for otherwise it could not be called *eternal* life.

---

[138] *Supra* note 14, p. 788.

But the second part of the definition is where we must part ways. Grudem explains further: "On the other hand, the second half of the definition makes it clear that continuing in the Christian life is one of the evidences that a person is truly born again. It is important to keep this aspect of the doctrine in mind as well, lest false assurance be given to people who were never really believers in the first place."[139] Thus, Grudem introduces the Reformed idea that there are multitudes of people who think they are Christians but are not. They are the so-called professors of faith, but not possessors of faith.

The Westminster Confession of Faith, in Article XVII, states the traditional reformed doctrine of the perseverance of the saints: "They whom God hath accepted in his Beloved, effectually called and sanctified by his Spirit, can neither totally nor finally fall away from the state of grace; but shall certainly persevere therein to the end, and be eternally saved." Again, this is not just about being eternally secure, but about having a lifestyle that evidences faith to the end. The Calvinist, Hoekema, explains this point with reference to the writings of fellow Calvinist John Murray:

> John Murray makes a strong plea for retaining the express "perseverance" rather than "preservation." The term "perseverance," he says, guards against the notion that believers are spiritually secure regardless of the extent to which they may fall into sin or become careless about their way of life. It is simply not biblical teaching to say that believers are secure regardless of how they live. The doctrine we are considering is the doctrine that believers *persevere*; it is only through the power of God that they are able to persevere, to be sure, but they do persevere. The security of believers is

---

[139] *Supra* note 14, p. 788.

inseparable from their perseverance; did not Jesus say, "He who stands firm to the end will be saved" (Matt. 10:22)? Murray, in fact, puts it as strongly as this: "Perseverance means the engagement of our persons in the most intense and concentrated devotion to those means which God has ordained for the achievement of his saving purpose."[140]

Dabney likewise explains that the doctrine of perseverance of the saints requires an outward showing of works evidencing salvation:

> This perseverance does not imply that a man may be living in habitual and purposed sin, and yet be in a justified state, because he who is once justified cannot come into condemnation. We heartily join in everything which can be said against so odious a doctrine. It is impossible, because the living in such a state of sin proves that the man never was, and is not now, in a justified state, whatever may be his names and boasts.[141]

Berkhof remarks that "[t]he name naturally suggests a continuous activity of believers whereby they persevere in the way of salvation" and then offers this definition: "Perseverance is that continuous operating of the Holy Spirit in the believer, by which the work of divine grace that is begun in the heart, is continued and brought to completion."[142] Strong also defines perseverance of the saints to include a lifetime of works, and like many Calvinists, views the doctrine as the "human" side of sanctification:

---

[140] Anthony A. Hoekema, *Saved by Grace*, William B. Eerdmans Publishing Company (1994), p. 236.
[141] *Supra* note 36, p. 688-89.
[142] *Supra* note 34, p. 274.

The Scriptures declare that, in virtue of the original purpose and continuous operation of God, all who are united to Christ by faith will infallibly continue in a state of grace and will finally attain to everlasting life. This voluntary continuance, on the part of the Christian, in faith and welldoing we call perseverance. Perseverance is, therefore, the human side or aspect of that spiritual process which, as viewed from the divine side, we call sanctification. It is not a mere natural consequence of conversion, but involves a constant activity of the human will from the moment of conversion to the end of life.[143]

In his systematic theology, the Calvinist, Culver, is emphatic on the works component of the doctrine:

The true doctrine (not the caricature often rejected by opponents of the supposed doctrine) means that the believer is kept in faith and obedience, partial and temporary lapses notwithstanding. It means that final apostasy does not take place, that sins committed in moments of neglect of the means of grace will be repented of rather than continued in. Those who live scandalous lives have no basis for assurance and are not to be received as Christians by the churches.[144]

Thus, it is evident that there is much more to perseverance of the saints than eternal security or "once saved, always saved." It should also be pointed out again that there are Calvinists that would only hold to eternal security and not the rest of the doctrine. Interestingly, most Calvinists that accept the

---

[143] *Supra* note 30, p. 881.
[144] *Supra* note 35, p. 767.

traditional view explained in all of the quotes above would defend their position as a natural and necessary conclusion from the doctrine of unconditional election, which all Calvinists hold to. Thus, there seem to be some irreconcilable conflicts among Calvinists as to this doctrine, much as there is regarding limited atonement. Our purpose here, though, is limited to addressing the traditional doctrine and its primary proof texts, but before we turn to those, we need to first consider whether the doctrine flows from the very definition of the term "faith."

When Trusting Christ Is Not Enough

The very essence of the gospel depends on how you define faith, and not everyone defines faith the same way. Reformed theologians typically differentiate between faith and saving faith. According to Robert Culver, there are three elements to saving faith:

> The first element, not to be neglected, is, indeed, *intellectual* assent — to the facts of biblical history and of redemption provided. This is sometimes called historical faith....

> The second element in saving faith is *appropriation*— of Christ as Lord and Savior.

> A third element in saving faith is *commitment* to Christ... And that is exactly what a contrite sinner does, having been convinced in mind that Jesus is, indeed, the Savior, and having received the Savior to himself — he commits himself, his hopes, ambitions and things to Jesus.[145]

---

[145] *Supra* note 33, pp. 717-18.

Note that it is Culver's third element that makes saving faith mean faith plus something else, namely the commitment of oneself to Christ. Obviously, every Christian should commit themselves to a life of obedience to Christ, but the issue at hand is whether they must do so in order to be saved in the first place. Wayne Grudem gets to same place as Culver, but by adding his definition of repentance to the required saving faith. He first defines the three elements of saving faith:

1. **Knowledge alone Is not enough.** Personal saving faith, in the way Scripture understands it, involves more than mere knowledge. Of course *it is necessary that we have some knowledge of who Christ is and what he has done*, for "how are they to believe in him of whom they have never heard?" (Rom. 10:14) But knowledge about the *facts* of Jesus' life, death, and resurrection for us is not enough....

2. **Knowledge and approval are not enough.** Moreover, merely knowing the facts and *approving* of them or *agreeing* that they are true is not enough. Nicodemus knew that Jesus had come from God... Nicodemus had evaluated the facts of the situation, including Jesus' teaching and his remarkable miracles, and had drawn a correct conclusion from those facts: Jesus was a teacher come from God. But this alone did not mean that Nicodemus had saving faith, for he still had to put trust in Christ for salvation; he still had to "believe in him."...

3. **I Must Decide to Depend on Jesus to save Me Personally.** In addition to knowledge of the facts of the gospel and approval of those facts, in order to be saved, I must decide to depend

on Jesus to save me. In doing this I move from being an interested observer of the facts of salvation and the teachings of the Bible to being someone who enters into a new relationship with Jesus Christ as a living person. We may therefore define saving faith in the following way: *Saving faith is trust in Jesus Christ as a living person for forgiveness of sins and for eternal life with God.*[146]

I agree with what I have quoted from Wayne Grudem above, but he then adds that repentance is also necessary for salvation and that "*repentance is a heartfelt sorrow for sin, a renouncing of it, and a sincere commitment to forsake it and walk in obedience to Christ.*"[147] Hodges likewise says that faith necessarily leads to good works and also speaks of saving repentance as entailing "[g]rief and hatred of sin, a resolute turning from it unto God, and a persistent endeavor after a new life of holy obedience."[148] Strong affirms that faith includes a "voluntary element" (so-called *fiducia*), which means: "Surrender of the soul, as guilty and defiled, to Christ's governance."[149]

By giving the term "faith" this special definition, which finds no support whatsoever in the lexical meaning of the term, Reformed theologians insist that salvation is by faith alone while also maintaining that no one can enter heaven without sufficient works (i.e., with faith alone). Reformed theologians go to great lengths to try to distinguish their view from the works-based salvation of Catholicism. Typical of Reformed theologians, R.C. Sproul comments in his book *What Is Reformed Theology?*: "For Rome justification is the result of

---

[146] *Supra* note 14, pp. 709-10.
[147] *Supra* note 14, p. 713.
[148] *Supra* note 39, pp. 479, 487.
[149] *Supra* note 30, p. 838.

faith plus works. In Reformed theology justification is the result of faith alone, a faith that always produces works."[150] But how can it be faith alone if it must necessarily produce works? For the Reformed theologian, it is a question of the quality of faith. There is saving, genuine or true faith and there is spurious or dead faith. As Sproul explains, saving faith always produces works:

> At issue here is the question of genuine faith. The Reformers taught that 'justification is by faith alone, but not by a faith that is alone.' True faith is never alone. It always manifests itself in works. Works that flow out of faith, however, are in no way the ground of our justification. They contribute nothing of merit before God. The only ground or basis of our justification is the merit of Christ. Nor is faith itself a meritorious work or the ground of our justification. Faith is a gift of God's grace, so it possesses no merit of its own.[151]

Likewise, in his *Concise Theology*, J.I. Packer explained that true faith always bears fruit:

> The truth is that, though we are justified by faith alone, the faith that justifies is never alone. It produces moral fruit ... it transforms one's way of living; it begets virtue. This is not only because holiness is commanded, but also because the regenerate heart, of which fiducia is the expression, desires holiness and can find full contentment only in seeking it.[152]

---

[150] *Supra* note 18, p. 71.
[151] *Supra* note 18, pp. 70-71.
[152] J.I. Packer, *Concise Theology: A Guide to Historic Christian Beliefs* (Wheaton: Tyndale House, 1993), 160.

Pillar Verses

The pillar proof text for the notion that saving faith means more than believing and necessarily entails a commitment of obedience is James 2:14 ff. Commenting on James 2, Sproul finds a distinction between saving and spurious faith:

> James is asking what kind of faith is saving faith. He makes it clear that no one is justified by a mere profession of faith. Anyone can say he has faith. But saying it and having it are not the same thing. True faith always manifests itself in works. If no works follow from faith, then the alleged faith is "dead" and useless. Abraham demonstrated his faith by his works. He "showed" he had true faith, thus "justifying" his claim to faith. Abraham's profession of faith is vindicated in his demonstration of his faith in Genesis 22.
>
> * * *
>
> At issue here is the question of genuine faith. The Reformers taught that "justification is by faith alone, but not by a faith that is alone." True faith is never alone.[153]

Similarly, in a section of his commentary on James captioned "empty confession," John MacArthur explains:

> The question **can that faith save him?** is not offered to dispute the importance of faith, but to oppose the idea that just any kind of faith can save. (cf. Matt. 7:16-18) The grammatical form of the question calls for a negative answer—"No, it cannot save." A profession of **faith** that is devoid of righteous **works** cannot

---

[153] *Supra* note 18, pp. 69-70.

save a person, no matter how strongly it may be proclaimed. As already noted, it is not that some amount of good **works** added to true **faith** can **save** a person, but rather that **faith** that is genuine and saving will inevitably *produce* good **works**.[154]

Since Reformed theologians place much reliance on James 2, we will examine the passage in detail. We should first consider a couple of preliminary matters. James uses the term "save" several times. Some Christians have a tendency to automatically read "save" to mean salvation from sin's penalty, but as J. B. Hixson explains, the term more often does not have anything to do with salvation from hell:

> The terms *save* [Greek *sozo*] and *salvation* [Greek *soteria*] carry the primary meanings of *rescue* and *deliverance*, respectively. The context must determine whether the deliverance in question is temporal in nature— such as deliverance from sickness or danger— or eternal in nature—that is, deliverance from the penalty of sin, namely, hell. For instance, the verb *save* [Greek *sozo*] occurs 109 times in the New Testament. Only forty-one of these occur in the context of eternal salvation. The remaining occurrences refer to temporal deliverance from physical harm, sickness or danger (fifty times); eschatological deliverance into the Messianic Kingdom (fifteen times); or eschatological deliverance at the Bema Judgment (three times). Similar data exist for the noun *salvation*.[155]

---

[154] John MacArthur, *The MacArthur New Testament Commentary: James* (Chicago: Moody Press 1998), 124.
[155] *Supra* note 73, p. 93.

Thus, when we find the word "save" in James, we cannot assume that he has in mind deliverance from hell, but must instead look to the context to determine the meaning. Secondly, we should observe that James is writing to Christians since he refers 15 times to his audience as brethren, and five other times refers to how we behave in relation to another brother or sister. However, many Reformed theologians assume a mixed audience of believers and non-believers. This makes no sense, of course, since Calvinism teaches that the lost people cannot understand the things of God, and that surely includes the book of James.

The purpose of James is to address practical Christian living with a view to rewards in heaven, and the central passage is James 1:19-21:

> James 1:19 Wherefore, my beloved brethren, let every man be swift to hear, slow to speak, slow to wrath: 20 For the wrath of man worketh not the righteousness of God. 21 Wherefore lay apart all filthiness and superfluity of naughtiness, and receive with meekness the engrafted word, **which is able to save your souls**.

Note the bolded language. James says that the engrafted or implanted word is "able to save your souls." This is frequently misunderstood to address the issue of our justification before God, in other words, being saved or delivered from the sin's penalty. But James does not say "save your spirits" or anything about receiving eternal life. The concept of the salvation of the soul was addressed in detail by Jesus, Peter, and the author of Hebrews, and it relates to the concepts of our inheritance or rewards to be received at the bema judgment. Because of the volume of that material, I have included an excurses in the Appendix on the salvation of the soul. Seeing that James is addressing the "salvation of the soul" and not salvation from sin's penalty is critical to rightly dividing the epistle, and especially the material in James 2.

When James says that God's word is "able to save your souls," the word soul is the Greek *psuche*. The working definition provided in the Appendix is "the temporal experience of human life," and as outlined there, the concept of the salvation of the soul has to do with the deliverance of our experience of life into eternity. And that happens as we are rewarded, or receive our share as co-heirs with Christ of his inheritance, in exchange for a life lived in obedience. It is not surprise, then, that James says that when received "with meekness" or humility the "engrafted word" of God is able to save our souls. The idea is not merely that we read the Word of God or commit some of it to memory, but it is engrafted or implanted within us, shaping who we are and how we think and live. A life lived on the basis of the engrafted word will vindicate the reality of our faith at the bema, and will translate into rewards or inheritance. This is why so much of James addresses practical Christian living. James' teaching in that regard is against the backdrop of our standing before Jesus and giving account for how we lived. We ought to live in such a way that our lives well-lived translate into rewards at the bema.

Moving forward, the more immediate context for James' statements beginning in 2:14 are his comments in 2:8-13:

> James 2:8 If ye fulfil the royal law according to the scripture, Thou shalt love thy neighbour as thyself, ye do well: 9 But if ye have respect to persons, ye commit sin, and are convinced of the law as transgressors. 10 For whosoever shall keep the whole law, and yet offend in one point, he is guilty of all. 11 For he that said, Do not commit adultery, said also, Do not kill. Now if thou commit no adultery, yet if thou kill, thou art become a transgressor of the law. 12 So speak ye, and so do, as they that shall be judged by the law of liberty. 13 For he shall have judgment without mercy, that hath shewed no mercy; and mercy rejoiceth against judgment.

Keeping in mind that James' practical instruction for Christian living is set against the doctrine of the salvation of the soul, James says that we need to fulfill the royal law, which is to "love thy neighbour as thyself." (James 2:8) Showing favoritism violates the royal law (James 2:8) and makes us guilty of violating the righteousness of "the whole law" (James 2:10). Beckoning back to James' central passage where he said to "be swift to hear, slow to speak" (James 1:19), James writes that we must speak and act "as they that shall be judged by the law of liberty." (James 2:12) The "law of liberty" is an apparent reference to the "royal law" that we love our neighbor as ourselves. The judgment in view is the only judgment faced by New Testament believers—the bema with a view to rewards. (see, e.g., Matthew 25:14-30, 1 Corinthians 3:11-15, 2 Corinthians 5:10) The standard of the Christian's judgment at the bema is explicitly set forth in 2:13: "For he shall have judgment without mercy, that hath showed now mercy; and mercy rejoiceth against judgment." In other words, our lives are measured against the royal law or law of liberty. But again, this is not with a view to our eternal destiny, but to rewards.

Before moving to the pillar passage in James 2:14, jump to 3:1: "My brethren, be not many masters, knowing that we shall receive the greater condemnation." Note there that James is still addressing this future judgment, and in 3:1 he refers to the fact that Christian teachers will be judged against a more demanding standard. Inexplicably, many commentators dislodge James 2:14 from the material before and after it, but James 2:14-26 falls between the judgment verses of James 2:12-13 and 3:1, and all of this addresses the same topic. Salvation from sin's penalty is not in view. All of these verses are telling believers that if they live a life of disobedience to the royal law they will be called to answer for it at the bema. And none of us should want that.

> James 2:14 What *doth it* profit, my brethren,
> though a man say he hath faith, and have not

> works? can faith save him? 15 If a brother or sister be naked, and destitute of daily food, 16 And one of you say unto them, Depart in peace, be *ye* warmed and filled; notwithstanding ye give them not those things which are needful to the body; what *doth it* profit? 17 Even so faith, if it hath not works, is dead, being alone.

James does not write in a vacuum, but against the background of his central passage in chapter 1 about right Christian living based on the word of God saving our souls, and the immediate context of being judged at the bema on the basis or standard of the royal law. He asks two rhetorical questions. First, James asks what it will "profit" a man who claims to have faith but not works. The obvious answer is there is no profit. Preliminarily, since we cannot profit or earn justification ("by the deeds of the law there shall no flesh be justified," Romans 3:20), James is not addressing justification but something we can earn (i.e., rewards). Second, James asks, "can faith save him?" James means can faith alone save the person who has faith but not works, and the answer is a resounding no.

When we understand a central purpose of the entire epistle as well as the immediate context before and after James 2:14-26 is the salvation of the soul at the judgment for believers, the passage makes perfect sense. At the bema, the issue is not whether we are bound for heaven or the lake of fire. The test is not whether we are real believers or we had fake faith. The standard is the royal law. Did we show mercy? This, of course, ties back to the central passage—that the engrafted word is able to save our souls. Recall that James followed "which is able to save your souls" (James 1:21) with: "But be ye doers of the word, and not hearers only, deceiving your own selves...But whoso looketh into the perfect law of liberty, and continue therein, he being not a forgetful hearer, but a doer of the work, this man shall be blessed in his deed." (James 1:22-25) At the bema, faithfulness will be rewarded. But a Christian that was not a doer of the royal law will not profit or earn a reward. Note that in 1 Corinthians 3, Paul explained that at the bema the "work" of our lives will be tested by fire as to "what sort it is," namely "gold, silver, precious stones" or "wood, hay, stubble." In other words, did this person lay up treasure in heaven or on earth, and "if any man's work shall be burned, he shall suffer loss: but he himself shall be saved; yet so as by fire." (1 Corinthians 3:15) James 2:14 is addressing that man, who has faith but no "work" worthy of earning a reward.

In the next three verses, James illustrates his point in a way that ties James 2:14 back to the standard at the judgment announced in 2:13. James says, "If a brother or sister be naked, and destitute of daily food, And one of you say unto them, Depart in peace, be ye warmed and filled; notwithstanding ye give them not those things which are needful to the body; what doth it profit? Even so faith, if it hath not works, is dead, being alone." (James 2:15-17) Notice first his reference to a brother or sister, terminology that only makes sense if this is an illustration of a Christian saying "depart in peace..." to another Christian. Second, when the term "dead" is used figuratively, as it is here, it carries the idea of something being useless or nonproductive. (See, e.g., Romans 4:19) What James is doing is illustrating in the most practical terms how our living out or not living out the royal law of loving thy neighbor as thyself will play out at the bema. If we have faith but fail to love our neighbor, then our faith does not have works of mercy ("being alone") and is therefore "dead" or useless when it comes to earning rewards at the bema (i.e., "he shall have judgment without mercy"). Faith alone will not result in rewards at the bema judgment. It is faith accompanied by works, faith that is visible to those around us, that will profit us at the bema as we are rewarded by Christ.

> James 2:18 Yea, a man may say, Thou hast
> faith, and I have works: shew me thy faith
> without thy works, and I will shew thee my

faith by my works. 19 Thou believest that there
is one God; thou doest well: the devils also
believe, and tremble. 20 But wilt thou know, O
vain man, that faith without works is dead?

James next deals with a hypothetical objector to what he
previously stated. This is a common literary device of raising a
hypothetical objection and addressing it. There is debate
about which words in 2:18-19 are the objector's words and
which are James' words in response; some take all of it as
James' words. But the "Yea, a man may say," clearly introduces
the objection. The objector's argument is essentially that faith
and works need not go together. Bear in mind there is no
indication in 2:14 or here that "faith" is belief in the gospel.
What is in view is the Christian's general belief in the Word of
God, including the royal law. James says if you accept the royal
law, you ought to live it out, i.e., do not be a hearer only. If you
are a hearer only, you will not be rewarded. The objector says
faith and works need not go together, and a person can show
their faith to another person apart from doing so by works
("shew me thy faith without they works"). The objector who
says, "I have works" but does not say he has faith, then argues
that he can "shew thee my faith by my works." The objector
then uses the example of someone who believes the Shema of
Deuteronomy 6:4, i.e., "there is one God." Note the example
is not someone that believes the gospel. And the one person
can believe "there is one God" and they "doest well," while the
"devils also believe" but it produces only trembling and not
well-doing.

To this argument that believing the Word of God and living it
out do not go hand in hand, James says: "But wilt thou know,
O vain man, that faith without works is dead?" (James 2:20)
And in response to the objector's example of the demons,
James offers to his audience the examples of Abraham and
Rahab. With regard to Abraham, we read:

> James 2:21 Was not Abraham our father
> justified by works, when he had offered Isaac
> his son upon the altar? 22 Seest thou how faith
> wrought with his works, and by works was faith
> made perfect? 23 And the scripture was
> fulfilled which saith, Abraham believed God,
> and it was imputed unto him for righteousness:
> and he was called the Friend of God. 24 Ye see
> then how that by works a man is justified, and
> not by faith only.

The answer to James' rhetorical question in verse 21 is
obviously yes, Abraham was justified by works when he offered
Isaac, but James does not use the term justified in the same
way Paul would years later in his epistles. We know from
Genesis 15:6, quoted by James in verse 23, that Abraham was a
genuine believer decades before he went on the mountain to
sacrifice Isaac, and moreover, that righteousness was imputed
to him on the basis of faith those many years ago apart from
works. The episode of the offering of Isaac occurred in
Genesis 22. Are we to understand that notwithstanding God's
statement in Genesis 15:6 that Abraham was not really saved
until Genesis 22? Of course not. Between those chapters
spanned many years and many failings by Abraham, but he
matured in his faith to the point that Abraham could say to his
party as he and Isaac went up the mountain: "...and I and the
lad will go yonder and worship, and come again to you."
(Genesis 22:5) Abraham had faith for many decades at this
point and had been justified *before God* (who alone can see
our hearts) no later than Genesis 15:6, but we know that by
Genesis 22 he had reached a point of maturity where his faith
was visible before men, and in that sense he was justified
before men.

> James 2:25 Likewise also was not Rahab the
> harlot justified by works, when she had
> received the messengers, and had sent *them*

> out another way? 26 For as the body without
> the spirit is dead, so faith without works is
> dead also. 3:1 My brethren, be not many
> masters, knowing that we shall receive the
> greater condemnation.

The sort of faith that is visible before men is the sort that produces works that are rewarded at the bema. In his second example, James recalls Rahab: "Likewise also was not Rahab the harlot justified by works, when she had received the messengers, and had sent them out another way?" The writer of Hebrews acknowledges that Rahab had faith when she received the spies. (Hebrews 11:31) But James refers also to her tricking the king and sending the spies out another way. Rahab's act of courage was faith that people could see.

Rather than distinguishing between saving and spurious faith, James simply addresses what will matter at the bema, the sort of belief in the Word of God that will be profitable there and result in a deliverance of our soul-life in the form of rewards. As James said in chapter 1, the Word must be received in meekness and engrafted. We must not be hearers only. James then adds that those who would step forward as teachers should do so with a keen awareness that at the bema judgment, where our being a doer of the Word and not a hearer only is assessed by Jesus with a view to rewards, the standard will be more strictly applied. It is imperative that those who publicly teach model what they teach. One final comment is that if James' concern really was saving versus spurious faith, in the sense of saving from sin's penalty, then surely he would have clearly presented the gospel in his epistle.

Another favorite proof text for the notion of spurious faith comes from John's Gospel:

> John 2:23 Now when he was in Jerusalem at the
> passover, in the feast day, many believed in his
> name, when they saw the miracles which he did.

> <u>24</u> But Jesus did not commit himself unto them, because he knew all men, <u>25</u> And needed not that any should testify of man: for he knew what was in man.

As the argument goes, these people did not truly believe, but were just smitten with the signs Jesus did and so he did not entrust himself to them. In the first place, we should take God's Word that "many believed in his name" at face value. If God had wanted to say they did not really believe, or believed with a spurious faith, he could have done so. Indeed, there is no example in John's gospel of God expressly stating that someone had spurious faith or any words to that effect. But more than that, the language employed here or its equivalent is utilized in the Gospel to indicate saving faith. John wrote in his prologue: "But as many as received him, to them gave he power to become the sons of God, *even* to them that **believe on his name**." (John 1:12) Indeed, "his disciples **believed on him**." (John 2:11) Then again in John 3:15-16: "That whosoever **believeth in him** should not perish, but have eternal life. For God so loved the world, that he gave his only begotten Son, that whosoever **believeth in him** should not perish, but have everlasting life." Accordingly, the phraseology in John 2:23 that they "believed in his name" means these people had saving faith in Jesus, having witnessed his miracles.

Reformed theologians infer spurious faith from Jesus' unwillingness to entrust himself to them. But that had nothing to do with the quality of their faith. There was great expectation at this time that Messiah would immediately implement his kingdom. In John 1:49, Nathaniel called Jesus the "King of Israel." The crowd welcomed Jesus in John 12 (the Triumphal Entry) as their King, and there is much emphasis on Jesus as the King of the Jews in the closing chapters. Of special relevance here, in John 6:15, we are told expressly why Jesus refused certain people: "When Jesus therefore perceived that they would come and take him by force, to make him a *king*, he departed again into a mountain himself alone." The issue in John 2 was not that they did not have saving faith, but that they would want him to do something (likely be installed as king) contrary to his mission that would take him to a Roman cross. Remember, the apostles also did not understand that until after the fact. And note that the verse does not say they had spurious faith, but only that Jesus would not "entrust Himself to them," i.e., remain with them, because he knew what they were thinking.

Accordingly, there is no basis for taking a text that says people believe in him, which is affirmed in John 3 to be what is required to obtain eternal life, and insist the text does not mean what it plainly says. This is one of the most blatant examples of Calvinists misusing a text to fit their theological commitment. Reformed theologians also find support in John 6:60-66:

> 60 Many therefore of his disciples, when they had heard this, said, This is an hard saying; who can hear it? 61 When Jesus knew in himself that his disciples murmured at it, he said unto them, Does this offend you? 62 What and if ye shall see the Son of man ascend up where he was before? 63 It is the spirit that quickeneth; the flesh profiteth nothing: the words that I speak unto you, they are spirit, and they are life. 64 But there are some of you that believe not. For Jesus knew from the beginning who they were that believed not, and who should betray him. 65 And he said, Therefore said I unto you, that no man can come unto me, except it were given unto him of my Father. 66 From that time many of his disciples went back, and walked no more with him.

Since John 6 was thoroughly addressed in the context of irresistible grace, I will simply remind the reader that the context in John 6 is dealing with genuine disciples versus the wannabe disciples that were following Jesus solely for a meal or to see a miracle. Reformed theologians equate discipleship with being a Christian, but obviously not all disciples believe (at least as John uses the word in his Gospel), as Jesus plainly states in verse 64. It is not that they trusted Jesus but later had their faith invalidated as spurious because the works did not follow. Instead, they never believed to begin with ("Jesus knew from the beginning who they were that believed not"). And there is no indication they ever professed faith. In fact, we can follow the wannabe disciples from the Feeding of the 5,000 through the entire discourse of John 6 and, despite Jesus' pleas to them to "believe on him" (John 6:29), they did not. There is no feigned or spurious faith in this text, just outright rejection of Jesus' invitation.

Reformed theologians also find great support in the story of Simon in Acts 8:9-25. The text plainly states in 8:13: "Then Simon himself believed also: and when he was baptized, he continued with Philip, and wondered, beholding the miracles and signs which were done." Simon later offered Peter money as if he could purchase the ability to do miracles. Peter responded: "Thy money perish with thee, because thou has thought that the gift of God may be purchased with money. Thou hast neither part nor lot in this matter: for thy heart is not right in the sight of God. Repent therefore of this thy wickedness, and pray God, if perhaps the thought of thine heart be forgiven thee." They argue that Simon's belief was spurious, but Peter is not suggesting that Simon is going to hell. Simon has committed a great sin and runs a risk of being temporally judged, just as had occurred in Acts 5 with Ananias and Sapphira in another money related incident. If Peter was telling Simon he was lost, then it seems doubtful he would admonish him to pray and "perhaps" God will forgive him. The point is that if he repents, perhaps God will not punish him temporally (i.e., kill him).

To be sure, there are other less significant verses that Reformed theologians appeal to in order claim a Biblical distinction between spurious and saving faith. But as we have seen, their key verses simply admit of no distinction between different kinds of faith. What is supported by the Bible and the lexical meaning of the words "believe" and "faith" is, as Charles Ryrie explains:

> Faith means confidence, trust, to hold something as true. Of course, faith must have content; there must be confidence or trust about something. To have faith in Christ unto salvation means to have confidence that He can remove the guilt of sin and grant eternal life.[156]

Ryrie also states that saving faith "is a reliance on the truth of the Gospel as revealed in the Word of God."[157] As Charlie Bing explains, believing is simply believing: "Let's be clear about what it means to believe. To believe something means that we are convinced or persuaded that it is true. We cannot almost believe something. We either believe it or we don't."[158] The New Testament does not distinguish kinds of faith, but the object of faith, and the faith that we may rightly call "saving faith" is the faith that is placed in Christ alone. Throughout John's Gospel, we see Jesus interacting with people and inviting them to believe in him without ever suggesting a commitment to a life of fruitfulness as a requirement for everlasting life, and without ever mentioning spurious faith. To Nicodemus, Jesus used the illustration of the raising of the bronze serpent in the wilderness where people only had to look to be delivered. And to the woman at the well, Jesus said: "If thou knewest the gift of God, and who it is that saith to thee, Give me to drink; thou wouldest have asked of him, and he would have given thee living water." (John 4:10) Jesus could have told her to ask for the water and promise a life of faithful service. This surely would have been

---

[156] Charles C. Ryrie, *Basic Theology* (Chicago: Moody Press, 1999), 377.

[157] *Supra* note *156,* p. 377.

[158] Charlie C. Bing, *Simply by Grace* (Grand Rapids: Kregel Publications, 2009), 40.

the place to do it, but Jesus never said it. If the Reformed theologians are correct, the content of Jesus' preaching was entirely inadequate to save her.

You might be thinking that if a commitment to a life of faithfulness is not included in the word "faith," then perhaps it is inherent in the concept of repentance. First of all, as Charles Ryrie notes, the term repentance simply means "to change one's mind" and context must answer the question of what specific concept we are to change our minds about.[159] The term certainly does not always mean a turning from sin since the Bible speaks of God repenting. It is beyond the scope of this book to do a complete analysis of the New Testament use of repentance, but I would point out that the term is rarely used (note that I did not say never used) in connection with receiving eternal life. John's Gospel was expressly written for evangelism and provides us with a good litmus test for whatever we believe is a requirement for salvation: "And many other signs truly did Jesus in the presence of his disciples, which are not written in this book: But these are written, that ye might believe that Jesus is the Christ, the Son of God; and that believing ye might have life through his name." (John 20:30-31) Since the Gospel of John claims for itself to contain sufficient content that a person reading it can believe and have "life through his name," whatever we think is necessary for salvation from hell must be defensible from John's Gospel.

Notoriously absent from John's Gospel are the words "repent" and "repentance." If repentance in the sense that Reformed theologians use the term (to indicate sorrow over sin and a commitment to obedience) were necessary for eternal life, why did John fail to record Jesus' use of the word even one time? The term does occur several times in messages in the synoptic Gospels, but it is typically in reference to the Jewish people

---

[159] Charles C. Ryrie, *So Great Salvation* (Wheaton: Victor Books, 1989), 92.

repenting from their sins because the Kingdom was at hand, which they knew from the Old Testament prophecies was to be characterized by righteousness. That is why John the Baptist's baptism is referred to as a baptism of repentance and his message was primarily directed at the Jews. But again, in examples that undeniably involve preaching eternal life to unregenerate people as we so often see in John's Gospel, repentance is not mentioned.

Moreover, Paul used the term only ten times in his epistles, once in reference to God's gifts and calling (Romans 11:29), twice in terms of Paul's writing a letter to the Corinthians (2 Corinthians 7:8), and typically in reference to repentance for believers. Of particular importance, Paul does not use the term in 1 Corinthians. Paul writes in 1 Corinthians 1:17: "For Christ sent me not to baptize, but to preach the gospel...." And then in 1 Corinthians 15, Paul spelled out exactly what he meant by "the gospel." If the Reformed theologians are correct, surely 1 Corinthians 15 would have been the place for Paul to spell it out, and indeed, its absence there makes Paul's explanation of the gospel in error if they are correct.

We do, however, find Paul's use of the term in his sermons recorded in Acts. In Acts 17:30, in the course of his sermon to the Athenians (Gentiles), Paul says that God has "now commanded all men every where to repent" in the context of his talking about their polytheism and idols and on the heels of his sentence in the prior verse: "Forasmuch then as we are the offspring of God, we ought not to think that the Godhead is like unto gold, or silver, or stone, graven by art and man's device." Paul's point is that these people who have an idol for every God, including the unknown god, need to repent (change their minds) about the notion that people can make gods out of sticks and stones and turn to the only true God that created them. We find in Paul's sermon in Acts 19 that he contrasts John's baptism of repentance to the believer's baptism: "Then said Paul, John verily baptized with the baptism of repentance, saying unto the people, that they should believe on him which should come after him, that is, on Christ Jesus. When they heard *this*, they were baptized in the name of the Lord Jesus." (Acts 19:4-5) In Acts 20:21, Paul characterized his preaching of the gospel as preaching a repentance or turning toward God: "Testifying both to the Jews, and also to the Greeks, repentance toward God, and faith toward our Lord Jesus Christ." And similarly, in Acts 26:20, we read: "But shewed first unto them of Damascus, and at Jerusalem, and throughout all the coasts of Judaea, and *then* to the Gentiles, that they should repent and turn to God, and do works meet for repentance."

While Paul clearly used the concept of repentance in his evangelism, it was a turning away from false concepts about God to the truth. We never find Paul suggesting that the sinner must clean up his life, or even commit to cleaning up his life, in order for Jesus to save him. You cannot clean your fish before you catch them. But to be absolutely clear, I am not saying that that repentance has no place in evangelism. The most striking example, of course, is Peter's sermon in Acts 2. Peter said in Acts 2:38: "Repent ye therefore, and be baptized every one of you in the name of Jesus Christ for the remission of sins, and ye shall receive the gift of the Holy Ghost." In the context of Acts 2, Peter preached that Jesus fulfilled prophecy by being resurrected, and that he ascended to the right hand of the Father. Then Peter exclaimed to his mostly Jewish audience: "Therefore let all the house of Israel know assuredly, that God hath made that same Jesus, **whom ye have crucified**, both Lord and Christ." (Acts 2:36) And their response to his Pentecost sermon: "Now when they heard this, they were **pierced in their heart**, and said unto Peter and to the rest of the apostles, Men and brethren, what shall we do?" (Acts 2:37) Thus, when Peter says repent, he is talking about the Jewish people changing their mind about Jesus, who claimed to be the Messiah, but whom they crucified as a blasphemer. Their repentance is to now believe that Jesus is exactly who he claimed to be. The issue, then, is not whether repentance is a part of salvation from sin's penalty, but what we mean by repentance.

Earlier in this book, I quoted the following succinct definition of the gospel: "Saving faith is the belief in Jesus Christ as the Son of God who died and rose again to pay one's personal penalty for sin and the one who gives eternal life to all who trust Him and Him alone for it."[160] To trust Christ and him alone, as the Son of God, for the forgiveness of our sins, necessarily entails a change of mind about several things, and different aspects of this are emphasized in different passages that use the terms repent or repentance, as we have seen. To generalize about the concept of repentance and its relationship to salvation from sin's penalty, what we can say is that a person has to change their mind about any ideas they have that are directly contrary to what is inherent in saving faith, and in that sense, repentance plays a role in salvation from sin's penalty.

I believe that the term repent is often not mentioned in the context of preaching the good news to unregenerate people in the Bible precisely because repentance is inherent in trusting him and him alone for the forgiveness of sins. Moreover, repentance does not mean the same thing for every person in every situation, which is why, when we see the term used, the context clarifies precisely what incorrect beliefs requires repentance. The crowd in Acts 17, for instance, needed to change their mind about there being many gods, but that certainly was not the case for Peter's audience in Acts 2. But the common Reformed view that the repentance that is necessary for salvation is a commitment to complete obedience to Christ is merely writing into the text something that is not inherent in the lexical meaning of the term or the context. The testimony of the Bible is that we can only clean up our lives if we are believers and as we are sanctified by the

---

[160] J.B. Hixson, *Getting the Gospel Wrong*, p. 84 (2008).

power and leading of the Spirit in our lives. The reality is that the new believer will sin soon enough, and that sin within minutes or hours surely calls into question any supposed whole-hearted commitment to complete obedience to Christ. This may entail a change of mind about our sinfulness, about polytheism, about Jesus' deity, about Jesus as the exclusive way to the Father, or any of a number of false ideas that are contrary to saving faith.

The view that the term "believe," as used in reference to salvation from hell, must include a commitment to complete obedience to Jesus is often referred to nowadays as *lordship salvation*. I have parked here on this issue of saving faith because lordship salvation is really the flip side of the coin from perseverance of the saints. Lordship salvation says that saving faith entails a commitment to obedience. Perseverance of the saints says that if the obedience is not consistently there to the end of a person's life, the original faith was spurious. These are really the same doctrines described from different perspectives, and to get at a proper Biblical definition of faith is to get at the root of the matter. If believing in the Bible just means believing, then lordship salvation and perseverance of the saints are both invalidated. But beyond their redefining faith to fit their theological commitment, proponents of perseverance of the saints and lordship salvation usually miss the critical distinctions between verses that address the faith required for salvation from sin's penalty and verses addressing discipleship or rewards.

While there is no question that all Christians should be devoted and maturing disciples, it is a mistake to take a verse addressing the requirements of faithful discipleship and turn those into requirements for salvation. Likewise, it is a mistake to take a verse that speaks to rewards at the bema judgment, or the possibility of a loss of rewards, and conflate that teaching with what is required for salvation. Because the New Testament says so much about discipleship and rewards, it would require an entire book to address the misunderstandings and abuses such verses. Charlie Bing's excellent book, *Grace, Salvation, and Discipleship: How to Understand Some Difficult Bible Passages*, does exactly that. For our purposes here, a few examples from the Gospels illustrate the importance of making these distinctions.

> Matthew 10:37 He that loveth father or mother more than me is not worthy of me: and he that loveth son or daughter more than me is not worthy of me.

> Luke 14:26 If any *man* come to me, and hate not his father, and mother, and wife, and children, and brethren, and sisters, yea, and his own life also, he cannot be my disciple.

Some argue these verses mean that if someone loves anyone more than Jesus, they are not saved. Any profession of faith was spurious. Of course, this would require the unsaved person, at the moment of trusting Christ, to know enough about him to love him more than anyone else including their spouse and children. It is more reasonable that that sort of relationship with Jesus develops over time in the life of a maturing disciple. And indeed, the context in both cases is discipleship, as Jesus expressly states in the Luke verse. The phrase "worthy of me" in Matthew 10:37 parallels "be my disciple" in Luke 14:26 and has the same meaning. The issue is not being worthy (i.e., meriting) of salvation, but being one of Jesus' disciples. Moreover, the Luke verse uses the idiom of hate to mean to love less. So the point in both passages is that being a disciple will require a decision that prioritizes the relationship with Jesus over others. In the first century culture, as in many parts of the world today, to openly follow Christ is to put one at odds with friends and family, which may lead to ridicule and persecution, being disowned, or in some places, murdered. This verse is about the cost of being a disciple.

> Matthew 16:24 Then said Jesus unto his
> disciples, If any *man* will come after me, let
> him deny himself, and take up his cross, and
> follow me.

We find similar statements in Matthew 10:38, Mark 8:34, Luke 9:23, and Luke 14:27, and those parallel passages should be similarly interpreted. Note here that Jesus speaks to his disciples, and that in the immediate context Peter makes his great profession of faith: "Thou art the Christ, the Son of the living God." (Matthew 16:16) Jesus responds that Peter is blessed because "flesh and blood hath not revealed it unto thee, but my Father which is in heaven." There is no question that Jesus' audience here is his apostles, and he speaks to them not about how to become a Christian but what a devoted disciple must do. He warns them "how that he must go unto Jerusalem, and suffer many things...and be killed" and then tells "his disciples" that in order to "come after me" (i.e., follow Jesus as a disciple), they must be prepared to "deny himself, and take up his cross, and follow me." The point is that being a devoted disciple will require them to set aside their personal agenda and pursue Jesus even if it entails reproach and suffering. And in this same context, the result of doing so or not doing so has nothing to do with their eternal destiny, but their rewards when Jesus returns. (Matthew 16:27) Note that the Appendix provides further exegesis of Matthew 16:24-27.

> Matthew 10:32 Whosoever therefore shall
> confess me before men, him will I confess also
> before my Father which is in heaven. 33 But
> whosoever shall deny me before men, him will
> I also deny before my Father which is in
> heaven.

The common teaching here is that if someone was unwilling to publicly proclaim Jesus, they either lose their salvation or never had it to begin with. The context in Matthew 10 is Jesus sending out his disciples and these two verses are part of his instructions about how they will be received. What they stand to lose for not boldly proclaiming the message of Jesus Christ is not salvation, but Jesus' commendation (one of the rewards) in the future. This is clear from the balance of the passage that addresses the keeping or losing one's soul-life (Matthew 10:39), a reference to the salvation of the soul that Jesus builds on in Matthew 16 and I discuss in detail in the Appendix. We keep our life by living in obedience so that our life translates into rewards or inheritance in heaven. Similarly, Jesus explicitly references gaining and losing rewards in 10:41-42. This passage illustrates the critical distinction to be made between rewards passages and salvation (justification) passages.

Next, we will move on to proof texts for the idea that the life of a true believer must necessarily be characterized by a consistency of fruitfulness until death. Before leaving this section, however, let me be very clear that none of the foregoing comments should be understood to suggest that it does not matter how we live. James' whole point in his epistle was that it matters a great deal in this time and at the bema. The New Testament teaches a host of adverse consequences for continued sin in the life of a believer, including an incapacity to mature in the word of God, the possibility of God's temporal judgment including illness and death, a loss of fellowship with God and the fruit of the Spirit, and a loss of rewards at the bema.

Some people like to throw around pejorative labels like "cheap grace" and "easy believism," but these are red herrings to avoid dealing objectively with the Biblical text. The term grace carries the meaning of a free gift and so it is absurd to speak of it being expensive or cheap. The Bible teaches that salvation is free to us because Jesus paid for it one hundred percent. As for easy believism, what makes believing difficult is not having to commit to a life of obedience, but having to humble oneself at the cross and coming to terms with the fact that we are sinners, hopelessly lost, and cannot do anything toward earning or meriting our salvation. Finally, John MacArthur and others insist that those that do not agree with them are teaching that mere mental assent to the historical facts of the gospel is all that is necessary for salvation. This is a blatant strawman argument. **What the dissenters are saying, and what I am saying, is that you must believe the historical facts of the gospel and affirmatively trust Christ for the forgiveness of sins on the basis of his finished work at Calvary.** With this important groundwork laid about the meaning of faith, we will look at some of the more common proof texts, but understanding that virtually any rewards or discipleship verse may find itself misplaced into a proof text list for perseverance of the saints.

Proof Texts for the Perseverance of the Saints

Calvinists tend to provide long string cites of proof texts for this doctrine, but almost all of the verses only go to the eternal security of the believer and not to perseverance in the faith. (e.g., John 6:39, 10:27-30; Ephesians 4:30) As indicated previously, the eternal security of the believer is not questioned. Therefore, the analysis of the proof texts will be limited to the primary texts that purportedly teach that a genuine believer's life must evidence "saving faith" to the end.

> Romans 8:29 For whom he did foreknow, he also did predestinate *to be* conformed to the image of his Son, that he might be the firstborn among many brethren. 30 Moreover whom he did predestinate, them he also called: and whom he called, them he also justified: and whom he justified, them he also glorified. 31 What shall we then say to these things? If God *be* for us, who *can be* against us? 32 He that spared not his own Son, but delivered him up for us all, how shall he not with him also freely give us all things? 33 Who shall lay any thing to the charge of God's elect? *It is* God that

justifieth. 34 Who *is* he that condemneth? *It is* Christ that died, yea rather, that is risen again, who is even at the right hand of God, who also maketh intercession for us. 35 Who shall separate us from the love of Christ? *shall* tribulation, or distress, or persecution, or famine, or nakedness, or peril, or sword? 36 As it is written, For thy sake we are killed all the day long; we are accounted as sheep for the slaughter. 37 Nay, in all these things we are more than conquerors through him that loved us. 38 For I am persuaded, that neither death, nor life, nor angels, nor principalities, nor powers, nor things present, nor things to come, 39 Nor height, nor depth, nor any other creature, shall be able to separate us from the love of God, which is in Christ Jesus our Lord.

This passage typically finds itself near the beginning of the list of Calvinists proof texts for the perseverance of the saints even though it is not mentioned. That the passage teaches the eternal security of the believer is certain, for that is explicitly taught in verses 38 and 39. But what of perseverance? Notice in verses 29 and 30 the order: foreknowledge, predestination, calling, justification, and glorification. Recall, Calvinists consider the perseverance of the saints to be the human side of sanctification, but where is sanctification mentioned in this passage? It is not. Paul is looking to the future resurrection in verse 29: "...he also did predestinate *to be* conformed to the image of his Son, that he might be the firstborn among many brethren." Jesus is said to be the "firstborn" with reference to his resurrection. The saints are all promised resurrection as well, so that in verse 30 Paul states that all that are justified will be glorified. But nothing here says that every believer will be conformed to the image of Christ throughout their mortal lives. In fact, this verse does not say that any believer will be completely conformed to Christ during their mortal life on this earth. There is nothing here about perseverance of faith.

> Romans 11:20 Well; because of unbelief they
> were broken off, and thou standest by faith. Be
> not highminded, but fear:

In Romans 11, Paul addresses the fate of national Israel and whether God has cast them away as His people. Paul explains in the opening of the chapter that God has not cast away national Israel: "I say then, Hath God cast away his people? God forbid. For I also am an Israelite, of the seed of Abraham, *of* the tribe of Benjamin. God hath not cast away his people which he foreknew...." (Romans 11:1-2) Indeed, there is a faithful remnant, meaning Jewish Christians. But Paul explains that the temporal judgment on Israel (cutting national Israel from the vine) has made way for the grafting in of the Gentiles. Verse 20 is not about perseverance of individual saints. Instead, the point is that national Israel "because of unbelief ... were broken off" and this allowed the Gentiles to be grafted in. As the grafted vine, they corporately "standest by faith," but Paul warns in verses 21 and 22 that the Gentiles can be cut off just as Israel was, and in verse 23 that Israel can be grafted in again. In verse 11, Paul explained that all of this has happened to provoke Israel to jealousy, that is, national repentance from their disbelief. Thus, what is in view in Romans 11 is not individual salvation but God's redemptive plan as it relates to the Jewish nation and the Gentiles corporately. There is no support here for perseverance of the saints.

> 1 Corinthians 1:8 Who shall also confirm you
> unto the end, *that ye may be* blameless in the
> day of our Lord Jesus Christ. 9 God *is* faithful,
> by whom ye were called unto the fellowship of
> his Son Jesus Christ our Lord.

This passage speaks of eternal security, not perseverance. In verse 8, we are not told that the believers in the Corinthian church will manifest faithful obedience "unto the end." Indeed, much of the epistle is written to address the fact that the church in Corinth had significant problems, strife, litigation, and fornication. What the verse states is that Jesus will confirm them unto the end. This is a straightforward promise of eternal security. And it is rooted not in their works, but as verse 9 states, in God's faithfulness. This passage does not teach the Calvinist doctrine of the perseverance of the saints.

> 1 Corinthians 13:7 Beareth all things, believeth all things, hopeth all things, endureth all things....
> 13 And now abideth faith, hope, charity, these three; but the greatest of these *is* charity.

This passage comes in the larger context of 1 Corinthians 12 and 13, in which Paul discusses the active Spirit gifts in the Corinthian church, concluding in chapter 13 that "charity" or love is more important than the exercise of these gifts. In chapter 13, verse 7, Paul is describing what Christian love should be, so that when he says Christian love bears all things and endures all things, he is not at all suggesting that all Christians endure in works or that all Christians have love that endures. Paul is admonishing the members of the Corinthian church to have this quality of Christian love in their lives. Of course, if they were already demonstrating this love in their lives, Paul would not need to address the issue as extensively as he does, but in view of the strife and disunity in the Corinthian church (symptoms of unloving attitudes), Paul hammers home the point.

Paul anticipates a time when the Spirit gifts will cease: "But when that which is perfect is come, then that which is in part shall be done away." (1 Corinthians 13:10) In contrast, Paul teaches in verse 13 that faith, hope and love will continue. The overall message of 1 Corinthians 13 is that those members of the Corinthian church should be more concerned about being loving toward their brethren than their gifts. Because the gifts will eventually cease, it will be their love toward one another that is the enduring quality that marks them as Christians. Nothing in this passage guarantees that they will in fact demonstrate love to the end. On the contrary, that is the apostle's appeal to his audience because it is not automatic. The passage is about Christian love, not perseverance.

> Philippians 1:3 I thank my God upon every remembrance of you, 4 Always in every prayer of mine for you all making request with joy, 5 For your fellowship in the gospel from the first day until now; 6 Being confident of this very thing, that he which hath begun a good work in you will perform *it* until the day of Jesus Christ:

The Calvinists frequently construe this verse as support for their perseverance of the saints doctrine. Verse 5 addresses the church's "fellowship in the gospel," a reference to their participation in Paul's missionary ministry, for which the entire epistles serves as a thank you letter. In context, verse 6 does not present the human side of sanctification, but instead only speaks of God's work. What Paul expresses in verse 6 is his personal confidence in what God will do through the church at Philippi corporately "until the day of Jesus Christ." Paul is not issuing a guarantee against any specific individual falling away, but is instead expressing his confidence in them corporately based on his prior experience of their participation in his ministry. When Paul says in verse 6 that "he which hath begun a good work in you," the good work is their participation in Paul's evangelistic ministry by providing for his needs, the fruit of which will have lasting significance. (cf. Philippians 4:10-17) Then verse 7 again confirms it is their partnership with him in the ministry that is in view: ".... inasmuch as both in my bonds, and in the defence and confirmation of the gospel, ye all are partakers of my grace." The word "partakers" means they shared in God's grace with Paul "in the defence and confirmation of the gospel."

Rather than assuring the Christians in Philippi that they cannot fall away, Paul specifically prays that their love will continue to grow: "And this I pray, that your love may abound yet more and more in knowledge and *in* all judgment; That ye may approve things that are excellent; that ye may be sincere and without offence till the day of Christ." (Philippians 1:9-10) A prayer like this would not make sense if the Philippians could not stagnate or fall away. Paul's words in this passage are encouraging words, but provide no guarantee of personal perseverance.

> 2 Thessalonians 3:3 But the Lord is faithful,
> who shall stablish you, and keep *you* from evil.

It is important to see the context for this passage in 2 Thessalonians 3:1-2: "Finally, brethren, pray for us, that the word of the Lord may have *free* course, and be glorified, even as *it is* with you: And that we may be delivered from unreasonable and wicked men: for all *men* have not faith." Paul has mentioned "unreasonable and wicked men" and then tells his audience that the Lord will keep them "from evil." When Paul says the Lord is faithful to "stablish" them, he is talking about the Lord strengthening them against persecution from evil men (or the evil one). This verse says nothing about a believer's ability to fall away from faith or cease to do works that evidence faith. This promise to these people of what the Lord will do for them to keep them from evil cannot be transformed into a guaranty against their falling away or a promise that they will always evidence works of saving faith in their lives.

> 1 Peter 1:5 Who are kept by the power of God
> through faith unto salvation ready to be
> revealed in the last time.

On a casual reading, this verse appears to speak to eternal security. While I agree the Bible affirms eternal security, that does not fit this context, and neither does perseverance.

Just as the inheritance of 1 Peter 1:4 is kept in heaven, so also are the heirs to the inheritance kept by the power of God "through faith unto salvation ready to be revealed in the last time." The word kept translates the Greek *phroureō* which means, according to Strong's, "to be a watcher in advance, i.e. to mount guard as a sentinel (post spies at gates); figuratively, to hem in, protect...." In other words, it has the sense of being guarded or protected. To understand the sense in which believers are kept or guarded / protected by the power of God through faith we note first that this protection is "unto" (with a view to or for the purpose of) the "salvation ready to be revealed in the last time." This is a salvation in the future, i.e., in the last time, and not justification, and this salvation relates directly to faithfully living in obedience and is called the salvation of the soul. The excurses in the Appendix addresses the entire prologue of 1 Peter and the doctrine of the salvation of the soul in detail.

The source of this protection is the power of God but the means of that protection is through his readers' faith. Thus, it seems best to understand that Peter was speaking of God's ongoing provision for His people while they lived by faith in obedience to God Word so that they would receive this future salvation, i.e., rewards or inheritance. It is clear from verse 6 that Peter anticipated his audience going through trials, and so he was not saying his readers were being kept from trials or the like. Rather, this verse speaks of their being kept through the trials, that is, strengthened and enabled by God to endure in faith unto the salvation ready to be revealed in the last time. The opposite of this would be their falling back in the face of adversity and trials. This understanding is confirmed by 1 Peter 4:19, which in the context of suffering and trials, states: "Wherefore let them that suffer according to the will of God commit the keeping of their souls to him in well doing, as unto a faithful Creator." Trials should cause us to lean in to God, not away, and when we do that He will strengthen us in the trials.

There is nothing here of perseverance, just a promise by God to enable and strengthen those who face trials in faith, with a view to their appropriating their share of the inheritance reserved in heaven for them.

> 2 Timothy 2:12 If we suffer, we shall also reign
> with *him*: if we deny *him*, he also will deny us:

Calvinists often quote this verse out of context to suggest that those who fall away from the faith ("deny him") go to hell ("he also will deny us"). The fact is that this verse has nothing whatsoever to do with salvation from sin's penalty, and indeed, the Calvinist ignore verse 13 because it explicitly rejects their position: "If we believe not, *yet* he abideth faithful: he cannot deny himself." Paul speaks of a Christian not believing, yet says that Jesus will remain faithful. But even if we ignore verse 13, verse 12 also does not teach the perseverance doctrine. This is a rewards verse that teaches that those who suffer persecution for Christ's sake will reign with him, i.e., the reward is the position of authority in the Kingdom. The remainder of the verse is a contrast. When it speaks of those that deny Jesus, it is not talking about those change their minds about who Jesus is or their faith in the gospel. Persecuted Christians are put to a choice of suffering for Jesus or denying him publicly (recall Peter's response by the charcoal fire in John's Gospel after Jesus' arrest). Those that deny Jesus to avoid persecution will suffer a loss of reward. The verse does not say anything about a loss of salvation or that the person that denies Jesus was never saved to begin with. This verse relates persecution and the believer's response to the issue of rewards.

> Galatians 5:21 Envyings, murders, drunkenness,
> revellings, and such like: of the which I tell you
> before, as I have also told you in time past, that
> they which do such things shall not inherit the
> kingdom of God.

Often Calvinists argue that in this verse Paul is teaching that people who are living in habitual sin are not saved. The argument Paul is making here is the same as he makes in 1 Corinthians 6:9-11 and Ephesians 5:3-5, and it will be helpful to examine these passages and then come back to Galatians 5:21. We must remember that the church in Corinth was having serious problems from strife and disunity to litigation and fornication. To these people, Paul writes: "Know ye not that the unrighteous shall not inherit the kingdom of God? Be not deceived: neither fornicators, nor idolaters, nor adulterers, nor effeminate, nor abusers of themselves with mankind, Nor thieves, nor covetous, nor drunkards, nor revilers, nor extortioners, shall inherit the kingdom of God." (1 Corinthians 6:9-10) In the next verse, Paul writes: "**And such were some of you**: but ye are washed, but ye are sanctified, but ye are justified in the name of the Lord Jesus, and by the Spirit of our God." (1 Corinthians 6:11) When Paul says "and such *were* some of you" he is referring to their past state prior to coming to Christ. Paul makes two things abundantly clear when he says "and such were some of you." First, verses 9 and 10 are a description of unsaved people. Second, the Corinthians are acting no different now as Christians than they did before they were saved.

Paul confirms his belief that the Corinthians are regenerate in verse 11, but he most certainly is not suggesting that they are living consistently in obedience to Christ. Indeed, just the opposite is true. Paul has rebuked them for their litigation (see 6:1-7), defrauding one another (6:8), fornication (5:1), pride about the fornication (5:2), carnality (3:3), and disunity (1:11), among other sins. Paul's appeal is that they live in a manner consistent with their position in Christ and not merely carry on as they did before. Christians can live a lifestyle that from the outside appears no different than it did before they were saved and the Corinthians prove the point. Accordingly, 1 Corinthians 6:9-11 teaches the opposite of perseverance of the saints, and Paul's use of nearly identical language in Galatians 5:21 and Ephesians 5:3-5 should be understood the same way.

In Ephesians 5, although there is no evidence of the sort of carnality problems present in the Corinthian church—but what we know of Ephesus at that time leaves no doubt—Paul voices a similar warning: "But fornication, and all uncleanness, or covetousness, let it not be once named among you, as becometh saints; Neither filthiness, nor foolish talking, nor jesting, which are not convenient: but rather giving of thanks. For this ye know, that no whoremonger, nor unclean person, nor covetous man, who is an idolater, hath any inheritance in the kingdom of Christ and of God." (Ephesians 5:3-5) Note that Paul says, "let it not be once named among you, as becometh saints." Once again, Paul describes non-believers and encourages the Ephesians not to live like lost people that are not even going to be in the kingdom. It is precisely because Christians are capable of rebelling against God that Paul deals with this issue. Paul's admonition is that they would live in a manner consistent with their position in Christ, which Paul dealt with extensively in Ephesians 1 and 2.

The point Paul makes in Galatians 5 is the same. He is contrasting the works (or fruit) of the flesh with the fruit of the Spirit and admonishing them to live right. Paul is teaching the very opposite of the Calvinists position, namely that it is possible for Christians to sin it up: "For, brethren, ye have been called unto liberty; only use not liberty for an occasion to the flesh, but by love serve one another. For all the law is fulfilled in one word, even in this; Thou shalt love thy neighbour as thyself. But if ye bite and devour one another, take heed that ye be not consumed one of another. This I say then, Walk in the Spirit, and ye shall not fulfil the lust of the flesh." (Galatians 5:13-16) Paul tells them not to "fulfil the lust of the flesh" and then illustrates this behavior with the list in 5:21 that describes the characteristic behavior of lost people, which believers are capable of doing. Living right is not automatic, but instead, they will have to walk in the Spirit. Far from teaching that Christians cannot fall into a life of sin, Paul knows that when Christians cater to the flesh they look just like lost people. All three of these passages prove exactly the opposite of the perseverance of the saints.

> Matthew 24:13 But he that shall endure unto the end, the same shall be saved.

This verse was saved for last, but it often heads the proof texts list. There are few better examples of a verse being so blatantly wrenched from its context than this one. This verse is part of the Olivet Discourse, and in it Jesus addresses Jewish believers that in the future would endure unto the end of the Tribulation. Those that do so will be saved. The term saved here does not speak of being delivered from the death penalty of sin, but of physical deliverance from the terrible judgments and anti-Semitism of this future time.

An Alternative View

Calvinists and many non-Calvinists hold to the doctrine of eternal security, which doctrine forms the "F" in NULIF and stands for *forever*. At the moment you have the life God provides in Christ Jesus, you will have it forever, hence the term "eternal life" used in Scripture. But that does not mean that every Christian will always be a good representative of Christ living a life consistent with his position in Christ. Just how bad a life can a Christian live?

Paul considers a hypothetical man at the judgment seat of Christ in 1 Corinthians 3. This man, when he stands before Jesus to make an accounting of how he used the time, talent and treasure given him, has zero to show for it:

> 1 Corinthians 3:11 For other foundation can no
> man lay than that is laid, which is Jesus Christ.
> 12 Now if any man build upon this foundation
> gold, silver, precious stones, wood, hay, stubble;
> 13 Every man's work shall be made manifest: for
> the day shall declare it, because it shall be
> revealed by fire; and the fire shall try every
> man's work of what sort it is. 14 If any man's
> work abide which he hath built thereupon, he
> shall receive a reward. 15 If any man's work shall
> be burned, he shall suffer loss: but he himself
> shall be saved; yet so as by fire.

This hypothetical man watches his life burn up in the sense that none of his works abide for eternity. He receives no reward. We must ask ourselves what his life looked like so that at the end of his days he had nothing left. This is a picture of a man who in every part of his life failed to live consistently for Christ, but Paul says his salvation is not in question. He "shall be saved, yet so as by fire." The reality is that Christians can live in rebellion to God, even for a prolonged period of time. Sampson is an obvious example of a child of God who was in a state of rebellion until the very end of his life, and even then it appears it was his appetite for personal revenge and not obedience to God that caused him to ask for his strength again.

Jesus' parable of the ten pounds in Luke 19 paints a similar picture. We read in Luke 19:12-13: "He said therefore, A certain nobleman went into a far country to receive for himself a kingdom, and to return. And he called his ten servants, and delivered them ten pounds, and said unto them, Occupy till I come." When the nobleman receives his kingdom and returns, one of the servants took the one pound and gained ten pounds, to whom the nobleman says, "Well, thou good servant: because thou hast been faithful in a very little, have thou authority over ten cities." (Luke 19:17) A second servant earned five pounds. We read, "And he said likewise to him, Be thou also over five cities." (Luke 19:19) Of course, Jesus is the nobleman, and these two servants will rule and reign with him in the kingdom as a reward for their faithful service. But a third servant had nothing to show for his time and he even makes a false accusation against the nobleman to cover for his own disobedience. Of him, we read: "And another came, saying, Lord, behold, here is thy pound, which I have kept laid up in a napkin: For I feared thee, because thou art an austere man: thou takest up that thou layedst not down, and reapest that thou didst not sow." (Luke 19:20-21) Regarding the nobleman's response, we read: "And he saith unto him, Out of thine own mouth will I judge thee, thou wicked servant. Thou knewest that I was an austere man, taking up that I laid not down, and reaping that I did not sow: Wherefore then gavest not thou my money into the bank, that at my coming I might have required mine own with usury? And he said unto them that stood by, Take from him the pound, and give it to him that hath ten pounds." (Luke 19:22-24)

What Jesus teaches, then, is that faithful service results in rewards in the kingdom, but what of the unfaithful servant, and what of those that sent the message to the nobleman that they would not have him to reign over them? (Luke 19:14) Listen to Jesus' commentary: "For I say unto you, That unto every one which hath shall be given; and from him that hath not, even that he hath shall be taken away from him. But those mine enemies, which would not that I should reign over them, bring hither, and slay them before me." (Luke 19:26-27) The faithful servants are rewarded and the unfaithful servants have no reward at all, but the enemies are slain. What is critical to note is that the unfaithful servants, who represent believers who have nothing to show for their lives at the bema, suffer the loss of any rewards but are not among those slain. Only those that sent the message that they would not have the nobleman reign over them are slain; they represent the lost people. Jesus taught the very same thing that Paul would later, namely that those believers who at the bema do not have any faithful service to show King Jesus are still saved (though as by fire!).

How we live as Christians has tremendous consequences, for time and eternity. And it may be that a person whose life never appears to bear fruit is not saved. But it is also the case that a Christian can live as a practical atheist for a long time and yet be saved. This is not to say that their life will have no fruit at all, but that we may not see the fruit in their lives. Rest assured, God knows what is there. Probably, most of us have experienced Christians that never seem to live for the Lord, and we may even have found ourselves questioning their salvation. For the Calvinist, since God decreed everything it follows that He decreed the Christian's works. But the Bible presents Christians as being able to live in rebellion. Sometimes it is rebellion for a portion of a person's life (like David), sometimes it is the latter part of their life (like the generation of Israel that died in the wilderness and did not enter the Promise Land), sometimes it is their entire life (like Samson), and sometimes it is a life of compromises (like Lot). But all of these had eternal life. Once you become rightly related to God through His Son, you are His *forever*.

The doctrine of the perseverance of the saints steals away our assurance of salvation. Since the mark of the true Christian is that they never fall away permanently from a life of good Christian works, how could anyone possibly have assurance in this lifetime? As long as they are living, there is the possibility of turning from the faith and never turning back. So on this view, the only assurance of salvation is when we get to heaven. But should not the best and only assurance we need be the promise of God himself in His word? Moreover, who is to say that a person's life has enough fruit to establish that their faith was not spurious to begin with? Does it take one good work each day or each month? And does not the new believer's first sin as a believer establish that his commitment to faithful obedience to Christ's commands was a less than total commitment? And who sets the standard anyway?

In this quagmire of confusion, the only sure thing is that Jesus set aside the legalism of the Pharisees, and yet people have found a way to put it back in, a Neo-Phariseeism for our time. The standard you must meet cannot be objectively defined or found in the Bible, but if you do not meet it, your faith was spurious. Is this life of self-doubt the life of peace Jesus promised us? The consistent testimony of the Bible is that salvation from sin's penalty is ours by believing. I think the Reformed theologians are concerned that if salvation is really free to those that trust Christ, apart from any commitment to obedience, then believers can live as they please without consequence. Surely God would not let sinners into heaven.

But is that not the point, that while we were yet sinners, Christ died for us. Paul wrote in Romans 6 that the grace of God is not a license to sin. Instead, God's grace toward us should be the greatest possible motivator to Godly living as we live with one foot in heaven's door, assured of our eternal destiny.

Concluding Thoughts on Perseverance of the Saints

This brings us not only to the end of our discussion on the perseverance of the saints, but the end of the TULIP as well. By this point, it should be evident to the reader that as you move from "T" to "P" the Calvinists have fewer and fewer purported proof texts and rely more and more on philosophical arguments and inferences from other parts of the TULIP. By the time you get to the "P", although the list of supporting verses for eternal security is admirable, there is simply not a single verse that even comes close to teaching a perseverance doctrine that is the human side of sanctification. The scant handful of verses cited for perseverance either teach nothing but eternal security or have nothing whatsoever to do with eternal security or perseverance.

If God does not program Christians to persevere, then we are genuinely responsible for how we live as believers. God's appeal to us is to grow in Christ and be transformed into His image, but God will not make us obey. And we should not look to our brothers and sisters in Christ whose lives do not appear to us to be bearing fruit and write them off as false professions. If a brother or sister is in a persistent sin, we need to guide them to repentance from that sin with meekness and in love. There is a real danger with the doctrine of perseverance. It is all too easy to impose legalistic standards in separating out all of the false and true professions. We tend to have PhD's in picking out the faults in others and a pre-school education in looking in the mirror. There is a temptation to make our perception of ourselves be the standard we apply, but the Bible does not teach us to make this judgment. Rightly understanding that Christians can choose to live outside of God's will and yet be saved reinforces to us our responsibility to encourage, admonish, mentor, bear one another's burden, and love as we seek to grow and help those around us grow as well.

Concluding Thoughts on NULIF (New Life)

Calvinism is a complex doctrine with myriad practical implications. I suggested in the first chapter that we sit as unbiased jurors and consider the claims and the evidence. Although Calvinists boast evidence for their philosophy from almost every page of Scripture, I have demonstrated that in fact they have very few verses (what we might call stronghold verses or supporting pillars) that even superficially lend credence to their doctrine, and upon careful analysis even those verses lend no evidentiary support. The proof texts of Calvinism fall far short of proving the TULIP. One by one, careful exegesis based on the context and proper meanings of the words unravels the proof texts and deconstructs Calvinism.

We should not think of this exercise in refuting Calvinism as merely academic. Calvinism strikes at the heart of the gospel message, and if there is any place where the Christian should take a stand, it is on the gospel. Simply put, Calvinism robs the gospel of its integrity. You cannot tell anyone that (1) God loves them, (2) the Son died for them, or (3) that they may trust in Christ for eternal life. If they are not elect, all three of those statements are lies. The gospel is now contingent good news, and for most people it is bad news. The reality is that at every step of trying to present the gospel and give people context for understanding their sin condition and need for Jesus Christ, the TULIP imposes upon us to caveat each statement. For example, I cannot, with integrity, tell anyone that Jesus loved them enough to die for them so that they might have eternal life if they trust him. I have no way of knowing if they are elect or not, and if they are not elect, then obviously I cannot tell them Christ died for them or that there is any good news for them. I cannot even tell people God loves them because He passed over most people. Moreover, I cannot tell people that they simply need to trust Christ. I have to try to explain the commitment they must make to obey Christ's commands, which they may know little or nothing of, so that they can get saved. And what if I become aware of a sin issue in their life after they professed Christ? Perhaps their commitment was inadequate, so what do I do then?

Moreover, Calvinism robs the gospel of substantive meaning. For the Calvinist, people are not ultimately saved because they have trusted Christ. They are saved because God picked them and His Son died for them, totally securing their salvation at the cross. We have to ask why the gospel is needed at all, especially if no one can ever believe on their own, and indeed there are Calvinists who take TULIP to its logical conclusion and openly teach that preaching the gospel and doing missions work are inconsequential. After all, God picked them, died for them, and will give them their faith, which they cannot reject. In this picture, the gospel of 1 Corinthians 15 is a mere prop. The gospel is reduced from an invitation to have a relationship with God into a mere declaration of a completed historical event predetermined in eternity past and devoid of the legitimate substance of a relationship because the elect individual is completely passive in the entire transaction.

Calvinism also robs the gospel of its assurance. Living under the mantra, "you are saved by faith alone but the faith that saves is never alone," I cannot know I am a child of God until I get to heaven and find out whether the fruit in my life was enough. Moreover, the logical consequence of the perseverance doctrine is that there always remains before me the possibility that I will fall away, that is, that I will start living in such a way that my conduct proves my profession of faith was spurious. What looked like Christian fruitfulness for decades might prove to have been mere emulation of the Christian walk. It is only a life of fruitfulness and obedience to the very end that is the Christian perseverance that validates salvation, and therefore, we cannot have assurance of eternal life until we are in heaven. We have a life of doubt, not peace.

Finally, Calvinism robs the gospel of love. The elephant in the room for Calvinists is why God did not simply elect everyone. There is a tremendous difference between the God that loved the world so much that He died for every sinner without exception so that any sinner could come and drink freely of the fountain of living waters and the God that only made a way for some. All we can say to the lost person is that God loves the elect and that may or may not be you and may or may not be your spouse, your child, your sibling, or your best friend.

Praise God that while the Bible does not teach TULIP, it does teach NULIF ("new life"). Mankind is naturally sinful ("N") in that all of us are born with a propensity to sin and do commit personal sin. But God has given unconditional grace ("U") toward the world in that He has made salvation available to everybody. When Jesus died on the cross, he paid the price for everyone. This is limitless atonement ("L"), and the good news is going to the ends of the earth inviting ("I") sinners to trust Christ for the forgiveness of sins so that they can live forever ("F") with God.

Chapter 9

Jesus and Calvinism

While there is no question that God has revealed Himself and His doctrine progressively in the Bible, most of the significant doctrines we find in the New Testament epistles were addressed at some level by Jesus as recorded in the four Gospels. Thus, while we do not get a complete prophetic picture without the Revelation, Jesus addressed prophetic and end times matters during his earthly ministry. (e.g., Matthew 24-25) Similarly, we get a more comprehensive ecclesiology with the completed New Testament cannon, especially as concerns the roles and requirements for deacons and elders, but Jesus began to teach on ecclesiology during his earthly ministry. (e.g., Matthew 16) Jesus also taught about the coming role of the Holy Spirit after he would depart (e.g., John 16:7-13), salvation through faith (e.g., John 3:16, 4:10-14), the doctrine of rewards (e.g., Matthew 16:24-28), discipleship (e.g., John 14-15), the future resurrection (e.g., Matthew 22:30-32), and the future judgment (e.g., Matthew 25:31-46).

With this in mind, we are constrained to ask, if Calvinism is the centerpiece of a Biblical soteriology, did Jesus teach any of it? It is telling that Calvinism leans so heavily on the New Testament writings other than the Gospels. In previous chapters, I addressed the primary TULIP proof texts from the four Gospels. In this chapter, we approach the question of Jesus and Calvinism from the other direction by exploring whether Jesus did and taught things that cannot be reconciled with Calvinism. This is an application of the hermeneutical circle referenced in the first chapter to test the TULIP principles against what Jesus said. Indeed, as we will see, Jesus said some outrageous things for a Calvinist to say.

The point of this brief exercise is that Calvinism presents itself as a system supported by lengthy citations to proof texts, but even a casual reading of the Gospels reveals serious conflicts. The hermeneutical circle reminds us that it is not acceptable for different verses in the New Testament to stand in conflict. If Jesus said things that cannot be reconciled with what we think the rest of the New Testament teaches about the TULIP, then we should accept Jesus' words and re-examine our system.

The Mission

Jesus described one of the purposes of his incarnation as "to seek and to save that which was lost." (Luke 19:10) He illustrated this by speaking of a man with 100 sheep who, when one was lost, left the 99 to find the one. (Matthew 18:12) The man rejoiced "more of that sheep, than of the ninety and nine which went not astray." (Matthew 18:13) When a Samaritan village would not receive Jesus into their village, his disciples asked if they should command fire to come down and devour the village. Jesus responded, "For the Son of man is not come to destroy men's lives, but to save them." (Luke 9:56) But from a Calvinist perspective, how could Jesus' mission possibly be to seek and save the lost? The TULIP Jesus, knowing only a very small percentage of humanity was elected for salvation, surely comprehended the limited scope of his mission.

Perhaps Jesus should have said, "to seek and save the elect." But that makes no sense of the man with 100 sheep that searched for the one lost sheep and rejoiced to find it. Why would Jesus rejoice in the TULIP reality? If TULIP is accepted, Jesus knew exactly who the elect were, where they were, and understood none were truly lost. In fact, there was neither reason to weep over the lost, which appears to be the reason Jesus wept at the tomb of Lazarus (John 11:35), nor rejoice over their being found, since all of it was predetermined. We hear Jesus say, "O Jerusalem, Jerusalem, which killest the prophets, and stonest them that are sent unto thee; how often would I have gathered thy children together, as a hen *doth gather* her brood under *her* wings, and ye would not!" (Luke 13:34) But does not Jesus' expression of sorrow at their hardness of heart ring hollow if he knew they "would not" because they could not?

The Healings

Jesus not only stated his purpose of seeking and saving the lost, but he preached to the masses beckoning them to believe on him and vindicating his message with signs. Indeed, he frequently healed people of "all manner of sickness and all manner of disease." (Matthew 4:23) This caught the public's attention so that "his fame went throughout all Syria: and they brought unto him all sick people that were taken with divers diseases and torments, and those which were possessed with devils, and those which were lunatick, and those that had the palsy; and he healed them." (Matthew 4:24) Matthew even saw Jesus' healings as a fulfillment of Isaiah 53:4:

> Matthew 8:16 When the even was come, they brought unto him many that were possessed with devils: and he cast out the spirits with *his* word, and healed all that were sick: 17 That it might be fulfilled which was spoken by Esaias the prophet, saying, Himself took our infirmities, and bare *our* sicknesses.

Not only that, Jesus gave his disciples "power against unclean spirits, to cast them out, and to heal all manner of sickness and all manner of disease." (Matthew 10:1) Jesus sent them out, instructing them to preach that the kingdom was at hand and "heal the sick, cleanse the lepers, raise the dead, cast out devils: freely ye have received, freely give." (Matthew 10:7-8) Indeed, as multitudes followed Jesus in Matthew 12, "he healed them all." (Matthew 12:15)

The miracles not only vindicated the message, but showed his ability to bring spiritual healing. When a paralytic was brought to him through a roof, Jesus said, "Son, they sins be forgiven thee." (Mark 2:5) This caused the scribes to think to themselves, "Why doth this man thus speak blasphemies? Who can forgive sins but God only?" (Mark 2:6-7) Reading their minds, Jesus responded, "But that ye may know that the Son of man hath power on earth to forgive sins, (he saith to the sick of the palsy,) I say unto thee, Arise, and take up thy bed, and go thy way into thine house." (Mark 2:10-11) As the author of Hebrews confirmed regarding the message of salvation (not just justification but sanctification), God confirmed the message through signs: "God also bearing them witness, both with signs and wonders, and with divers miracles, and gifts of the Holy Ghost, according to his own will?" (Hebrews 2:4)

So the point is this. If Jesus only purposed to save a small group of people who would be given their belief in him based on election, then why did he heal everyone who came to him for healing without exception? We find no example of Jesus turning away anyone who asked for healing. The reason is because Jesus proclaimed himself, by these miracles, both capable and willing to bring spiritual healing to everyone who came to him in faith. Thus, the words of Revelation 22:17, "and whosoever will, let him take the water of life freely." Is it not much more probable that Jesus physically healed all that asked (or asked on behalf of someone who could not ask) because he viewed the spiritual healing as also available to all?

On a more fundamental level, why would TULIP Jesus heal anyone, or authorize and direct the Twelve to do so? Or even if it be accepted (but unexplained) that he must heal some to fulfill prophecy, why heal the masses? After all, the elect would be saved because God would give them faith at the moment of His choosing. They needed no convincing with evidence; they needed to see no vindicating miracles. They would reject all of that until God gave them faith.

Sin Cities

Jesus also taught things that cannot be true in a TULIP framework. For example, he frequently talked about those that reject his revelation being judged more harshly than the famous sin cities of the Bible. In fact, had those sin cities received the special revelation that first century Israel received during Jesus' earthly ministry, they would have turned to God. We read of that harsher judgment in Matthew 10:

> Matthew 10:12 And when ye come into an house, salute it. 13 And if the house be worthy, let your peace come upon it: but if it be not worthy, let your peace return to you. 14 And whosoever shall not receive you, nor hear your words, when ye depart out of that house or city, shake off the dust of your feet. 15 Verily I say unto you, It shall be more tolerable for the land of Sodom and Gomorrha in the day of judgment, than for that city.

We must ask, why is the judgment harsher? Of course, the answer is that the audience that rejected Jesus' words delivered through his disciples had superior special revelation that Sodom and Gomorrah did not have. But why does that matter? After all, Sodom, Gomorrah and the homes that would reject the disciples, all did so for the same reason—their inhabitants are not elect. Whether they heard the good news one time or fifty times, their response could only be to reject it. So again, why is the judgment harsher?

Jesus even "began...to upbraid the cities wherein most of his mighty works were done, because they repented not." (Matthew 11:20) And again, the reason was that they had more revelation—specifically in the form of "mighty works"—than the sin cities. But here, Jesus went further. It was not just that the judgment would be harsher for the first century cities that rejected him; Jesus said that had the sin cities experienced the additional revelation they would have repented (e.g., like Nineveh did):

> Matthew 11:21 Woe unto thee, Chorazin! woe unto thee, Bethsaida! for if the mighty works, which were done in you, had been done in Tyre and Sidon, they would have repented long ago in sackcloth and ashes. 22 But I say unto you, It shall be more tolerable for Tyre and Sidon at the day of judgment, than for you. 23 And thou, Capernaum, which art exalted unto heaven, shalt be brought down to hell: for if the mighty works, which have been done in thee, had been done in Sodom, it would have remained until this day. 24 But I say unto you, That it shall be more tolerable for the land of Sodom in the day of judgment, than for thee.

This presents a substantial dilemma. Tyre and Sidon rejected God's Word because their inhabitants were not elect—they could do nothing else. But Jesus did not say they *possibly* could have believed with additional revelation like that provided to Israel during Jesus' earthly ministry. Jesus said Tyre and Sidon "would have repented long ago in sackcloth and ashes." Jesus says those towns full of non-elect people would have done what non-elect folks cannot do. And that is outrageous for a TULIP Jesus to say. But there is more.

In the next chapter of Matthew, the pivot chapter where the Jewish leadership accuses him of doing his miracles by Beelzebub, Jesus pronounced judgment on that generation because they rejected the greater revelation while the sin city Nineveh responded in faith to the minimal revelation delivered through the prophet Jonah:

> Matthew 12:39 But he answered and said unto them, An evil and adulterous generation seeketh after a sign; and there shall no sign be given to it, but the sign of the prophet Jonas: 40 For as Jonas was three days and three nights in the whale's belly; so shall the Son of man be three days and three nights in the heart of the earth. 41 The men of Nineveh shall rise in judgment with this generation, and shall condemn it: because they repented at the preaching of Jonas; and, behold, a greater than Jonas *is* here. 42 The queen of the south shall rise up in the judgment with this generation, and shall condemn it: for she came from the uttermost parts of the earth to hear the wisdom of Solomon; and, behold, a greater than Solomon *is* here.

Jesus' words again conflict with TULIP—indeed, his words reject TULIP's most fundamental premise that those that do not believe cannot believe because they are not elect. No amount of evidence will change their total inability. But Jesus specifically called out that generation for not believing when the people of Nineveh believed based on much less revelation.

He called them out for not believing when the queen of Sheba traveled a great distance to hear Solomon's wisdom while most of the Jewish people rejected Jesus' words.

The Calvinist must insist that Jesus called them out in this way knowing they could not respond, but that makes a mockery of Jesus' words and efforts to convince his audience. The faithful men of Nineveh and queen of the South would only "rise in judgment with this generation...and condemn it" because that generation could believe and failed to do so. If they could not believe, it is absurd for Jesus to repeatedly compare them to the sin cities, and especially Nineveh.

Shutting People Out

Jesus also taught that false teachers may keep people out of the kingdom: "But woe unto you, scribes and Pharisees, hypocrites! for ye shut up the kingdom of heaven against men: for ye neither go in *yourselves*, neither suffer ye them that are entering to go in." (Matthew 23:13) Jesus also accused the Jewish leadership of building on Israel's history of killing God's messengers (prophets) by hiding the truth from people.

> Luke 11:49 Therefore also said the wisdom of God, I will send them prophets and apostles, and *some* of them they shall slay and persecute: 50 That the blood of all the prophets, which was shed from the foundation of the world, may be required of this generation; 51 From the blood of Abel unto the blood of Zacharias, which perished between the altar and the temple: verily I say unto you, It shall be required of this generation. 52 Woe unto you, lawyers! for ye have taken away the key of knowledge: ye entered not in yourselves, and them that were entering in ye hindered.

Jesus said the "lawyers" had "taken away the key of knowledge" through their Pharisaical doctrine (see Luke 11:46) and thus "hindered" people "that were entering in" the kingdom. But how can this be? If they were not elect, they could never enter the kingdom and there is no sense in which anyone could hinder them. And if they were elect, they would enter the kingdom, and no one could stop them by any means.

Not only did Jesus accuse some people of hindering others from being saved, Jesus said it is harder for rich people to be saved than poor people. And so circumstances like personal wealth hinder people from coming to Jesus: "Verily I say unto you, That a rich man shall hardly enter into the kingdom of heaven. And again I say unto you, It is easier for a camel to go through the eye of a needle, than for a rich man to enter into the kingdom of God." (Matthew 19:23-24) We see this play out with the rich young ruler of Luke 18. Jesus told him to "sell all that thou hast, and distribute unto the poor, and thou shalt have treasure in heaven: and come, follow me." (Luke 18:22) This made the young man "sorrowful" because "he was very rich." (Luke 18:23) In response to that, Jesus made the statement about it being difficult for rich people to enter the kingdom (e.g., "for it is easier for a camel...than for a rich man to enter into the kingdom of God" (Luke 18:25)). But this is an absurd statement for a TULIP Jesus to make. Elect people will believe, rich or not. The rest will reject Jesus, rich or not.

Hearing Jesus talk to the rich young ruler, the disciples asked, "Who then can be saved?" (Luke 18:26) Jesus responded: "The things which are impossible with men are possible with God." (Luke 18:27) If Jesus had in mind election, this would have been an opportune time to answer his disciples plainly. But if Jesus' answer was that rich people get saved because God elects them, then in what sense can it be easier for poor people to be saved? Surely it is no more burden for God to elect one person as another. The simplest reading is usually the best. Jesus was telling his disciples (and us) that many rich people trust in their money and possessions and that keeps them from the kingdom, which has nothing to do with being elect or not.

Believing the Words

In Luke 16, Jesus told of a person who went to hades but "in hell he lift up his eyes...and seeth Abraham afar off" and asked for mercy. (Luke 16:23-24) The man then asked if Abraham "wouldest send him to my father's house" so he could "testify" to his five brothers, "lest they also come into this place of torment." (Luke 16:26-28) Abraham's response was that "if they hear not Moses and the prophets, neither will they be persuaded, though one rose from the dead." (Luke 16:31) But why would Jesus even speak of persuasion? After all, the elect will believe the gospel when God makes them believe and not a moment before, and the rest can never believe, no matter how convincing or persuasive the messenger. Yet Jesus' point here was that if the writings of Moses and the Prophets were rejected, so also would be the evidence of resurrection. Like Jesus, Paul also preached with a view to convincing or persuading his audience. (e.g., Acts 18:4, 19:8, 28:23, 2 Corinthians 5:11) As a Calvinist, Paul surely must have known he could never persuade anyone through convincing and well-structured arguments of the truth of the gospel. But this again raises the question of why the Bible says Paul attempted to persuade people?

Just as troubling, the apostle John wrote of the preceding materials in his Gospel: "But these are written, that ye might believe that Jesus is the Christ, the Son of God; and that believing ye might have life through his name." (John 20:31) John recorded things Jesus said and did to convince his readers that Jesus is the Christ, the Son of God, so that they might have life through his name. But again, the elect will believe at the precise moment in time of God's choosing, and when they believe, it will not be because they were persuaded by evidence.

They cannot be persuaded except that God give them faith, but if God is giving them their faith, then surely God's gift of faith does not need Paul's or John's persuasive assistance to nudge the recipient of God's gift of faith into the light. Said another way, John wasted most of twenty chapters providing detailed proofs of Jesus being the Christ the Son of God as if his readers needed persuading so that they might believe and have eternal life. John could have dropped these extraneous matters and simply presented the bare historical facts of the gospel, that Jesus is the Son of God who died for their sins and rose again, and urged them to trust Jesus and him alone as their sin bearer. (1 Corinthians 15:1-4)

However, as we read the evangelistic New Testament writings like the four Gospels, the writers attempted from different perspectives to persuade their audiences who Jesus is and the salvation he provides. Matthew, for example, wrote from a Jewish perspective and sought especially by his arguments to persuade Jewish people about Jesus. More than that, the sermons in the New Testament attempt to be persuasive, whether through reliance on Old Testament passages as Peter did in Acts 2 and Stephen did in Acts 7, or on cultural matters as Paul did in Acts 17 as he spoke at Mars Hill. In a TULIP world, all of these writings and sermons should only have presented the bare gospel with no wasted efforts on persuasive arguments. Once the bare message of the gospel is provided, the matter is in God's hands. He would give them faith, or not, based on His predetermination and not the eloquence or cleverness of the instrument He used to deliver the gospel message. And all of this points to the big elephant in the room—why have any gospel message at all? Why engage people in the Great Commission? God could simply save whom He wills at the moment of His choosing without any messenger.

Believing the Works

In John 10, Jesus interacted with the Jewish leadership that rejected his testimony that "I and my Father are one." (John 10:30) Indeed, they would stone him for what they viewed as blasphemy (John 10:31), so Jesus asked, "Many good works have I shewed you from my Father; for which of those works do ye stone me?" (John 10:32) Their response was that it was not his works, but his blasphemous words, by which he "being a man, makest [himself] God." (John 10:33) In responding to that, Jesus said: "If I do not the works of my Father, believe me not. But if I do, though ye believe not me, believe the works: that ye may know, and believe, that the Father *is* in me, and I in him." (John 10:37-38) Said another way, Jesus told them that even if they reject his words, they should believe based on his works that validate his claim to be the Son of God. But as with what Jesus said about rich people coming to faith, his words here are irreconcilable with Calvinism. If they are elect, when the Spirit efficaciously calls them, they will believe the message. It is not possible that the efficaciously called could reject Jesus' words but be convinced by his works. If they are non-elect, however, they can believe neither Jesus' words nor his works.

Parables

Next, we observe that after the turning point in Matthew 12 where some Jewish leaders accused Jesus of doing miracles by the power of Satan, Jesus began teaching in parables. Jesus' stated purpose was to conceal and reveal. The famous parable of the soils (Matthew 13:3-9) introduced the parables that followed, and the purpose of the parable was to teach about comprehension. Because Jesus' use of parables as recorded in Matthew 13 was a turning point in how he taught, his "disciples came, and said unto him, Why speakest thou unto them in parables?" (Matthew 13:10) See Jesus' response—it was to conceal and reveal:

> <u>Matthew 13:11</u> He answered and said unto them, Because it is given unto you to know the mysteries of the kingdom of heaven, but to them it is not given. <u>12</u> For whosoever hath, to him shall be given, and he shall have more abundance: but whosoever hath not, from him shall be taken away even that he hath. <u>13</u> Therefore speak I to them in parables: because they seeing see not; and hearing they hear not, neither do they understand.

In other words, Jesus used parables to teach the mysteries of the kingdom to his disciples but conceal it to those that had rejected him. To him that had faith, more revelation would be given (especially about the kingdom), but to him that did not have faith, even the revelation they had received would come to nothing, just as in the examples in the parable.

From a TULIP perspective, the non-elect cannot believe the gospel. And more than that, many Calvinists teach that the non-elect cannot even comprehend it because if they could understand it, then they could believe. But in Matthew 13, Jesus began teaching parables for the express purpose of concealing from the lost people that had already rejected him the deeper truths of the kingdom he wanted to share with his disciples. Yet if the non-elect cannot even understand the gospel, then certainly it was not necessary for Jesus to use parables to conceal from them the mysteries of the kingdom. Said another way, what Jesus confirmed in Matthew 13 was that the lost Pharisees of Matthew 12 could comprehend the good news but having rejected it, the deeper truths of the kingdom would be withheld from them by masking them in parables.

Conclusion

The principles of TULIP Calvinism constrain its advocates to hermeneutical gymnastics to avoid the plain implications of Jesus' teachings. But all of the inconsistencies fall away if we simply accept what Jesus said at face value. Jesus really did come to seek and save that which was lost. Jesus told Nicodemus: "And as Moses lifted up the serpent in the wilderness, even so must the Son of man be lifted up: That whosoever believeth in him should not perish, but have eternal life." (John 3:14-15) Anyone who was bitten by a serpent could simply turn to look at the bronze serpent Moses displayed and they would be healed. A person might have chosen not to look, but there was no inability to look. To this, Jesus compared his gospel: "And I, if I be lifted up from the earth, will draw all men unto me." (John 12:32) Anyone could believe in him for spiritual healing just as centuries earlier anyone could look to the bronze serpent for physical healing.

Chapter 10

Learning, Listening and Talking

As this study comes to a close, it behooves us to briefly consider the matter of speaking to people with whom we disagree. As I have interacted with people about the issues covered in the preceding chapters, many of them had in mind someone they wanted to be better equipped to discuss these issues with. That is a good thing, and we ought always to be willing to share the truth. Paul said, "Preach the word; be instant in season, out of season; reprove, rebuke, exhort with all longsuffering and doctrine." (2 Timothy 4:2) But the Bible also says a great deal about how Christians ought to speak to others. Candidly, how some Christians speak publicly about political and Bible issues is an embarrassment and a reproach. If I had to sum up everything the Bible says about our speech in a single word, that word would be humility. It is the key to learning, listening, and talking in a manner that honors Christ and edifies the hearer.

Learning the Word with Humility

Recall Jesus' words, "for I am meek and lowly in heart." (Matthew 11:29) As Jesus was humble, so also we are called to humility. In fact, "the fruit of the Spirit is love, joy, peace...meekness...against such there is no law." (Galatians 5:22-23) Yet I would suggest that humility is among the scarcest of jewels even among Christians. Paul admonished his disciple Timothy to "follow after righteousness, godliness, faith, love, patience, meekness." (1 Timothy 6:11) He similarly instructed his disciple Titus to show "all meekness unto all men." (Titus 3:2) Perhaps the greatest passage on this topic is in Philippians 2, where the Apostle Paul said, "Let nothing be done through strife or vainglory; but in lowliness of mind let each esteem other better than themselves...Let this mind be in you, which was also in Christ Jesus: Who, being in the form of God, thought it not robbery to be equal with God: But made himself of no reputation, and took upon him the form of a servant, and was made in the likeness of men: And being found in fashion as a man, he humbled himself, and became obedient unto death, even the death of the cross." (Philippians 2:3-8)

Jesus is the second person of the triune Godhead, yet at a moment in history he took on the form of a human being and set aside the independent use of his divine attributes, humbling himself in obedience even to the point of permitting himself to be nailed to a cross. Paul told the Philippians to have the same "mind" or attitude as Jesus had. And do not miss Paul's statement in Philippians 2:9: "Wherefore God also hath highly exalted him...." Jesus was humble and God exalted him. Jesus said, "And whosoever shall exalt himself shall be abased; and he that shall humble himself shall be exalted."

(Matthew 23:12) Peter wrote, "...be clothed with humility: for God resisteth the proud, and giveth grace to the humble. Humble yourselves therefore under the mighty hand of God, that he may exalt you in due time." (1 Peter 5:5-6)

So what does humility have to do with engaging the Word of God? Simply put, proud people are not teachable. Paul warned the Romans, "Be not wise in your own conceits." (Romans 12:16) The Proverbs warn, "Seest thou a man wise in his own conceit? There is more hope of a fool than of him." (Proverbs 26:12) In other words, the prideful are worse off than fools. Pride works in pernicious ways in relation to learning the Word of God. Proud people already know everything. Paul warned that "knowledge puffeth up" and the proud believe they already have the knowledge they need. (1 Corinthians 8:1) Yet God's Word says that if someone "seemeth to be wise in the world, let him become a fool, that he may be wise." (1 Corinthians 3:18) The Bible learning process requires that we jettison the world's wisdom that we all have as we come into a right relationship with God, and replace such "wisdom" with God's wisdom. But this means admitting there are areas where our thinking and our conduct are wrong, and it takes humility to do that. It takes humility to be like the Ethiopian, who when asked if he understood what he was reading from Isaiah, said, "How can I, except some man should guide me?" (Acts 8:30)

The Bible says, "Give instruction to a wise man, and he will be yet wiser: teach a just man, and he will increase in learning." (Proverbs 9:9) Wise people are teachable and fools are not. As Christians, no matter how much Bible we may think we know and no matter how much time we have put into diligent study, we must remain humble in order to remain teachable. Some Christians seem to know something of the Bible but they stopped learning long ago and are unaware of it. May that not be us! We must always remain learners, looking to God by His Holy Spirit not only to teach us more, but to correct us in areas where our thinking is not in line with His thinking.

(2 Timothy 3:16) We must expect God to use not only those we think are the greatest Bible teachers ever, but those we mistakenly assume have nothing to teach us, and indeed even our enemies. Learning should lead to change; to learn we must be willing to let go of bad thinking even where we may have invested time and energy into that bad thinking or passed along our bad thinking to others. We have to be humble or we are done growing.

Listening and Talking

This book was not written to encourage strife, or even to encourage debate for the sake of the debate. Paul wrote, "Do all things without murmurings and disputings." (Philippians 2:14) The "disputings" refers to arguing. It is one thing to have a conversation in the right spirit, discussing what we believe and why, and quite another to argue or to debate with an intent of showing someone else how smart we are or how stupid we believe they are. Yet I have found that many Christians, all of whom suppose they are spiritually mature, prove the opposite through their manner of speech when they talk with those with whom they disagree, including the things they say on blogs or Facebook and other social media posts. We must be reminded that the Bible says a great deal about how we speak to one another, and our conversations with those with whom we disagree must comport with what the Bible says about our speech, or else we should not have those conversations.

The book of James contains five chapters on practical Christian living, and all five chapters address the issue of speech. The key verse is James 1:19: "Wherefore, my beloved brethren, let every man be swift to hear, slow to speak, slow to wrath." He continued, explaining, "if any man among you seem to be religious, and bridleth not his tongue, but deceiveth his own heart, this man's religion is vain." (James 1:26) James was addressing the person who believes they are spiritually mature but cannot control their speech. What they say and how they say it reveals a lack of maturity and their own self-delusion concerning their spiritual maturity. Someone might protest, "it is just when someone makes me mad that I mouth off." But the Bible says that circumstances do not create our spirit, they just reveal it. We must be mindful of what we say and the spirit with which we say it, especially when we interact with those we disagree with. Paul wrote: "Let us therefore follow after the things which make for peace, and things wherewith one may edify another." (Romans 14:19) And again, "Let no corrupt communication proceed out of your mouth, but that which is good to the use of edifying, that it may minister grace unto the hearers." (Ephesians 4:29)

So with this background in mind, I offer some recommendations about interacting with other believers about Calvinism, and more broadly about any theological matter where we disagree. First and foremost, do so with humility. As we can only learn the Bible with humility, we can only teach it effectively with humility. You (and I) do not know everything there is to know about the Bible or soteriology or even Calvinism; we have not arrived. In the specific context of instructing Timothy about how to approach correcting believers to whom he ministered in the area of doctrinal error, Paul wrote: "And the servant of the Lord must not strive; but be gentle unto all *men*, apt to teach, patient, In meekness instructing those that oppose themselves; if God peradventure will give them repentance to the acknowledging of the truth." (2 Timothy 2:24-25)

Our conversation with someone with whom we disagree should not be a fight or heated argument ("must no strive"), but our approach should be "gentle," for the purpose of teaching, with patience and humility. Even if the other person gets a bit testy or excited, our side of the conversation should be calm, reasoned, and respectful. I received a phone call out of the blue a couple of years ago from someone who wanted to challenge some statements I made in a sermon. We talked for good while and there were places in the conversation where this person was very emotional, and others where he interrupted me. At the end of the call, he made the comment that usually when he has these kinds of conversations, the other person ends up saying some harsh words and hanging up on him. He thanked me for talking through the issues even though he still disagreed with me. Having these types of conversations in an appropriate manner and with a gentle spirit ought to be the rule and not the exception.

Second, recalling James 1:19, we must be good listeners. We can have a reasoned and profitable discourse without monopolizing the conversation and without interrupting. And if we are humble enough to understand that God might use the other person to teach us something, then we will be good listeners. In fact, many of our responses ought not to be about telling the other person why they are wrong, but asking them questions based on what they have said. It is a good practice to use their own words in your questions. That shows you are listening. And it goes to the fact that our first goal should be to understand what the other person believes and why. We need to get an idea of where they are coming from before we launch into telling them they are wrong. We need to understand precisely the point at which we disagree, and sometimes we will find that our actual area of disagreement is narrow, or even that we are in agreement but just articulating our views differently. To do that, we must sincerely listen to the other person. Bear in mind that if we are not listening, then we are not really having a conversation. Our listening tells the other person they have value and what they have to say is important.

Next, if you know the conversation is going to be one of strong disagreement, it may be profitable to suggest some ground rules to cabin the conversation. Let me be specific here. Proof texting is a poor substitute for intellectual discourse. Anyone can commit a list of verses to memory and spout them off. But as I have tried to stress in this book, the only way to deal with this type of "evidence" is one verse at a time. My usual ground rule is that we select a single verse to discuss and cabin our conversation to the book within which that verse occurs. I usually ask the other person to pick the verse. So for example, if they want to discuss how they think John 3:16 supports some part of TULIP, I ask them to agree that until we exhaust our conversation about John 3:16 and move to another verse, we limit our conversation to John's Gospel. While whatever John teaches must be consistent with the other Bible writers, I do not need Paul or Peter to derive a best contextual-based understanding of John 3:16. I want to approach the issue first from a Biblical Theology perspective, and not a Systematic Theology perspective.

What I want to avoid is the "moving the goalposts" problem that so often defeats the utility of these conversations. If we do not cabin ourselves to the verse at hand and its immediate context, then what usually happens as we get close to the end zone is someone starts citing proof texts from other books and, in my example, John 3:16 gets left behind without any resolution. We can talk about any of those other verses, but should do so in an orderly fashion. We should take them one at a time and consider them carefully in the context of the book within which they are written. But if every time the person we are talking to feels cornered they retreat by citing new verses elsewhere in the Bible and derailing the conversation, we will never get anywhere. We will just keep running the ball toward the end zone only to have it moved on us again. Other ground rules I usually state, at least with someone I do not know or do not know well, is that: (1) I have no interest in debating but am happy to discuss what I believe and why; (2) let's listen to one another and not talk over one another; and (3) our speech should be edifying and respectful. Remember, the assault weapon of choice for Christians is our words, but it should not be that way.

The next thing I would briefly mention is what I call the Facebook folly. I have allowed myself more than a few times to get caught up in discussions on Facebook where multiple people are interacting on a hot button issue. If we were all in a room together speaking to one another, it might work, but it just takes one "keyboard warrior" on social media to ruin it all. All of the things I referenced before about humility, listening, and edifying go out the door. Social media (and blogs) are usually a poor vehicle for this kind of discussion, and the non-Christian that reads what we or those we are interacting with have written is not seeing an example of Christlikeness. Conventional wisdom is that we should not talk about politics and religion, but that is wrong. As believers we ought to be able to have profitable discussions about hot button issues without going to war, but the best way to do so is in person, or if that is not possible, then by phone or videoconference. We should generally avoid debates on social media because it almost always results in Christians writing mean-spirited things they should be ashamed of. Recall what I said about the Christian's assault weapon of choice. We need to know that what the Bible says about the tongue applies to our social media posts. Jesus said, "That every idle word that men shall speak, they shall give account thereof in the day of judgment." (Matthew 12:36) Giving an account for our social media posts ought to be a sobering reality check.

Finally, we are to be stewards of our time. Paul wrote, "Redeeming the time, because the days are evil." (Ephesians 5:16) We ought to use our time well. As with money, our time must be budgeted and wisely spent. It is easy to get bogged down in fruitless conversations that are a waste of time. This is one of the central reasons I discussed above setting some ground rules for theological conversations. If someone always moves the goal post on us, that conversation is wasting time better spent elsewhere. That conversation can spin in circles all day as every verse supposedly has some other verse to prop it up, and the conversation just moves like a ball in a pinball machine, never focusing and never resolving anything. We also need to recognize that some people are just disputers. They are eager to debate for the sake of debating, but it becomes apparent in the conversation that the qualities the Bible requires of us (listening, humility, gentle spirit) are not there. Cut your losses and exit that conversation gracefully.

While just about every Bible issue gets debated, not all issues are reasonably debatable. Paul exhorted Timothy, "Neither give heed to fables and endless genealogies, which minister questions, rather than godly edifying which is in faith: so do." (1 Timothy 1:4) If we interact with other people about Bible issues, we are going to come across what I can only describe as theological "flat earthers." They have private interpretations (see 1 Peter 1:20) that require just about everyone to be wrong for them to be right. They love debating, speak with great confidence (as fools do), and have an air of intellectualism about them, but their views are so far "off the deep end" that there is not even a sensible starting place from which to engage in a profitable conversation. And they have zero interest in the evidence. You might as well attempt a reasoned discourse with a brick wall expecting it to move for you. This book has relied on the metaphor of a courtroom where a jury hears and weighs the evidence. Some people want to fight and have no interest in the evidence; they are the willfully biased that I discussed in the first chapter. We are best to flee theological flat earthers and not waste our time.

Concluding Thoughts

Now, you might ask as this point whether I have had Calvinists change their minds as a result of our conversations, and the answer is yes. But it has almost always not been immediate. The same is true of other contentious theological issues. And I should add, I have frequently learned something from these conversations. Almost everyone has something they could teach us. A good conversation complying with what

Paul told Timothy in 2 Timothy 2:24-25 will often be profitable, but that may not be immediately apparent. However, showing you can inflict a verbal beat down, constantly interrupting the other person, or retreating to the use of ad hominem like a politician (insults and personal attacks against the other person) will never edify anyone and you will have to answer for it at the bema judgment. I once had someone come to me about three years after our conversation. I had forgotten most of what I said, but it planted seed as it were and he wanted me to know that he had abandoned Calvinism. Any time we are talking about the Word of God, we must leave the results to Him. But what we can control is how we deliver the message, and it ought always to be done the right way, in the right spirit, and for the purpose of edification. And in so doing, if we listen, it may be that God has something for us to learn as well.

One final thought. The reader might assume that Calvinism is my proverbial soapbox. But actually, my soapbox issues (we all have them) are effective teaching and discipleship and encouraging Christians to adopt children. Obviously, I think understanding TULIP is important or I would not have written this book, but we need to be mindful not to let one issue so consume us so that we cannot effectively minister to other people outside the scope of our soapbox issue. Probably we would all be best served if our soapbox were the Great Commission.

I pray that this study has enhanced your understanding of the love and sovereignty of God and firmed your conviction that God loved the world so much that He gave His Son for the world so "that whosoever believeth in him should not perish, but have everlasting life." God is good, "world" really and truly means the world, "whosoever" really and truly means whosoever, and by the blood of Jesus, any sinner can be saved by faith. "Unto him be glory in the church by Christ Jesus throughout all ages, world without end. Amen." (Ephesians 3:21)

Appendix

Excurses on the Salvation of the Soul

The purpose of this excurses is to build out in more detail the New Testament doctrine of the salvation of the soul. Understanding this issue is key in properly interpreting the book of James, and especially the portion of James 2 relied on by Calvinists in teaching the "P" in TULIP. Beyond that, this is information all Christians ought to be aware of. The doctrine is the central point of 1 Peter and so I will build the excurses around a basic exegesis of the prologue of 1 Peter with a focus on the "salvation of the soul" taught about there. But to be clear—this doctrine is pervasive in the New Testament. A proper understanding of this issue, which is bound up with the concept of the bema judgment for believers, our inheritance, and rewards, is often critical in distinguishing whether a particular passage is speaking to salvation from the death penalty of sin or addressing believers about a discipleship issue. With this in mind, we turn to 1 Peter.

> 1 Peter 1:3 Blessed *be* the God and Father of our Lord Jesus Christ, which according to his abundant mercy hath begotten us again unto a lively hope by the resurrection of Jesus Christ from the dead,

Following his greeting (vv. 1-2), in what formed the prologue to the book (vv. 3-9), Peter set out the primary subject matter of his epistle, namely their **lively hope**. He began his introduction of this significant concept by praising God, writing **blessed *be* the God and Father of our Lord Jesus Christ**. The reason for giving **God** adoration and praise is that **according to his abundant mercy** He **hath begotten us again**. The phrase **begotten...again** is the Greek *anagennaō* and is used only twice in the New Testament, here and in 1 Peter 1:23. The words translated "born again" in John 3:3 are different. Peter unmistakably spoke of a new birth, sourced in God's great **mercy** (not human effort), and it was God alone that provided this new birth. The word **mercy** is the Greek *eleos* meaning (according to Strong's) "compassion (human or divine, especially active):--(+ tender) mercy." Paul employed the same term when he wrote: "But God, who is rich in **mercy**, for his great love wherewith he loved us, even when we were dead in sins, hath quickened us together with Christ, (by grace ye are saved;) And hath raised us up together, and made us sit together in heavenly places in Christ Jesus." (Ephesians 2:4-6)

Much could be said from other places in the Bible about God's mercy and our justification, but we will see in what follows that Peter focused not so much on how or why this new birth was accomplished but on the purpose for which **God** gave us this new birth. In short, Peter spoke to the issue of how believers should live in light of the new birth. We must bear in mind that Peter's target audience was composed primarily of

Jewish believers, and so his central concern in this epistle was not the gospel and how to "get saved" from sin's penalty, for he affirmed plainly that they were already born again. Rather, it was the purpose and implications of their having been granted the new birth that Peter intended to unravel for his audience, and by application, for us as well. Peter answered the question, "What next?" His focus was on their sanctification. You have been born again and made a child of God, but what comes next? Shall you wait for the day when you are given a harp, a halo and a cloud to rest upon? Or is the reality of the Christian life something far more sobering and spectacular that we are to engage immediately after becoming Christians.

Peter explained first that his readers were born again **unto a lively** or living **hope by the resurrection of Jesus Christ from the dead**. The preposition **unto** is again the familiar *eis* and is flexible but frequently indicates purpose, so that something is "unto" or "to" in purpose, i.e., with a view to or for the purpose that. That sense will become apparent in this prologue. Peter said they were given a new birth "with a view to" something or "for the purpose that" something. We need to understand what that "something" is. And he began by saying the something is a **lively** or living **hope**.

The Bible never guarantees, and indeed denies, that the Christian life will be an easy one. From the earliest times, there was persecution and even martyrdom. Jesus told his disciples, "If the world hate you, you know that it hated me before it hated you." (John 15:18) And aside from persecution, Christians face trials just like everyone else. God does not prevent all trials, but instead uses them to grow us. (e.g., James 1:2-4) Notwithstanding the difficulties and sorrows we may face, the Bible does say a great deal about this concept of **hope**, which Peter will build out. But we do enough for the moment to observe that it is not an empty or uncertain **hope**, like "I am hoping for good weather" or "I hope the fish are biting today." Rather, our **hope** is rooted in the veracity of God and the certainty that what God says is true. Indeed, as someone has said, reality ever conforms to the Word of God. "[L]et God be true, but every man a liar." (Romans 3:4) The concept of **hope**, then, is an unwavering conviction that impacts how we live. We see this illustrated by Abraham's hope in the veracity of God's promise to him that he would be a father of nations: "Who against hope believed in hope, that he might become the father of many nations, according to that which was spoken, So shall thy seed be." (Romans 4:18)

Peter said the new birth was with a view to a **lively** or living **hope**. So we must seek to understand in what way this **hope** is **lively** or living? The opposite would be a dead **hope**, in other words, a **hope** that is useless, i.e., a hope that does not make a practical difference in our lives. This living **hope** is intended to change us now. It is helpful to consider how the author of Hebrews linked the faith that fuels the Christian life to a **hope** rooted in the Word of God: "Now faith is the substance of things hoped for, the evidence of things not seen." (Hebrews 11:1) The eleventh chapter of Hebrews reviews many examples of Christian endurance—believers whose lives in the present were reoriented around God's Word about the future so that they endured in faithfulness. These examples include Enoch, Noah, Abraham, Moses and others. They all experienced changed lives because of their firm conviction about the veracity of God's Word to them. Although God's Word to them primarily concerned future blessings or future events, their lives changed in the present because they believed God and reoriented their lives around this trust in what God told them. Their hope changed them, and this is the **lively hope** that Peter said is a purpose of the new birth. But **hope**, like faith, requires content, which we will address momentarily.

We are not merely saved from sin's penalty, but our new birth is with a view to our being transformed by a **lively hope** that is made possible **by the resurrection of Jesus Christ from the dead. Jesus** rose victorious over sin and death. Because he lives, we also live. This is the substitutionary life of Christ. This living **hope** Peter explained is an aspect of the "newness of life" and "reign[ing] in life" that Paul taught in Romans. We need to understand that what Peter had to say is central to the Christian life. The next verse addressed the content of this **lively hope** that is to transform us.

> 4 To an inheritance incorruptible, and undefiled, and that fadeth not away, reserved in heaven for you,

Peter explained that the new birth is with a view to our having a living hope, which in turn is with a view **to an inheritance incorruptible, and undefiled, and that fadeth not away**. Thus, it is the **inheritance** that defines the specific content of the hope Peter made the subject of his epistle. But what is this **inheritance?** Remembering that Peter's audience was composed of Jewish believers, this term **inheritance** carried a special meaning to them. Upon hearing the term, they would immediately think of the **inheritance** God promised to national Israel in the Old Testament as He freed them from bondage in Egypt and guided them to the Promise Land, i.e., their inheritance in their time.

Peter made a spiritual application of the familiar Jewish concept of **inheritance**, just as the writer to Hebrews did with the concept of "rest" (inheritance) in the Promise Land. (Hebrews 4) To get hold of the New Testament concept of **inheritance** we need to also understand the notion of heirship, because only heirs receive of the **inheritance**. The Jewish people in the Old Testament understood the concept of heirship, and in particular, that the firstborn son received a double portion of the inheritance from his father. (Deuteronomy 21:17) In the New Testament, we learn that upon his resurrection, Jesus was declared Son, in fulfillment of Psalm 2. (Psalm 2:7-8; Acts 13:33) This declaration of Jesus as Son was a legal declaration (Hebrews 1:5) that Jesus "hath [been] appointed heir of **all things**." (Hebrews 1:2) In Paul's writings, Christians are said to be "in Christ," and indeed, in Christ "we have obtained an inheritance." (Ephesians 1:11) We are qualified to inherit because we are heirs through Jesus Christ: "Wherefore thou art no more a servant, but a son; and if a son, then an heir of God through Christ." (Galatians 4:7) And not just heirs, but joint-heirs in Jesus' inheritance of all things: "And if children, then heirs; heirs of God, and joint-heirs with Christ; if so be that we suffer with *him*, that we may be also glorified together." (Romans 8:17)

Peter did not quantify exactly what is included in the **inheritance**, but he explained it is heavenly and permanent. The **inheritance** is **incorruptible, and undefiled, and that fadeth not away**. The meaning of **incorruptible** is that it is not subject to decay with the passage of time. The **inheritance** is also **undefiled**, meaning it is not soiled in any way. Not only that, it **fadeth not away**, meaning it is eternal in its duration. Reading these words, it is apparent that Peter had in mind Jesus' words in Matthew 6:19-21 where, in the Sermon on the Mount, Jesus talked about this issue of inheritance in terms of laying up treasure in heaven, i.e., investing our lives in the things of God and, by so doing, laying up in heaven our inheritance:

> Matthew 6:19 Lay not up for yourselves treasures upon earth, where moth and rust doth corrupt, and where thieves break through and steal: 20 But lay up for yourselves treasures in heaven, where neither moth nor rust doth corrupt, and where thieves do not break through nor steal: 21 For where your treasure is, there will your heart be also.

Recall that the Sermon on the Mount was directed at Jesus' disciples. (Matthew 5:1-2) He sought to teach them in practical terms about experiential righteousness as contrasted to the empty legalism of so many Jewish religious leaders at that time. Jesus taught them to invest their lives in the things of God and not the accumulation of worldly wealth. I must hasten to add at this point that Jesus was not prohibiting the exercise of diligence and wisdom in financial planning, such as maintaining a savings account or 401K. For Solomon taught that we can learn wisdom from the ant because even ants have the sense to store up food for winter. (Proverbs 6:6 ff.) But clearly, Jesus taught his disciples to be rich toward God.

Since our lives do not consist of our possessions, we should not invest our lives in the acquisition of things that have only temporal value, but instead lay up treasures in heaven. The **inheritance** Peter referred to is the very same "treasures in heaven" Jesus taught about. We will put more meat on the bones in the notes that follow, but we note that this issue of laying up treasure is not limited to financial giving. Rather, it is about obedience to God's Word and the investment of one's life to the things of God, for time and eternity, and that takes many forms. It may be various avenues of service in the local church and generally ministering to those in our respective spheres of influence. But it is broader than that, and in my view would include matters like pouring yourself into the Biblical rearing of your children and caring for elderly parents.

Peter added that this **inheritance... [is] reserved in heaven for you**. The term **reserved** is in the Greek perfect tense, indicating past completed action with continuing consequences. We may have little treasure on earth, but the **inheritance** of the Son that we will share in is safely **reserved in heaven**. But does this mean that the Christian life results in "participation ribbons" for every believer? In other words, can we live any way we please and then all share equally in this **inheritance** in the world to come? The short answer is a resounding "NO." Or as Paul might say, "God forbid...." (Romans 6:1-2) The treasure is **reserved in heaven** yet Jesus plainly taught to "lay up for yourselves treasure in heaven," by which he spoke to the issue of appropriating the treasure to our account by our faithful living. We will build out more details about how this **inheritance** is personally appropriated as we continue through Peter's prologue.

> 5 Who are kept by the power of God through
> faith unto salvation ready to be revealed in the
> last time....9 Receiving the end of your faith,
> *even* the salvation of *your* souls.

Just as the inheritance is kept in heaven, so also are the heirs **kept by the power of God through faith unto salvation ready to be revealed in the last time.** The word **kept** translates the Greek *phroureō* which means, according to Strong's, "to be a watcher in advance, i.e. to mount guard as a sentinel (post spies at gates); figuratively, to hem in, protect...." In other words, it has the sense of being guarded or protected. A common interpretation is that Peter here taught "eternal security," that is, that a justified or regenerate person cannot lose their justification. While this author agrees the Bible teaches eternal security, what Peter addressed in this context is something different.

To understand better the sense in which believers **are kept** or guarded / protected **by the power of God through faith** we note first that this protection is **unto** (with a view to or for the purpose of) the **salvation ready to be revealed in the last time.** This is a **salvation** in the future, i.e., **in the last time**, and not justification, and as will be further discussed below, this **salvation** relates directly to faithfully living in obedience and is called the **salvation** of the soul. The source of this protection is the **power of God** but the means of that protection is **through** his readers' **faith.** Thus, it seems best to understand that Peter was speaking of God's ongoing provision for His people while they lived by **faith** in obedience to God Word so that they would receive this future **salvation.** It is clear from verse 6 that Peter anticipated their going through trials, and so he was not saying his readers were being **kept** from trials or the like. Rather, this verse speaks of their being **kept** through the trials, that is, strengthened and enabled by God to endure in **faith unto** the **salvation ready to be revealed in the last time.** The opposite of this would be their falling back in the face of adversity and trials. This understanding is confirmed by 1 Peter 4:19, which in the context of suffering and trials, states: "Wherefore let them that suffer according to the will of God commit the keeping of their souls *to him* in well doing, as unto a faithful Creator."

In verse 9, Peter further identified this **salvation** as the **salvation of your souls** that he anticipated his audience **receiving**. The Greek verb translated **receiving** is *komizō*, which has the sense of receiving a wage or something earned. Since we do not earn our salvation from sin's penalty, justification is not the **salvation** in view. But what is this **salvation of** the soul? For some, any reference to **salvation** brings to mind **salvation** from sin's penalty, i.e., justification. But the word translates the Greek *soteria*, a very flexible term that means a rescue or deliverance. When we encounter this term, or the word *sozō* (to save), we must ask what we are being rescued or delivered from, and what we are being delivered to.

We find varied examples including rescue or deliverance from the penalty of sin (Acts 16:31; Ephesians 2:5-8); from a sickness (Matthew 9:21; Mark 5:34; Acts 14:9); from sleep (John 11:12); temporal deliverance from a perverse generation (Acts 2:40); from bondage in Egypt (Acts 7:25); from drowning (Acts 27:20, 31); from dying (Matthew 8:25); from death on the cross (Matthew 27:42); of the soul (1 Peter 1:9). For this reason, to merely assume when we find the words save, saved or **salvation** that deliverance from the penalty of sin is at issue is misguided. As already indicated, the **salvation** Peter had in mind was not the rescue from sin's penalty that occurred at the moment they believed the gospel and trusted Christ as their sin bearer. Instead, there is a future aspect to this **salvation** and it will be received as one receives a wage. At this point, we would benefit from briefly looking at this concept of the **salvation** of the soul in the larger New Testament context.

In 2 Corinthians 5:10, Paul taught about a future judgment of believers, sometimes referred to as the bema judgment: "For we must all appear before the judgment seat of Christ; that every one may receive the things *done* in *his* body, according to that he hath done, whether *it be* good or bad." Paul referenced believers appearing before the judgment seat (bema) of Christ to be recompensed based on their works. Note that Paul's use of "receive" is the same Greek verb we find in 1 Peter 1:9. In 1 Corinthians 3:11-15, Paul elaborated on this future judgment for believers:

> 1 Corinthians 3:11 For other foundation can no man lay than that is laid, which is Jesus Christ. 12 Now if any man build upon this foundation gold, silver, precious stones, wood, hay, stubble; 13 Every man's work shall be made manifest: for the day shall declare it, because it shall be revealed by fire; and the fire shall try every man's work of what sort it is. 14 If any man's work abide which he hath built thereupon, he shall receive a reward. 15 If any man's work shall be burned, he shall suffer loss: but he himself shall be saved; yet so as by fire.

The stuff of our lives is pictured as being tested by fire, and either it burns away like wood, hay and stubble, or it survives into eternity with eternal consequence and value. This judgment is not about heaven and hell, nor about whether they have trusted Christ for the forgiveness of sins, but about faithfulness, which will determine whether rewards are received. This is clear because Paul contemplates a hypothetical man whose life has nothing of eternal value to show for it (it all burns up), but he "shall be saved; yet so as by fire."

This teaching on rewards (or inheritance) for faithful endurance was taught not only by Paul, but Jesus taught on the subject. On the heels of Peter's great confession in Matthew 16:16 ("Thou art the Christ, the Son of the living God"), Jesus addressed rewards for faithful endurance:

> <u>Matthew 16:24</u> Then said Jesus unto his disciples, If any *man* will come after me, let him deny himself, and take up his cross, and follow me. <u>25</u> For whosoever will save his life shall lose it: and whosoever will lose his life for my sake shall find it. <u>26</u> For what is a man profited, if he shall gain the whole world, and lose his own soul? or what shall a man give in exchange for his soul? <u>27</u> For the Son of man shall come in the glory of his Father with his angels; and then he shall reward every man according to his works.

The Bible teaches that justification is by faith alone in Christ alone, but to be a faithful disciple will cost us. Throughout this passage, the Greek term *psuche* is translated as "life" or "soul." Although some take the English word "soul" to mean spirit it almost never carries that meaning in our Bibles. The term "soul" almost always refers to the conscious experience of our lives. Dr. Harry Leafe defined the "soul" as the temporal experience of human life. It is not merely being alive, but that which we do and experience. We see plainly in the scripture that our experience of life can be restful, physical bliss (Luke 12:19) as well as "exceeding sorrowful, even unto death." (Matthew 26:38) Broadly speaking, our soul consists of our thoughts (1 Corinthians 4:3-5), words (Matthew 12:36-37) and actions (Romans 2:6), all of which will be judged.

To his audience Jesus said, "If any man will come after me...." He was not speaking figuratively, but of literally pursuing after him in his earthly ministry as a disciple, as Peter did. The disciple must deny himself, subjecting his will to Jesus' will, his plans to Jesus' plans, etc. When Jesus spoke in verse 25 of "save" and "lose," he spoke to his believing apostles (except Judas Iscariot), and the point Jesus made is that a disciple chooses between (life no. 1) the life Jesus has for him or her and (life no. 2) the life they might otherwise pursue to serve their own self-interest. You cannot have both, Jesus explained, and indeed "whosoever will save his life [no. (2)] shall lose it [no. (1)]." And in contrast, "whosoever will lose his life [no. (2)] for my sake shall find it [shall save no. (1)]." One life can be saved or delivered into eternity, being rewarded and having continuing significance and eternal value, while the other will last no longer than our short time sojourning here. The point Jesus made in Matthew 16 is that a man that chooses to invest his life in pursuing earthly treasures, even to the point (hyperbolically) of gaining the whole world, will profit nothing from it in the world to come. For when "the Son of man shall come in the glory of his Father with his angels... he shall reward every man according to his works."

Note that Jesus frequently taught about rewards. (e.g., Matthew 5:12, 6:1, 10:42, 19:21; Mark 9:41, 10:21; Luke 6:23, 12:33-34, 18:22) Jesus' Parable of the Pounds (Luke 19:11-27) illustrates the doctrine. There, a nobleman was to journey to a far country to receive a kingdom, then return. For that interim period of his absence he left his ten servants with ten pounds, and then "when he was returned, having received the kingdom, then he commanded these servants to be called unto him, to whom he had given the money, that he might know how much every man gained by trading." (Luke 19:15) The first had gained ten pounds, to which the king said, "Well, thou good servant: because thou hast been faithful in a very little, have thou authority over ten cities." (Luke 19:17) Each servant was rewarded in accordance with how that servant used their allotted money, but one servant only returned the pound without any gain. (Luke 19:20) To that servant, the master said, "Take from him the pound, and give it to him that hath ten pounds...For I say unto you, That unto every one which hath shall be given; and from him that hath not, even that he hath shall be taken away from him." (Luke 19:24-26) This pictures a loss of rewards, not salvation, as Luke 19:27 makes clear: "But those mine enemies, which would not that I should reign over them, bring hither, and slay them before me."

We will either be rich toward the world, and then at the bema judgment as Paul described it, all will be burned away and our only reward will be smoke, or we will be rich toward God. In that case, we will lay up treasure in heaven and thus reap an inheritance in the future. Jesus well understood our tendency to invest in things of the world rather than of God when he warned in Luke 12:15: "Take heed, and beware of covetousness: for a man's life consisteth not in the abundance of the things which he possesseth." He then told the parable of the rich fool who, in the face of material blessings, invested in bigger barns so he could gain more and more. Hear the fool's thinking: "And I will say to my soul, Soul, thou hast much goods laid up for many years; take thine ease, eat, drink, *and* be merry." (Luke 12:19) In contrast to his perspective, we must heed God's rebuke: "But God said unto him, *Thou* fool, this night thy soul shall be required of thee: then whose shall those things be, which thou hast provided?" (Luke 12:20) And then Jesus' commentary, which ties the parable back to his teaching in Matthew 6:19-21 about laying up treasure in heaven: "So *is* he that layeth up treasure for himself, and is not rich toward God." (Luke 12:21)

Putting the pieces together, Jesus taught about the salvation of the soul-life in Matthew 16, and so it is no surprise to find that Peter taught this doctrine in 1 Peter 1:9. Jesus' half-brother James taught the same doctrine in James 1:21 ("save your souls") and the writer of Hebrews addressed the issue in Hebrews 10:39 ("the saving of the soul"). These concepts of saving the soul, laying up treasures in heaven, and our inheritance are all tied together. Dr. Harry Leafe (himself a Calvinist) summarized these verses in his book *Running to Win*:

> It is difficult for grace-oriented believers to think in terms of earning anything from God. Certainly, salvation from the penalty of sin is a free gift of God's grace. However, Peter now tells us that we attain (Gr. *komizō*) as the goal of our faith "the salvation of our souls" (v. 9).

> Clearly, the salvation of verse 5 is the same as
> verse 9, "a salvation ready to be revealed in the
> last time." Recall...that *komizō* means "to
> receive something that is due, or to get for
> oneself by earning."

> The point is clear. Our share in the inheritance
> is determined by that portion of our soul-life
> that is saved or delivered into eternity. And
> *that* salvation is demonstrated by our good
> works or, as Peter put it, the *proven character*
> of faith. We receive inheritance on the basis of
> our *demonstrated* faith (good works). And that
> is what "salvation of the soul" is all about![161]

Conventional wisdom is that "you cannot take it with you"
when this mortal life ends. But there is a sense in which we
can. How we invest our lives will determine whether, at the
bema, we are rewarded. When we invest our lives so that we
are "rich toward God," the outcome at the bema will be that
that aspect of our lives will translate into rewards or
inheritance. And in that sense, our experience of life, our soul-
life, is saved or delivered into eternity as we exchange our
experience of life for our inheritance, the treasure in heaven
that we appropriated over a lifetime of faithfulness. Verses 6-7
will build on this understanding of the salvation of the soul.

> 6 Wherein ye greatly rejoice, though now for a
> season, if need be, ye are in heaviness through
> manifold temptations:

Peter said that we **greatly rejoice** in the inheritance that will be
revealed in the last time, but **now for a season, if need be, ye
are in heaviness through manifold temptations**. The **if** is what
is known in Greek grammar as a first class condition and has
the notion of "since." It assumes the reality of what is said.

---

[161] Leafe, G. Harry, *Running to Win,* Second Edition (Biblical Studies Press
2004), 18.

While they have reason to **rejoice**, they also must suffer for a short time in **manifold** or various **temptations** or trials. The word **temptations** here is not about being tempted to sin, but enduring trials, and can include persecution as well as the normal trials of life (e.g., illness, financial struggles). The question is why is it necessary that they suffer, which is answered in the next verse.

> 7 That the trial of your faith, being much more precious than of gold that perisheth, though it be tried with fire, might be found unto praise and honour and glory at the appearing of Jesus Christ:

Peter next explained the significance of trials in the life of a believer. The noun **trial** is the Greek *dokimion,* which Strong's defines as "a testing; by implication, trustworthiness:--trial, trying." The word can refer either to the test or to the genuineness or proven character of that which is tested, depending on the context in which it is used, and the term could be used, for example, of testing coins for genuineness and testing pottery against defects. The related verbal form of this word, *dokimazō,* means to test with a view to approval. Certainly, Peter was not saying that trials are more valuable than **gold**. Rather, it is the results or responses to those trials as our faith is **tried with fire** and proven that is more valuable. We understand that **gold** is earthly treasure with transient value, while our good works is heavenly treasure with permanent value.

Peter's metaphor is that the quality of precious metals (like **gold**) is **tried with fire** to remove the impurities (the dross) and purify the product to make it more valuable. So also the trials of life prove and refine our **faith**, as we exhibit **faith** responses to the trials, and the product of that testing—our **faith** responses—is **much more precious** or valuable **than of gold that perisheth**. Peter was not talking about determining whether someone is a "true believer," or separating real **faith** from fake

faith, but instead, that the trials will show what we really believe. Our **faith** responses made on the basis of the Word of God will inherently take the form of thoughts, words and actions. In different ways, every day of our life presents new challenges, some small and others large. As believers engaged in God's training program we are to handle the challenges on the basis of God's Word and His wisdom. Dr. Leafe summarized the role of trials in the salvation of our soul-lives:

> The trials Peter has in mind are designed by our heavenly Father to prove the character of our faith (not destroy it!). To be sure, trials also demonstrate lack of faith. But the issue here is the *proven character* (Gr. *dokimion*) of our faith, said to be "more valuable than gold – gold that is tested by fire, even though it is passing away." The clear implication is that gold, in this analogy, has only temporary value, while the *proven character* of faith has eternal value. This is further expressed in the outcome – such proven faith results in "praise and glory and honor when Jesus Christ is revealed."

* * *

> Clearly, then, the trials we experience in life are designed to test our faith, and of necessity, the testing involves our thoughts, words and actions. This being the case, will we then evaluate our circumstances on the basis of God's Word – a biblical worldview – or on some other basis, whatever that might be? Will the intent of our words be to minister and to build up those around us? Will the purpose of our actions be to demonstrate our faith in Christ? If these responses issue from faith in God and His Word, then they become what Peter calls the *proven character* of our faith.

357

> And that proven faith will be demonstrated
> and rewarded "when Jesus Christ is revealed,"
> an event of great importance....[162]

Recall that Peter said our inheritance is reserved in heaven and we are to live by faith with a view toward a salvation to be revealed in the last time. Consistent with that, our **faith** responses will translate **unto praise and honour and glory** (part of our rewards) when Jesus returns, and that is why it is more valuable than **gold**. The word **praise** means commendation, as Jesus may say, "Well done, thou good and faithful servant." (Matthew 25:21) The word **honor** means exaltation, and may have to do with our place of authority in the world to come. Again, think of Jesus' words, "Well done, good and faithful servant; though hast been faithful over a few things, I will make thee ruler over many things: enter thou into the joy of the lord." (Matthew 25:23) Finally, the word **glory** means reputation, and here it is the recognition of a race run well, a life that was rich toward God rather than earthly pursuits.

Before leaving this verse, we must comment that it is especially the **trials** that reveal and grow our faith. We see elsewhere (e.g., James 1:2-4; Hebrews 12:1-11) that God uses the challenges and trials of life to grow us. It seems that when everything is going smoothly, our faith is not tested as strenuously, nor do we have the same opportunity for growth by applying the Word of God to real life issues. And so Peter focused on how the **trials** fit into God's training program for us and give us the opportunity to lay up treasures in heaven, that is, to appropriate our inheritance in real time as we live by **faith**. But there are a couple of caveats. First, many Christians face trials because they are obnoxious, which is not a spirit gift! They perceive the response of others to their bad attitude and bad behavior as related to their being a Christian, but such is not persecution. Second, some Christians face trials but do not do so on the basis of God's Word. Either because they do

---

[162] *Supra* note 161, pp. 15-17.

not know God's Word, or because they choose to set aside God's Word, they face the trials on the basis of self-sufficiency and worldly wisdom, and the results show. There is no laying up treasure in heaven when the result of the testing does not reflect proven character. Moreover, sometimes when you fail the test, you get to take it again.

> 8 Whom having not seen, ye love; in whom, though now ye see *him* not, yet believing, ye rejoice with joy unspeakable and full of glory:

In reference to the return of Christ and echoing Christ's words in John 20:29, Peter remarked that while they had not **seen** him, they **love** him. The **love** they have is volitional love (Greek *agapaō*), a love necessarily exhibits itself in action. Jesus used the same term in John 14:21 when he said: "He that hath my commandments, and keepeth them, he it is that loveth me: and he that loveth me shall be loved of my Father, and I will love him, and will manifest myself to him." Though his readers had not physically **seen** Jesus, their faith motivated their **love** for him, seen in how they lived, and especially how they lived during the trials they faced.

Thus, Peter said, **though now** they **see him not, yet believing** (moved by faith in what Jesus said), they **rejoice with joy unspeakable** (i.e., indescribable, beyond words) **and full of glory**. In a life full of trials, these Christians **rejoice** in Jesus Christ because of their firm conviction of his imminent return and the revealing of their inheritance in Christ as they enter the Kingdom. It bears saying here that a great many Christians fail to experience this **joy** in a real, tangible sense. These are not just words on a page. God expects us to experience a persistent and overwhelming **joy** rooted in our conviction of things future, things associated with the return of Christ, and especially receiving his approval and commendation as we receive of our inheritance. It is no exaggeration to say that many Christians are not even aware of this inheritance, or if they are, they do not care. We do well to get our myopic focus away from things of the world and toward the things of God, for therein is the key to **joy**.

> 9 Receiving the end of your faith, *even* the salvation of *your* souls.

The rejoicing of verse 8 does not happen in a vacuum. As already seen in Peter's prologue to this point, the rejoicing is rooted in love for the Saviour and a focus on his return and his rewarding the saints with the inheritance that is reserved in heaven for them. But more than that, the rejoicing is accompanied by an understanding that how we live now presently affects our future. Peter said that as their faith was being tested, and the assumption is that they were meeting the trials with proper faith responses, they were presently **receiving** or appropriating **the end** or final outcome **of** their **faith** lived out, **even the salvation of** their **souls**. As they lived, facing life on the basis of **faith**, specifically trusting the content of God's Word and applying God's Word moment by moment to the challenges of life in this fallen world, they were, to use Jesus' words from the Sermon on the Mount, laying up treasure in heaven.

They chose in each moment to live by faith or by the flesh, and thus chose to invest that moment with God and exchange it for heavenly treasures. To say it a different way, they were presently appropriating **(receiving)** the inheritance that would be revealed to them at the return of Christ. And insofar as they appropriated that inheritance during this lifetime, they were presently **receiving the end** or product or outcome of their **faith** life, namely the exchange of their present soul-lives (the temporal experience of life, i.e., the substance of their lives—thoughts, words, actions) for an eternal inheritance. Peter did not delineate the precise nature of this inheritance, but it is critical we understand that we are sharing in Jesus' inheritance, and he inherited everything. (Hebrews 1:2) Jesus will exercise complete dominion in the world to come, and we will share in that.

This makes how we live serious business. While we are saved by grace, the idea that how we live now does not have consequences for time and eternity is absurd. One of those consequences is whether we will be rewarded at the return of Christ or just fill the room with smoke as the substance of our lives, all earthly pursuits, burns up. In that event, our **souls** will not be exchanged at the bema for rewards, yet as Paul explained in 1 Corinthians 3, that person is still saved, though as by fire.

Do not miss what Peter was saying in the big picture. God is working through our lives, including especially in the trials, to produce faith responses as we live on the basis of the Word of God, and God rewards us in the process. As Peter indicated in 1 Peter 2:2, it is by the Word of God that we grow. But what does this mean for the Christian that refuses to engage the Word of God as a daily life practice? What of the Christian that will squander their life away on worldly pursuits and largely ignore the Word of God? It means they will meet the challenges of life on the basis of their self-sufficiency, falling back on worldly wisdom, and will make a mess of things. But worse than that, they will be embarrassed at the bema as nothing in their mortal life translated into something permanent in eternity.

Index

Index

Index

Index

Index

Index

Index

Index

Index

About the Author

HUTSON SMELLEY resides in Houston, Texas with his wife and children. He holds advanced degrees in mathematics, law and Biblical studies, and is an adjunct professor at the College of Biblical Studies. He can be contacted at: proclaimtheword@mac.com

www.proclaimtheword.me